BIBLEALIVE

*A Guide to Discovering the Ageless Vitality
of the Bible for Teachers and Students*

BIBLE ALIVE

A Guide to Discovering the Ageless Vitality of the Bible for Teachers and Students

Including Sunday School Lessons

Sara Ann Lincoln, D.A.

Come now, and let us reason together …
Isaiah 1:18

Let me never be found extending my arm for a handout; but
let me always be found extending my arm for a hand up!
Sara Lincoln

BIBLEALIVE
A GUIDE TO DISCOVERING THE AGELESS VITALITY OF
THE BIBLE FOR TEACHERS AND STUDENTS

iUniverse books may be ordered through booksellers or by contacting:

iUniverse
1663 Liberty Drive
Bloomington, IN 47403
www.iuniverse.com
1-800-Authors (1-800-288-4677)

ISBN: 978-1-4917-5369-9 (sc)
ISBN: 978-1-4917-5370-5 (e)

Library of Congress Control Number: 2015900789

Print information available on the last page.

iUniverse rev. date: 4/27/2015

All Bible quotations are from the King James Version unless otherwise indicated.

The textbook of Christian Science, Science and Health with Key to the Scriptures by Mary Baker Eddy, is frequently referred to in this book by its common name, Science and Health.

ACKNOWLEDGMENTS

I'd like to thank the many people who helped and encouraged me over three years get my book into its final form and ultimately published. Without them, this work would never have come to fruition.

First, many thanks to Mike Hedge, who patiently persevered in helping me rework many passages, helped me write several new chapters that were not in the original work, and for following this project through to completion.

Next, Shirley Corbitt for her untiring efforts in reading each of the seven drafts and working with me on further clarifications.

Also, these friends were of great help to me in encouraging me during the writing of this book: Barbara, Bettie, Bonnie, Chaylee, Crystal, Daphne, Ginny, Glenn, Jeanne, Jennifer, Joan, Katie, Kim, Marianne, Merrily, Paula, Robin, Sandy, Sheila, Tom, Tony, and one friend who edited early versions of the book suggesting revisions as well as additions—whom we shall call tomodachi-sama (which means "honored friend" in Japanese).

CONTENTS

INTRODUCTION
BIBLEALIVE—FACETS OF A GEM

Spiritually considered, rising thought is the major theme in the Bible. As we move through the Bible, we see how Spirit, God, calls all to rise from personal, materialistic motives to God-inspired service and revelation. Looking at some of the facets of this gem called the Bible, we can learn how to learn, how to be blessed by wisdom, and how to bless others.

How can we ask better questions during Bible study and avoid the trap of not asking questions—especially the right questions? Who are some of the major thinkers who led and keep leading mankind into a fuller understanding of the man created in the image and likeness of God—the God/man, creator/creation relationship? Let us remember that the term *man*—God's man—means man and woman.

What can we understand about ourselves as "image" that will equip us to detect and discard the false or graven images the Second Commandment warns us about? Dr. Lincoln notes that another insightful book, *Science and Health with Key to the Scriptures* by Mary Baker Eddy, has helped her find the spiritual light of the Bible and provide answers to questions we've wondered about for many years: Why and how does thought rise? What is image? What is really real? What is life? Who am I? Why am I here? These are a few of the questions that we all ask silently or audibly.

With more than thirty years of Bible study and teaching experience, Dr. Sara Ann Lincoln is uniquely qualified to help you find answers to these questions through her unique book *BibleAlive: A Guide to Discovering the Ageless Vitality of the Bible for Teachers and Students.*

This hymn, adapted from a poem by John Burton, describes the approach of *BibleAlive* to Bible study:

Holy Bible, book divine,
Precious treasure, thou art mine:
Mine to tell me whence I came;
Mine to tell me what I am;

Mine to chide me when I rove,
Mine to show a Savior's love;
Mine thou art to guide and guard;
Mine to give a rich reward;

Mine to comfort in distress,
With a Savior's tenderness;
Mine to show, by living faith,
Man can triumph over death.

(Hymn No. 114, *Christian Science Hymnal*, © 1932, renewed 1960, The Christian Science Board of Directors. Used with permission.)

PART I

LEARNING TO QUESTION

1

WHAT'S SO GOOD ABOUT TEACHING THROUGH QUESTIONING?

Jesus *taught*. More words in the Gospels are devoted to his teachings than to his healings. Perhaps Jesus could have found a quiet retreat with free room and board where he could "write a book" or whatever was the equivalent of scrolls. *God's Good Will for Man: Find It and Prove It Today!* Could that have been the title?

The religious leaders in Jesus' day relied on the written word of the Old Testament and interpreted it in their synagogue sermons. Why didn't Jesus write rebuttals to the interpretations that the Pharisees and Sadducees put on Scripture instead of preaching to the people?

Jesus' choice to transform human consciousness through teaching with the spoken word further exalted the profession of teaching. His choosing to teach through parables set this standard for teaching: the teacher should enable listeners to discover implied questions and answers. Observers of society's progress in discovery and invention understand that discoverers and inventors ask questions: Why? Why not? How?

Why did Jesus choose to preach rather than write? In Jesus' time, few people had the ability to read or write. He chose to preach and reached multitudes. Fourteen hundred years later in Europe, the printing press began to make books more widely available and gradually increased the number of people learning to read. This skill would later enable people to read the Scriptures for themselves and judge whether the words that were being interpreted in sermons were based on the Bible. Some of these sermons were written by men ensconced in the inherited perception of God as judge, judging mankind as sinful and condemning them to hell, and the prison called fear, defeat, and hopelessness.

A careful choosing of verbs can strengthen teaching. Verbs in a sentence are second in importance only to the message itself. English teachers everywhere should do their best to inculcate the importance of strong verbs in writing. The moral, ethical, and spiritual purposes of a piece of writing shine forth through the use of strong verbs.

Abraham Lincoln demonstrated this fact in one of the most powerful pieces of writing in American history, delivered as a speech in 1863, the "Gettysburg Address." He appealed to the crowd with such strong verbs as *brought forth, conceived, dedicated, created, engaged, hallow, struggled, consecrated, advanced, resolve.* He did not ask any questions, but he implied the great question, Can we "resolve that these dead shall not have died in vain,—that this nation, under God, shall have a new birth of freedom,—and that government of the people, by the people, for the people, shall not perish from the earth"?

Strong, active verbs and verb phrases are as essential to speaking as they are to writing. Jesus' Sermon on the Mount (Matthew 5–7) vibrates with these verbs. A fellow Bible student counted thirty-six directives for action, calling it a "sermon of verbs," urging all listeners to take action: rejoice … let your light shine … think not that I am come to destroy … bring thy gift to the altar … be reconciled to thy brother … pluck out … love your enemies … forgive us our debts … lead us not into temptation … deliver us from evil … lay up treasures in heaven … take no thought for your life … consider the lilies of the field … seek ye first the kingdom of God … judge not … cast out the beam in thine own eye … do unto others as ye would have them do unto you … build your house upon the rock.

Jesus "taught them as one having authority" (Matthew 7:29). That authority sounded forth in his choice of verbs.

Is *is* a strong verb? It seems to have been weakened by overuse. You might say it got worn out from substituting for strong verbs. Correctly used, *is*, in all its forms, is a most powerful verb: I am, you are, they are, he/she is, it was, it will be. This big little *be* verb conveys reality: this is the way things are. In the King James Version of the Bible, Moses heard God say, "I AM." Jesus directed his followers, "Be ye therefore perfect, even as your Father which is in heaven is perfect" (Matthew 5:48).

Yield and *let* are strong spiritual commands. Every prophet encountered these spiritual commands. Each one had to yield up human fear and human will. Each one had to learn how to let God's will be done. To yield is to let "thy will be done on earth as it is in heaven" (Matthew 6:10). For the Christian, *yield* and *let* are waymarks in the path to understanding Truth. To yield requires strength but at the same time provides strength. *Science and Health with Key to the Scriptures* describes what the thinker is to "let":

> Let the "male and female" of God's creating appear. Let us feel the divine energy of Spirit, bringing us into newness of life and recognizing no mortal

nor material power as able to destroy. Let us rejoice that we are subject to the divine "powers that be." Such is the true Science of being (p. 249:5–10).

And in the New Testament, Paul admonished, "Let this mind be in you, which was also in Christ Jesus" (Philippians 2:5).

Mortal-no-mind, knowing nothing, says, Let mortality have its way with man. Mind, God, declares, Let immortality have *its* way with man. Actually, as is stated in *Science and Health*, "The divine understanding reigns, is all, and there is no other consciousness (p. 536:8–9). So, "Let the words of my mouth, and the meditation of my heart, be acceptable in thy sight, O Lord, my strength, and my redeemer" (Psalm 19:14).

Socrates, the great teacher at the height of Greek civilization, taught through questions. The Socratic method has been honored and practiced for centuries as an effective tool of education.

Martin Luther generated a seismic shift in religion. He questioned the truth and morality of selling indulgences in order to raise funds to rebuild St. Peter's. The church did not permit questioning. This priest publicized his protest against excesses in the Roman Catholic Church through the ninety-five theses he nailed to the church door in 1517, but he had very likely been explaining the problem through his teachings before he bravely recorded his findings. Maybe one of his assignments to students was this: "Make a list of ten questions to be answered by the Roman Catholic Church hierarchy, and predict their responses."

A great religious thinker in American history was Mary Baker Eddy. A questioning heart led her to discover the nature of reality; namely, that reality is as spiritual as its creator, God. She taught her discovery through a question and answer method. Her teaching notes were eventually encapsulated in her book *Science and Health* in the questions-and-answers chapter entitled, "Recapitulation."

Is there a contest between the relative effectiveness of writing and verbal teaching? Hardly. They reinforce each other. Writers teach and teachers write. Both speak, and both may utilize the question-and-answer approach. Questions stimulate thought. Statements are more likely to activate thought only if one strongly supports or opposes them. Questions deliberately rouse thought and response, and they lead to discovery.

Lecturing is a method of teaching, but I am biased against it as the predominant method of teaching. Having been in the classroom setting long enough to obtain master's and doctoral degrees, I know lecturing. I experienced it as unquestioningly as breathing. It was "the way things are"! Few college professors contested the assumption that *teaching* meant *lecturing*. If asked, they might have argued, "This is the way it's done when you want to convey information and interpretation." From personal experience, I know that lecturing works—when it propels one into seeking and questioning.

In the intimate setting of a Sunday School class, lecturing turns students off. At least that's what I have observed. An entertaining "lecturer" might keep students' attention, but does this lecturing most certainly lead to the students' deeper commitment and questioning quest to learn more? As I see it, lecturers (especially in Sunday School) are so much dead weight when their main aim is to tell what they know.

I would have Sunday School superintendents challenge teachers whose primary approach is lecturing after this manner. Students deserve the best. Superintendents can engage all teachers in the process of questioning their teaching methods and measuring them against a sincere and deep assessment of how the great teachers and transformers of human thought have taught. It just might lead them to a revised and renewed appreciation of the importance of a questioning approach.

My method of teaching by questioning did not evolve because I sought to influence other teachers but because I believed (believe) strongly that young people can learn and apply critical thinking skills to reading the Bible and other books on religion and spirituality. Socrates, the prophets, Jesus, Mary Baker Eddy, and others you can probably name exemplified methods of teaching worthy of every Sunday School teacher's consideration.

The Word of God and the teachings of Christ Jesus spread beyond Jerusalem in the first century CE (Common Era), largely through the work of the apostle Paul. Did Paul mainly lecture or did he do significant questioning in his dozen or so letters to the churches? That question might make an instructive study for an individual or a Bible study group. What responsibilities did he lay out for church members?

In my experience, the teaching goes the deepest and stays the longest when the questioning approach is used. Indoctrination goes deep and stays long, but *indoctrination is not teaching.* It is incumbent upon the teacher to provide facts and background as needed, *but the teacher's main task is to inspire deep thought on the part of the students,* and to accustom them to the fact that deep thought and fresh questions are the most natural and necessary things they can practice in their lives and share with others.

What's so good about the questioning approach is that it *facilitates* deep thought, avoids dulling mentality with rote learning, and rescues the victim of indoctrination. Indoctrination does not stimulate original thought; it replaces and restricts thought.

Did you ever experience indoctrination, Sara? Some may see a fine if not invisible line between earnest and structured teaching of the principles of one's religion and indoctrination.

As I considered this question, I remembered a prayer I was taught as a young girl. I don't know if I learned it in my "mainline" Protestant Sunday School or if my parents found it somewhere and taught it to me, but here's the way it went:

> Now I lay me down to sleep.
> I pray the Lord my soul to keep.
> But if I die before I wake,
> I pray the Lord my soul to take.

I would now call that a very poor model of a "children's prayer." It preys upon a subtle fear of death and fear of God as *judge*. Furthermore, it does not emphasize God's tender, constant care.

If I had been taught more vigorously about questioning when I was growing up, surely I would have questioned the implications of that early prayer. As young people grow in their ability to ask questions, they will not be so readily influenced by negative characterizations of Deity.

Compare that prayer, for example, to two children's prayers penned by Mary Baker Eddy for parents to teach to their children. They are found in her *Miscellaneous Writings 1883–1896*, page 400:

**Mother's New Year Gift to
the Little Children**

> Father-Mother God,
> Loving me, —
> Guard me when I sleep;
> Guide my little feet
> Up to Thee.

To the Big Children

> Father-Mother good, lovingly
> Thee I seek, —
> Patient, meek,
> In the way Thou hast, —
> Be it slow or fast,
> Up to Thee.

Adults today can challenge themselves to gain more skills in questioning so as to become better models to the young people they influence. My point here is not merely to encourage you to employ questions and answers as a way of teaching, although I do believe it is the most efficacious method and was practiced by Socrates, Christ Jesus, and Mary Baker Eddy. In addition to using questions and answers in teaching, Sunday School teachers should enjoin their students to constantly ask questions themselves and seek meaningful answers, accepting answers that agree with their intuitive sense of what is right or wrong.

The right way—and wrong way—to question

A group of Jewish leaders asked Jesus, "What is the first commandment in the law?" (see Matthew 22). This was, perhaps, a sarcastic question. They knew that Jesus had studied the law of Moses with the Pharisees in the synagogue and that he knew the answer to the question. But they were apparently hoping that he would say something like, "I am the son of God, and I speak the Word of God, so you should listen to me." This would have given them more grounds to accuse him. They did not want information; rather they wanted to put him down with this sarcastic question. But Jesus answered correctly, stating the first and great commandment was to love the Lord thy God with all thy heart, soul, and mind, and that the second was "like unto it, Thou shalt love thy neighbor as thyself" (verses 38, 39).

Another example of questioning was when the Jews brought Jesus before Pilate to have him crucified (see John 18:37, 38). Pilate listened to the Jews' accusations and then questioned Jesus, "Art thou a king then?" This was not a sarcastic question; I believe Pilate was sincere. He could have asked, "Art thou a king, ha-ha," as if it was a sarcastic joke. But I think he sincerely wanted to understand what kind of kingdom Jesus was talking about. His intent was not to shame him but to learn.

Jesus responded, "Thou sayest that I am a king. To this end was I born, and for this cause came I into the world, that I should bear witness unto the truth."

Pilate, striving to understand Jesus, asks, "What is truth?" and the Bible tells us "when he had said this, he went out again unto the Jews, and saith unto them, I find in him no fault *at all*."

A sincere question shows respect; it seeks information or understanding. Did Jesus ask questions? Look in Matthew, and find some questions that Jesus asked. What would you say that Jesus' purpose was in asking the question you selected?

Has anyone ever asked you a sarcastic question intended to put you down or show you up? How did that make you feel? How did you respond? Has mortal-no-mind ever pushed you aside and made you appear to ask a sarcastic question of a friend? What if a dishonest, sarcastic question comes out of your mouth before you can stop it? What can you do? Can you at that moment name what kind of question that was, and apologize? If not then, later? Is it really all that important what kind of questions we ask and *how* we ask them? (Discuss.)

2

WHAT'S THE RISK OF NOT QUESTIONING?

The risks of not questioning are the numbing of thought, the decline in humane behavior, and the disintegration of society. Many of the world's wars and tragedies have occurred because people have not questioned the motives and purposes of their leaders, who themselves are often misled by a perverted reading of the Scripture and often in the name of Christianity.

Are there perversions of that responsibility called *teaching*, in which young people are taught to hate and destroy? Adolph Hitler wasn't the first to pervert teaching in this way. Well before him, the Crusades, which were often instigated by the papacy against Middle Eastern cultures, killed tens of thousands of people. Several hundred years later were the colonization of the New World and the Spanish conquest of the Mayan, Inca, and Aztec civilizations. Later the American Indians were virtually wiped out by the "white man." And slavery was instituted in the American South.

Today, we have terrorists in the Middle East who, in the name of Allah, virtually "imprison" women and enforce a strict code of conduct; they often kill those who oppose them, whether they be individuals or nations, such as when the terrorists flew into the towers of the World Trade Center, killing thousands.

Equally alarming, American evangelical churches in Africa are promoting government-sponsored anti-gay laws there that require friends, family members, and professionals, such as clergy or doctors, to report those who are gay. If they fail to do so, they can be punished by death.

Religious leaders have claimed to believe in and practice the Golden Rule: "Do unto others as you would have them do unto you," or, as expressed in the Islamic Sunnah, "No one of you is a believer until he desires for his brother that which he desires for himself."

Tragically, thoughtful people of many faiths are now observing that there are self-licensed religious leaders who indoctrinate their followers with hatred. They distort their perceptions and values and defy all that's humane in human communication by "inspiring" them to become agents of human destruction. Is this really what the Scriptures teach?

The prophet Malachi asked (ca. 500 BCE), "Have we not all one father? hath not one God created us? why do we deal treacherously every man against his brother, by profaning the covenant of our fathers?" (Malachi 2:10).

We need clear-thinking people to reign in the runaway extremism of some religious groups. Is it important that we do this? The survival of humanity's freedom to debate, act, and learn from experience how to guarantee the rights of all humans and how to value diversity is at stake. Thousands throughout history left their homes and countries in order to escape tyranny and find freedom of religion, which is inexorably linked to freedom of thought, freedom of the press, freedom of speech, freedom from molestation, and freedom from distorted and disastrous interpretations of these freedoms—and the Scriptures.

Evil has also been perpetrated by many self-professed religious leaders, groups, and individuals against other groups, whether they are believers or nonbelievers, straight people or gays, white people versus people of color, young versus old, and rich versus poor. The lowest form of thought is always trying to convince itself it is superior to someone else. That is why it is absolutely incumbent upon all of us who value true questioning and clear thinking—and a clear conscience—to prepare our young people to detect, avoid, and expose manipulators of thought.

When you think about it, have there been situations in your own life in which you wish you had asked questions before proceeding with some unkind act?

Individual willingness to ask questions stimulates collective thought in a positive way, advances humane behavior, and protects and strengthens society. At the very least, we should challenge our leaders by asking, "Do your beliefs and actions comply with the Golden Rule?" And if they profess to be Christian, ask if they obey what Christ Jesus called the Great Commandment: "Thou shalt love the Lord thy God with all thy heart, and with all thy soul, and with all thy mind. This is the first and great commandment. And the second is like unto it, Thou shalt love thy neighbour as thyself" (Matthew 22:37–39).

The following is a petition and commitment that can help unite thinkers in all religions:

The Daily Prayer

> "Thy kingdom come;" let the reign of divine Truth, Life, and Love be established in me, and rule out of me all sin; and may Thy Word enrich the affections of all mankind, and govern them! (*Church Manual* of The First Church of Christ, Scientist, p. 41)

PART II

MAJOR FIGURES AND THEMES IN THE BIBLE

3

ADAM AND EVE—THE SEQUEL

In this chapter I shall attempt to show that human thought is ever on the rise. It's not uncertainty or conflict that is rising. *Thought* is rising, and that's where you come in.

The following is another layer of the story about Adam and Eve. Do we really need another layer? Yes, because I just can't see leaving Adam in the doleful dumpster. You might wonder why anyone would care about these fictional symbols, but even though they *are* fictional, still many adults feel they are under "the curse of Adam." How stultifying! Perhaps it's time to explore further dimensions.

Let's suppose that Adam and Eve were actually human beings, not just legend. Would it be taboo to say so? Their story is a myth (more accurately, it is termed an "allegory"), but myth or allegory, it doesn't mean *lie*. A myth is just a fictional story, an explanation for something that has endured for centuries.

Why question the legend or try to supplant it with another story? Because Adam and Eve fell from grace, not into invisibility but into *fame*. According to the story, God rejected them, but they have lived on in the imaginations of writers and readers for centuries. It seems they lived on and live still as gods, knowing good and evil. The question then arises, Were they damned—or deified?

Can we write a human story about mythical characters? Sure. Washington Irving constructed a story about Rip Van Winkle, and Mary Shelley constructed a story about a larger-than-life character, Frankenstein. Biographers of historical figures face a similar dilemma: what, if anything, in the historical figure's history is true, and what has become mythologized, placing a taboo on further or unconventional interpretation?

According to the myth, Adam and Eve did become like gods, knowing good and evil and passing down to all descendants—to all mankind—an inheritance of accepting good *and* evil, a capacity for defying the one God, good. This myth much later became the substance of innumerable sermons. Religious leaders declared to their congregations, "This is the sorry state you are in as descendants of Adam and Eve. Like them, you are cut off from the presence and approval of God, and you can only hope for mercy when you die. But Jesus Christ may be able to prepare you to receive that 'undeserved' mercy."

Adam and Eve may seem to linger as mortal personalities knowing good and evil, with a much stronger influence than the vision of mankind in the *first* chapter of Genesis, who was created in the image and likeness of God. I must, therefore, choose *daily* between thinking that man has an inheritance of good *and* evil as stated in the second chapter, and the knowledge that man was created in the image and likeness of God—completely good, as the first chapter of Genesis sets forth when God pronounced all that He had made "very good." I thank God, our Father-Mother, who oversees and guarantees this creation of perfect man in God's likeness and who sent His Son to awaken us from the "Adam dream."

Can I question the traditional interpretation of Adam and Eve? I can. I can focus attention on the true story of man in Genesis 1—man endowed with dominion, the male and female created in God's own image (Genesis 1:26, 27). By agreeing to a divine identity, I learn to say, Adam and Eve did not fall on me. I am not suffering mental and physical damage. God did and does raise me to see suffering as a mental imposition to be put off. I am enabled to put on a robe of right thinking—rising thought—and to claim continuing ascension as God's "very good" creation.

How can truth-seekers keep rising as God's image and likeness if, in fact, every seeker is actually a sinner pinned down by an impenetrable load of damnation? Who wants to tackle *that* question? Everyone must grapple with that question, it seems to me, so here is a story about the redemption of mankind's alleged human parents. Perhaps it will help shift the focus away from Adam and Eve as eternal symbols of—and excuses for—*fallen* man. My story is called, "Adam and Eve—the Sequel."

The sequel to the story of Adam and Eve

In this discussion I go beyond the symbolism of disobedience and damnation and, instead, imagine Adam and Eve as actual people who kept on learning after they left the Garden of Eden. My basic theme is *thought rising* and learning from our mistakes. Adam and Eve exemplify thought rising and its beneficial effect on successive generations of enlightened thinkers, such as Noah, Abraham, and Jacob.

But the Adam story is a fable, you may say, devoid of facts and foundation, so it's problematic to treat Adam as a person, like Jacob. More than a fable, it's a *myth*. Not myth as a lie, but myth as one particular and enduring explanation.

The incentive and context for my refiguring of the Adam and Eve story is Sunday School, where I taught teenagers for more than twenty years. Elements of the Adam and Eve and Jacob/Israel stories appear frequently in Sunday School discussions. Because I prefer to teach through questions that generate discussion, I have devised questions that explore the continuing implications of the *influential serpent* in Genesis 2, and *disobedience redeemed* due to thought that began rising with the birth in Genesis 4 of Adam and Eve's third son, Seth, about whom we hear very little (verse 25).

This essay presents my record of discovery. It's not written for students, but I have them in mind as I pose fourteen questions that I hope students and teachers are asking, even if they are not articulating them at this moment. I'm inviting Sunday School teachers and anyone else to come and reason together with me about the sequel of Adam and Eve because the Adam and Eve story and its fallout have oppressed Christians for centuries.

Every culture has a "first man and woman" story. According to many scholars, the first Bible story, penned by the Hebrews about 1000 BCE, was about Adam and Eve—their "fall" in the garden of Eden, disobedience, and expulsion. But what is the rest of the history of this couple? They bore a son Cain who became a murderer, and a son Abel who was murdered by his brother Cain. Cain was "cursed from the earth" and condemned to be "a fugitive and a vagabond" (see Genesis 4:11–12). Later, Seth was born to Adam and Eve. Seth in turn had a son named Enos, and "then began men to call upon the name of the Lord" (Genesis 4:26), showing a shift in thought from self-satisfaction and indifference to acknowledgment of a power superior to their own—a divine will.

After several generations, Enoch was born, and he, along with his wife (who is not mentioned), begat Methuselah. "And all the days of Methuselah were nine hundred sixty and nine years" (Genesis 5:27). "And all the days of Enoch were three hundred and sixty and five years: And Enoch walked with God: and he was not; for God took him" (Genesis 5:23–24). This phrase, "and he was not, for God took him" implies to me that Enoch ascended. What dramatic progress in just a few generations, from expulsion … to ascension!

This rise from the physical to the ageless and spiritual is the natural progression of humans. Luke, for example, delineates the genealogy of Jesus, "being [as was supposed] the son of Joseph" (Luke 3:23–38).

The author of Genesis 6 describes the view of an anthropomorphic God and his displeasure with man (verses 5–13). "God saw that the wickedness of man was great in the earth, and that every imagination of the thoughts of his heart was only evil continually … And the Lord said, I will destroy man whom I have created from the face of the earth … But Noah found grace in the eyes of the Lord."

Noah's son Shem was especially blessed above his brothers (Genesis 9:26–27). From Shem descended the line leading to Abraham. Abraham's thought was definitely "on the rise" because of what he heard God telling him to do in Genesis 12—leave the known world of many gods and go to a yet-to-be-revealed land of the one Almighty God.

This spiritualization of thought, represented by Enos, Enoch, Noah, and Abraham, makes it obvious to me that the human race, as perceived by the Hebrews, was not on a downward spiral instigated by Adam and Eve. It was not condemned to endless sinning, but rather exalted to endless progression. Ascending thought is the law of being because God, Life, is the law of being.

Over a period of more than a thousand years, these men perceived and added to an up-ward-moving concept of God: Abraham, Isaac, Jacob/Israel, Joseph, Moses, Joshua, David, Elijah, Elisha, Isaiah, and Jeremiah. These men showed that Truth was ever guiding, caring, and transforming human consciousness, while at the same time destroying false images of thought. Love's pure fire consumed only the "tares," not the "wheat." It's a *puri*-fire"! Each of these men identified himself as an eyewitness, or an *"I-witness"* to God's presence with men—the great I AM as revealed to Moses (Exodus 3:14).

The prophet Isaiah described God's life-preserving words in this way:

> I have made the earth, and created man upon it: I, even my hands, have stretched out the heavens, and all their host have I commanded. I have raised him up in righteousness, and I will direct all his ways ... I the Lord speak righteousness, I declare things that are right ... Look unto me, and be ye saved, all the ends of the earth: for I am God, and there is none else (Isaiah 45:12–13, 19).

Unfortunately, innumerable religionists through the centuries have earned their keep by arguing for the sinful nature of man, ignoring the facts of Genesis 5 and ignoring the lights that were no doubt shined on their damned interpretation over the centuries, revoking it. Finally, a permanent light appeared in this dark sky regarding man's inheritance, as prophesied by Isaiah:

> I the Lord have called thee in righteousness, and will hold thine hand, and will keep thee, and give thee for a covenant of the people, for a light of the Gentiles; To open the blind eyes, to bring out the prisoners from the prison, and them that sit in darkness out of the prison house ... Behold, the former things are come to pass, and new things do I declare (Isaiah 42:6, 7, 9).

Jesus Christ taught not only the perfectibility but also the present perfection of man in God's image and likeness. These teachings, which proved that it is the nature of man to "turn to the Lord," walk with God, and "ascend," cannot be ignored, will never be forgotten, can never be discarded, and need to be acknowledged and protected.

As Paul wrote to the Corinthians, "God, who commanded the light to shine out of darkness, hath shined in our hearts, to give the light of the knowledge of the glory of God in the face of Jesus Christ" (II Corinthians 4:6).

Even before the birth of Jesus, the Christ was calling human consciousness to wake up, come forth from condemned and condemning states of thought, and receive and bring forth good. What a spiraling up and out toward infinity—within. It is God's, Life's, line, one straight upward-pointing line. It is not the down–up–down–up of doubt/hope, sorrow/joy, and defeat/triumph. True living has always meant ascending.

How can this brief history of the sinning, limited, mortal Adam-man and the spiritual, pure, and unlimited Christ-man be woven into Sunday School lessons for teenagers? I'm glad you asked. Do you have more questions than answers? Here are some points to consider.

The Adam and Eve story: Genesis 2:6–5:32

Below are some questions about the book of Genesis and the story of Adam and Eve. Let's be rational, reason together, and respond to these questions one at a time.

1. *Genesis* **means beginning. What began in the book of Genesis?**

Two separate and distinct creations by two Gods with opposite natures. The God of Genesis 1 is a God of order, harmony, light, and goodness, and His creation, including man, reflects His nature. The God of Genesis 2 is a God of good *and evil*, or discord, conflict, materiality, and fear; and *His* creation—Adam and Eve, the serpent, and the garden of Eden—reflect Him in their duplicity, lies, guilt, fear, and death.

2. **When was the Adam and Eve story written? (Genesis 2:6 through 5:32)**

Scholars believe this story of a material creation appeared when David was king of all Israel, around 1000 BCE.

3. **When was the story of true and spiritual creation written as given in the first chapter of Genesis?**

Some scholars believe it was written in late 500 BCE—about four hundred years *after* the story of Adam and Eve.

4. **Why do you think the Adam and Eve story appeared about four hundred years before the story of spiritual creation? (Genesis 1:1 through Genesis 2:5)**

Thought that sits still and does nothing may have seemed easier than thought that rises—reaches up and ascends. I'm continuing to "seek and find," and I hope you will join me.

5. **What followed in the wake of Adam and Eve?**

Everything was cursed—the ground, Adam, Eve, and the serpent. Before Adam and Eve left their paradise, God "cursed" the serpent, condemned it to eat dust, and declared that the seed of the woman shall bruise the serpent's head and the serpent shall bruise his heel (see Genesis 3:14–15). It would seem that the serpent knew how to disguise itself, appearing to be a fellow being, worthy of a hearing.

6. **And what does this mean for us? Are we guilty or innocent?**

We must keep crushing the head of the serpent—evil (the temptation to feel guilty and condemned)—even as it tries to bite our heels when we turn away from material sense and march forward in our God-given dominion, to the kingdom of heaven within. Man, created in the image and likeness of God, is forever innocent.

7. **Does this imply perpetual warfare between goodness and evil?**

God forbid! And God did forbid! According to the true story of creation, God gave man dominion "over every creeping thing" (Genesis 1:26). Dominion is not to be interpreted as domination but includes loving care, goodness, and consideration rather than exploitation and destruction.

8. **What happened to Adam and Eve after they involuntarily left the garden of Eden?**

Something good must have happened to Adam and Eve after they left the garden of Eden, because good things happened after the birth of their third son, Seth (see Genesis 4:25–26).

9. What did Adam and Eve learn during the next 930 years? (See Genesis 5:5.)

Perhaps they learned that God, good, is spiritual, not material or to be found in matter. Perhaps they also learned that God is Love and loving, and hence began to practice what came to be known as the Golden Rule: do unto others as you would have them do unto you. This Golden Rule—or something quite similar to it—has been incorporated into most world religions.

10. Did the writers of the Adam and Eve story regard man only as a sinner?

The writers of the Adam and Eve story appeared to regard man as a learner needing continuing education. These writers told about the third son, Seth, and the ascending (not the sinning) thought of man, culminating in the ascension of Enoch.

The nature of sin and sinner

Sin cannot be a fact, because God, good, didn't make anything unlike Himself; therefore sin must be unreal. Sin is a belief that something can overpower God, good. Sin claims that mortals did, indeed, invert God's creation and call it material. This claim of sin is that man is born a sinner and is therefore guilty, and that man is material now with only a tenuous hope of receiving a spiritual nature in the hereafter.

Creation seems to fall but does not actually fall. The sun seems to set, but it's the earth that's moving. Most theology teaches that man is born into matter. The five material senses reinforce this belief, and people attending church repeat this notion and accept it as normal and natural. But Christ Jesus, our way shower, looked about at the sick and sinning and saw only God's creation as sinless, whole, and free. He transformed both the body and the thought of those he healed by understanding what God did, and did not, create.

The following is a poem by Emily F. Seal. She offers a question for all Christians to ask. Note that the answer in the first verse reveals that man is not a sinner but is "His beloved son."

> What is thy birthright, man,
> Child of the perfect One;
> What is thy Father's plan
> For His beloved son?
>
> Thou art Truth's honest child,
> Of pure and sinless heart;
> Thou treadest undefiled
> In Christly paths apart.

Vain dreams shall disappear
As Truth dawns on the sight;
The phantoms of thy fear
Shall flee before the light.

Take then the sacred rod;
Thou art not error's thrall;
Thou hast the gift of God—
Dominion over all.

(Hymn No. 382, *Christian Science Hymnal*, by Emily F. Seal. Used
courtesy of The Mary Baker Eddy Collection.)

Some religious leaders, including media evangelists, assert that man is a sinner. Does that
mean man is not only dirty but dirt itself—like Adam, made of the dust? Does that mean
that God, infinite good, created man bad? Surely religious leaders want to preach the Word
of God, not the words of fear and human opinion. The Bible, the Word of God, presents
many examples of what God thinks of man. The author of Genesis, Chapter 1, declares that
God made man in His own image and likeness. And in the story of Job, several "learned
friends" (friends?) argued that Job was destitute and diseased because he was guilty. But
Job held on to a higher hope and heard Elihu say, "God hath made man upright, but they
have sought out many inventions."

Jesus looked at sinners but beheld the child of God, and he said to all, not just to his disciples, "Be ye therefore perfect, even as your Father which is in heaven is perfect" (Matthew
5:48). I would like to think religious leaders look for words that reflect the Word of God
as presented throughout the Bible. They do not look to fear or human opinion. Indeed,
mankind has much to be repented of, and much to rule out in consciousness. But people
are not helped to achieve this goal by being labeled as sinners. In the following verses, Paul
repeatedly reminds Christians to remember who they are and act accordingly.

- If any man be in Christ he is a new creature: old things are passed away; behold, all
  things are become new (II Corinthians 5:17).
- What? Know ye not that your body is the temple of the Holy Ghost which is in you,
  which ye have of God, and that ye are not your own (I Corinthians 6:10).
- In Him we live and move and have our being (Acts 17:28).

Another description of God's view of man is found in I John 3:

Behold, what manner of love the Father hath bestowed upon us, that we
should be called the sons of God: therefore the world knoweth us not,

because it knew him not. Beloved, now are we the sons of God, and it doth not yet appear what we shall be: but we know that, when he shall appear, we shall be like him; for we shall see him as he is. And every man that hath this hope in him purifieth himself, even as he is pure.

Man is not a sinner, but is the idea of God, forever expressing and reflecting what God knows and does. God is Truth, and "Truth is made manifest by its effects upon the human mind and body, healing sickness and destroying sin" (*Science and Health*, p. 316:9).

11. Are there any lies about Adam and Eve that all of us are still dealing with?

Yes, the lie that evil did have an origin and is real, and that we must look for the origin of particular evils in our own lives. In other words, we must find someone or something to blame. The apostle Paul knew all too well the importance of focusing on what is true and good. Thank God, Paul received the light of the Christ and learned to live by this spiritual creed he gave us:

> Finally, brethren, whatsoever things are true, whatsoever things are honest, whatsoever things are just, whatsoever things are pure, whatsoever things are lovely, whatsoever things are of good report; if there be any virtue, and if there be any praise, think on these things. Those things, which ye have both learned, and received, and heard, and seen in me, do: and the God of peace shall be with you (Philippians 4:8–9).

12. Why do these lies about the nature of men and women persist, and how are you and I dealing with these lies?

These lies persist only if one believes the serpent. The serpent is allegedly biting man's heel as man moves forward and upward. You and I know better. The author of Psalm 91 says that God shall "give his angels charge over thee, to keep thee in all thy ways. They shall bear thee up in their hands, lest thou dash thy foot against a stone. Thou shalt tread upon the lion and adder; the young lion and the dragon shalt thou trample under feet" (verses 11–13).

As I yield to the care of God's angel messages expressed as my thought, I trample the serpent of limited, evil thinking and disable it. I must play my part in proving that God's will is all good for all mankind all the time. This is demonstrating that God's will is done "as in heaven, so on earth."

In depictions of the Adam and Eve saga in classical art, the serpent is materialized as a *snake*, a member of the animal kingdom, which can sting or squeeze the life out of man. The serpent's attributes, however, are entirely mental, not physical.

The term *animal magnetism*, according to Merriam-Webster.com, is defined as "a mysterious force claimed by Mesmer to enable him to hypnotize patients; a magnetic charm or appeal." Perhaps you remember learning in school that man also belongs to the *animal kingdom*.

One time I was talking about animal magnetism in Sunday School with my students. A ten-year-old asked me if animals were bad, clearly disapproving of linking good animals to bad magnetism. I assured him that the term *animal magnetism* did not condemn animals. I alluded to the fact that parents have been heard to say to children, "You are eating like an animal!" Or, "You're acting like an animal." The Merriam-Webster online dictionary describes *animal* as a person who behaves in a wild, aggressive, or unpleasant way," and some synonyms would include brutish, untamed, physical, and sensual. An animal is less refined and less socially responsible than a human.

A serpent is not only a snake but also a creature or "a treacherous person; an insidious enemy," according to Dictionary.com. Lies, deception, and malice describe the mental tactics of the serpent in the garden of Eden to separate God from His creation. Conceptually and artistically, however, this serpent has always been depicted as physical, an animal, and a living thing.

This depiction has tempted humans through the centuries to look for the material form (the person) instead of looking at the evil *mentality* that would harm them. Yes, *mentality* implies a material person with a mind, as does *creature.* That which is mental seems to be embodied, but is actually disembodied until a person agrees to embody it. Either way, one needs to destroy evil thoughts to be rid of them.

What would harm humans is not other humans (other living things) but simply a mistaken sense of *mind* or mentality as being mortal and evil. But God, good, is *divine* Mind—the Mind that the apostle Paul said was in Christ Jesus.

Christ Jesus thoroughly taught his followers how to find and claim their true spiritual nature as the way to redeem their apparent human nature. In his Sermon on the Mount, he commanded, "Be ye therefore perfect, even as your Father which is in heaven is perfect" (Matthew 5:48). He was not commanding them to have perfect material bodies, but to be perfect in *thought*, to identify only with perfect motives and acts. He didn't expect them—or us—to be perfect *in spite of* having material natures, but *because of* having *spiritual* natures.

Blame

One of the serpent's other deceptive tactics is to tempt us to blame something or someone for evil. In Genesis 3, Eve blamed the serpent for their disobedience, but Adam blamed Eve.

This unenlightened "blame game" has persisted among humans, especially in the oppression of women. All over the world, women are excluded from educational, professional, and other opportunities. Traditionally, in many Christian churches, synagogues and mosques, women have been excluded from leadership positions.

Note that God does not specify that "male and female"' are unequal, but equal, made in His image and likeness: "And God said, Let us make man in our image, after our likeness: So God created man in his own image, in the image of God created he him; male and female created he them" (Genesis 1:26–27).

This declaration in Genesis 1 does not provide any basis for inequality or blame for anyone or anything, but full equality and love—expressing God's nature—in and for all His harmless creation.

Even Jesus' disciples had to learn this lesson (see John 9:1-3). When they came upon the man "blind from his birth," the disciples looked for someone to blame, asking Jesus, "Master, who hath sinned, this man, or his parents, that he was born blind?" Christ Jesus responded, "Neither hath this man sinned, nor his parents: but that the works of God should be made manifest in him"—in other words, "Don't blame the man or his parents. Regard the situation as an opportunity, a call, to see the works of God made manifest."

Blame illustrates thought sliding downward, contrary to the pattern of thought rising, as was exemplified by Enos, Enoch, Noah, and Abraham. Blame is the action of mortal mind, the mistaken concept of man's actual Mind, God, that tries to impose blame in order to divert attention from its own error and hypocrisy.

13. How "original" was the sin?

People talk about "original sin." Instead of obeying and trusting God, Adam and Eve believed the serpent's promise, and they ate of "the tree of knowledge of good and evil" (Genesis 2:17), hoping to "be as gods, knowing good and evil" (Genesis 3:5). Their disobedience could better be called their sin or first sin. The popular label, *original sin*, implies that people would be reproducing a sinful original indefinitely, and indeed, people have been led to believe that they are copying Adam and Eve and disobeying God. No. People choose either to ignore sin or simply to deny it. No one is merely a helpless, thoughtless printed piece of matter spewed out by a machine making billions of copies.

When Christ Jesus told his disciples to pray "after this manner," he included the line "And lead us not into temptation, but deliver us from evil" (Matthew 6:13). Fourteen modern translations of the Bible (1961–2008) use the term *evil one* in this verse, whereas only four translations use the term *evil*. Can there be an "evil one" alongside the one God? If God is infinite good, any "evil one" would be a liar and usurper.

Because sin doesn't have an origin, it can't be original. Sin can only be an unthinking dream or a moment of forgetfulness, and God would make neither of those! Sin is like suddenly wondering whether it's Tuesday or Wednesday. The truth is quickly determined, and the momentary uncertainty is forgotten. All of us want to know Truth, God, so we refuse confusion; we refuse sin.

Was it original and clever to defy the command of the Lord who was providing all good to Adam and Eve? No. Sin was not original in the sense of being first *or* of being clever.

Unlike Adam and Eve, our Bible friends in Genesis and Exodus—Noah, Abraham, Jacob/Israel, Joseph, Moses, and Joshua—all chose to obey God. Their thought and spiritual understanding kept rising. Might Adam and Eve also have chosen good, and could that have been when their son Seth was born? Thought kept on rising for many generations, and finally Enoch was able to bypass death by ascending.

Later, the prophet Elijah left earth's scene by the same route. He ascended, and Elisha witnessed it. If we make good choices by knowing that God is the Life and Mind of man, we, too, will keep rising and ascending, coming into fuller knowledge of our spiritual nature and ability to obey Jesus' command to heal the sick, cast out devils, and raise the dead (see Matthew 10:8).

14. Was there resurrection? What was their resurrection?

So, did Adam and Eve wake up and rise up? For the sake of "Adam and Eve—The Sequel," let's say they did. Evidence that they could have is that Jesus knew himself to be the Son of man as well as the Son of God. Jesus was not slipping into a dual identity when he identified himself both ways. I think he knew that the Christ-man came first and ensured that the Adam-man as well as the Jesus-man would rise from the deadened Adam thought and ascend in his thinking.

The "refigured" Adam and Eve, the people, made good choices that lifted them up. Adam and Eve, the symbols and so-called originators of mortal man, seem permanently locked into the stereotype called fallen man.

Let us remember that the term *man*—God's man—means man and woman. It's not man that's clay or dust watered by mist and then hardened. *Thought* is the clay, ever malleable, still and now. This poem by Mary Alice Dayton is set to music in the *Christian Science Hymnal*:

Eternal Mind the Potter is,
And thought th' eternal clay:
The hand that fashions is divine,
His works pass not away.
Man is the noblest work of God,
His beauty, power and grace,
Immortal; perfect as his Mind
Reflected face to face.

Mortal mind (or, as I like to call it, *mortal-no-mind)* stiffens when required to yield, but its rigidity dissolves like an icicle exposed to the sun. Stanza three of the hymn above affirms, as do we,

God's will is done; His kingdom come;
The Potter's work is plain.
The longing to be good and true
Has brought the light again.
And man does stand as God's own child,
The image of His love.
Let gladness ring from every tongue,
And heaven and earth approve.

(Hymn No. 51, by Mary Alice Dayton, *Christian Science Hymnal*. Used courtesy of The Mary Baker Eddy Collection.)

Probation and progression

Probation and progression comprise the two-rail track of ascending thought. What inspires the journey? It must be a revelation in human consciousness of absolute truths about our spiritual identity. This idea inspires us to call the serpent *sense* and its material sense testimony *untrue*. The result is always, eventually, correction of thought, removal of the material sense testimony, and the realization in human experience that divine Love meets the human need, always. Did Adam and Eve, the people, get onto this two-rail track?

The awakening to true identity is instant as well as constant, illustrating progression and probation. While he was on earth, Jesus' understanding kept rising higher. In his ascension, he continued to rise.

Those of us in Sunday School learning about Adam and Eve need to recognize that the characters and stories in the Bible are not just storybook tales with morals. These Biblical characters are our good friends. Can we interact with them in the same way we interact with our friends at school? I ask God to show me what I need to learn from the apparent motives and acts of these Bible friends, as well as from school, family, and church friends; don't you?

Speaking the Truth...

Since the days of Abraham and the dawning realization that there is only one Almighty God, attempts have been made to corrupt and pervert true religion, which nurtures discovery of the relationship between perfect God and perfect man. May enlightened religionists always be stepping up to tell how the correct understanding of God and man enables them to heal themselves and others!

There are clergy who insist on the sinfulness of man. Are they "speaking the truth"? They could get a better perspective from the Shepherd's point of view as depicted in the Bible. Jesus said,

> The thief cometh not, but for to steal, and to kill, and to destroy: I am come that they might have life, and that they might have it more abundantly. I am the good shepherd: the good shepherd giveth his life for the sheep. But he that is an hireling, and not the shepherd, whose own the sheep are not, seeth the wolf coming, and leaveth the sheep, and fleeth: and the wolf catcheth them, and scattereth the sheep. The hireling fleeth, because he is an hireling, and careth not for the sheep. I am the good shepherd, and know my sheep, and am known of mine (John 10:10–14).

Don't all of us have an obligation to mankind to refuse the lie of the Adam dream? Wouldn't this refusal add to the mental force that deflates the balloon of hateful preaching, the preaching of hate? Some of the old, less enlightened thinking of the Old Testament is still carried forward today by those who preach an anthropomorphic God who can love and hate, but this is in stark contrast to what Genesis 1 and the New Testament teach about God. The Gospel of John says, "God is a Spirit" (John 4:24), and I John 4:16 states, "God is love" and that "now are the sons of God" (I John 3:2).

Individuals are becoming more alert, and society as a whole is rising to resist the disservice of bigoted or merely charismatic spokespersons.

Protestant as well as Roman Catholic churches are being more careful not to tolerate sexism, racism, and commercialization from the pulpit. Sexism and racism are distortions that stereotype humans and relegate all to limited roles in the progress of mankind. Placing arbitrary limitations on some is obviously antithetical to progress for all.

A Muslim, by definition, is "one who surrenders to God." A Christian is "one who professes belief in the teachings of Jesus Christ." The journey toward purer *surrendering* and *professing* is either aided or distorted by the clergy of any religion.

Is warfare needed? Yes, but what kind of warfare and against what? Let no one imagine he or she is "conquering sin" by eliminating those who think differently or do not bend to his or her will. Let us help save mankind from self-destruction by correctly defining this sin we are to conquer—in thought—through mental warfare on the side of good.

Every human must fight the good fight of yielding, surrendering, to the fact of perfect God and perfect man. The prophet Ezekiel said, "For I have no pleasure in the death of him that dieth, saith the Lord God: wherefore turn yourselves, and live ye" (Ezekiel 18:32).

Some religious leaders justify their dim view as being God's view. They highlight passages in the Bible where God initially condemns "man," who broke away from God to become his own boss and set his own rules.

Does any religion other than Christian Science highlight passages where God awakens man out of the dream of separation from God (Genesis 2) and wakens thought to claim his (or her) original unity with God as His image and likeness (Genesis 1)? Many passages in other books of the Bible also awaken man out of the dream of separation from God. For example, "As for me, I will behold thy face in righteousness: I shall be satisfied, when I awake, with thy likeness" (Psalm 17:15).

And also, Psalm 103 praises God, good, and His continual blessings:

> Bless the Lord, O my soul: and all that is within me, bless his holy name. Bless the Lord, O my soul, and forget not all his benefits: Who forgiveth all thine iniquities; who healeth all thy diseases; Who redeemeth thy life from destruction; who crowneth thee with lovingkindness and tender mercies; Who satisfieth thy mouth with good things; so that thy youth is renewed like the eagle's (verses 1–5).

God keeps doing these things, and blessed is the one who knows all that God is doing as expressed in the Psalms:

- forgiving all iniquities
- healing all diseases

- redeeming from destruction
- crowning with lovingkindness and tender mercies
- satisfying the mouth with good things
- executing righteousness and judgment for all that are oppressed
- making known His ways
- being merciful and gracious

Judgment and destruction

Awakening from the Adam dream means mentally accepting and holding to the Truth, God's perfect view of His spiritual offspring. Does God judge and destroy? Yes, God judges and destroys the darkness called sin, disease, and death. But no, God does not destroy *man*, even though he or she seems to dream on. God judges each man and woman to be a true image and likeness, now and forever.

Rising thought is rational as well as unselfish, protective, and creative. The serpent incites extremism, but men and women are at fault who neglect or refuse to handle the serpent of evil and hatred and tread it underfoot. Men and women must demand higher thought and action from themselves and from their religious leaders. Mortals must assert their freedom and dominion, not ignore it or be uncertain about it.

All are being called upon to focus again on the Golden Rule, which is recognized and professed in all major religions. Many describe the Golden Rule as the basis for universal human rights. When it is lived, it is evidence of God governing His creation. Christ Jesus said it this way in Matthew 7:12: "All things whatsoever ye would that men should do to you, do ye even so to them: for this is the law and the prophets." Islam words it this way: "No one of you is a believer until he desires for his brother that which he desires for himself" (Al-Bukhari and MuslimSunnah.com). The Golden Rule leads the way out of the Adam dream, which says God is both good and evil and therefore so is man. It reveals, instead, the man created by the all-good, all-loving God of the first chapter of Genesis, who created man in His image and likeness, "and God saw everything that He had made, and behold it was very good" (Genesis 1: 31).

"Adam and Eve—The Sequel," and their heritage: A summary

We need not return to the garden of Eden, for we have moved onward and upward, as did our human progenitors, to a more perfect and permanent place—the consciousness of God.

Adam and Eve are more than just symbols of humans defying God and demanding minds of their own. I like to think of these individuals as symbols of rising thought yielding more and more to the one divine Mind, God. I have presented this story of "Adam and Eve—The Sequel" because mankind needs to know that it is not cursed.

With this new understanding could not Adam and Eve—if they had been real—have turned away from sin, blame, and curse and grasped something of what the Biblical prophets and the Messiah would later make clear: man—male and female—created in God's image and supplied with dominion over all evil.

Thought kept rising through the generations after the Adam and Eve allegory. Thought keeps rising today like the irresistible ocean tide, lifting every ship in the sea, every boat in the harbor. There is no "yesterday"; there is just *yes*—today. The zenith of rising thought was the resurrection of Jesus, and now we all can "sing of Easter gladness that rejoices every day":

> Let us sing of Easter gladness
> That rejoices every day,
> Sing of hope and faith uplifted;
> Love has rolled the stone away.
> Lo, the promise and fulfillment,
> Lo, the man whom God hath made,
> Seen in glory of an Easter
> Crowned with light that cannot fade.
>
> (Hymn No. 171, by Frances Thompson Hill, *Christian Science Hymnal*,
> © 1932, renewed 1960, The Christian Science Board of Directors. Used
> with permission.)

In my version of "Adam and Eve—The Sequel," both Adam and Eve learned more about the fatherhood and motherhood of God, which illustrates the transforming power of God, who is Love. Again, we learn—we continue learning—that the history of a human family does not devolve into persistent problems or extreme conditions. These problems and conditions are felt as attacks on one's mind-body, which disturb, disrupt, or dis-ease.

In my hypothetical version, Adam and Eve modeled, as we also model, the rising thought of resurrection, rising in stages from death to life. Each stage calls for a yielding to perfect God and the perfect idea of *man as His image and likeness*. Each stage includes the ongoing effort to dismantle any "stage" on which *mortal no-mind* would act out a drama of sin and suffering, a drama that particularizes and individualizes the dream of *mortal no-mind* and evil—a belief in a creator opposed to God.

But in the words of this song, here's what God, the great I AM is doing for me and you:

> I am holding you, I am knowing you.
> I am minding you, and causing you.
> I am blessing you, and cherishing you,
> My own image, expression, reflection so true.

("I Am Holding You," Susan Mack, © 2009 The Solo Committee. Used with permission.)

Why did you celebrate Adam and Eve?

I have celebrated Adam and Eve not because I want to create a better human origin or better parents. I do not inherit from any humans, only from Father-Mother God. I have tried to follow the command, "Mark the perfect man, and behold the upright: for the end of that man is peace" (Psalm 37:37) where *mark* means to pay attention to, take notice of, or consider.

My end, their end, is peace that has no end. For as long as I am aware of human beings, I must see them as rising in self-knowledge, in the knowledge of perfect selfhood. Jesus is ever the ultimate teacher, showing each of us how to better express the Christ-man, or the "ideal" man that Jesus presented.

Now let's summarize what we have learned from the myth of Adam and Eve and their heritage:

1. Their first son was a murderer. Their second son was murdered. Their third son reversed this downward spiral and set in motion an ascending thought. Enoch ascended.

2. Noah obeyed God and kept mankind afloat.

3. Abraham heard the call to leave the land of many gods and go to the land of one Almighty God.

4. Jacob struggled but accepted a more spiritual view of man and received the new name of Israel. Soon he was reunited with his brother, Esau.

5. King David united a divided nation and wrote many psalms about man's relationship to God.

6. The prophet Isaiah rejected the image of an anthropomorphic God and prophesied the coming of the Messiah.

7. Christ Jesus taught and proved that man is spiritual, not material; man is one with God.

8. The apostle Paul urged man to have the mind of Christ.

Now let's look at what happens when we accept the second story of creation—the allegory of the "fall" of Adam and Eve—as true:

1. False teachers in many major religions deny the essential goodness of men and women. They teach that God condemns some of His creation to hell; therefore, as spokespersons for God they feel entitled to do the same.

2. Individuals are becoming more alert, and society as a whole is rising to resist the disservice of bigoted or merely charismatic spokespersons for any religion.

3. For more than two thousand years, people have been arguing for and against the sinful nature of men and women. Through our thoughts as well as our words, we are either part of that argument (the Adam dream) or we choose not to participate and deny it with the truth.

4. Some church leaders believe and try to convince others that sin, disease, and death are real, but that God might help you accept these conditions—"with grace"—or might deliver you.

5. Some cultures and religions have been weakened because they do not give men and women the same rights. The struggle goes on, but Christianity has righted many of these wrongs and will eventually right them all through the conviction that every man and every woman has the right to pursue involvement and advancement in any and every field of worthy endeavor.

Are you ready to confirm what you've learned by filling in some blanks? Let's summarize what we've said about Adam and Eve and their heritage (for answers, see the list above).

1. Their first son was a m_____. Their second son was m_____. Their third son reversed this downward spiral and set in motion an ascending thought. Enoch a_____.

2. Noah o_____ God and kept mankind afloat.

3. Abraham heard the call to leave the land of m_____ g_____ and go to the land of one Almighty God.

4. J_____ struggled but accepted a more spiritual view of man and the new name of I_____. He was ready to be reunited with his b_____, Esau.

5. King D_____ united a divided nation and wrote many p_____ about man's relationship to God

6. The prophet Isaiah rejected the image of an anthropomorphic _____. He prophesied a Messiah.

7. Christ Jesus taught and proved that man is s_____, not m_____; man is one with God.

8. The apostle _____ instructed us to have the mind of Christ.

4

THE TOWER OF BABEL, ABRAHAM, CHRIST JESUS, JOHN THE REVELATOR, AND THE TOWERING REVELATION GIVEN TO MARY BAKER EDDY

The Tower of Babel: What it might mean

The Tower of Babel, built on the plain of Shinar, never was finished. It could not be completed, because it did not include God. The tower expressed the people's fear of being forgotten—or perhaps their desire to be seen as *special*.

The Tower of Babel was not intended to exalt God and therefore had no foundation. Having no foundation, it crumbled. The Tower of Babel portrays the vanity of self-glorification and the failure of men without God. Did the Tower of Babel represent a stage in human thought as it coped with the flood that had destroyed the earth?

The Tower of Babel: What it looked like

The author of Genesis 11 may have had in mind a Babylonian temple tower, or "ziggurat." One such ziggurat was known to have existed before 1000 BCE (Before the Common Era; CE refers to the advent of Christ Jesus). It was like a step pyramid, three hundred feet square and rising three hundred feet into the air. The top was reached by a stairway. The specific phrase *Tower of Babel* does not appear in the Old Testament. The descendants of Noah said, "Let us build us a city and a tower … lest we be scattered …" (Genesis 11:4). The tower came to be known as Babel because "the Lord did there confound the language of all the earth" (Genesis 11:9). There is neither stone nor lime on the Plain of Shinar, so bricks were used. Babylonia was the land (country), and Babylon was its political and religious center. (See *The New Westminster Dictionary of the Bible*, H. Gehman, The Westminster Press, Philadelphia, Pennsylvania, 1952.)

The Tower of Babel: The story in Genesis 11

The sons of Noah "went forth from the ark" after it rested on high ground. Some settled the fertile land between two rivers, the Tigris and the Euphrates. As they settled, they desired to build a city and a tower to distinguish their city, a tower "whose top may reach unto heaven; and let us make us a name, lest we be scattered abroad upon the face of the whole earth" (see Genesis 11:4–9). Apparently their motive was not to make known the one God but to ensure their own survival and identity. At any rate, the author of Genesis perceived that the Lord came down to see the city and the tower, which the children of men built.

> And the Lord said, Behold, the people is one, and they have all one language; and this they begin to do: and now nothing will be restrained from them, which they have imagined to do. Go to, let us go down, and there confound their language, that they may not understand one another's speech (Genesis 11:5–7).

The original purpose in building the city and the tower "whose top may reach unto heaven" was for the descendants of Noah to make themselves "a name, lest we be scattered abroad upon the face of the whole earth." Ironically, this fate was precisely the result of their attempt: "So the Lord scattered them abroad from thence upon the face of all the earth: and they left off to build the city" (Genesis 11:8).

The author of Psalm 48 wrote of "the city of our God … the mountain of His holiness," not of a plain in Shinar. Perhaps the author had heard of the demise of the materialistic city and tower of Babylon. The collection of psalms grew from about 1000 to 165 BCE, a period of about eight hundred years (see "Bible Time-Line" from *The Reforming Power of the Scriptures, A Biography of the English Bible,* by Mary Metzner Trammel and William G. Dawley, The Christian Science Publishing Society, Boston, 1996).

Babel/Babylon

Babel, the Hebrew word for Babylon, was a city from prehistoric times. It was a primary region of Nimrod's kingdom (Nimrod was a great-grandson of Noah; see Genesis 10:8–10). Built on the ruins of an older city, the city of Babylon was the splendid capital of Nebuchadnezzar in about 500 BCE. Various historians describe the city: two walls, one hundred gates made of massive brick towers, and timber houses up to four stories high. The Euphrates River flowed through the city, and there is a field of the ruins of Babylon in the suburbs of modern Baghdad (*The Anchor Yale Bible Dictionary,* New York, Doubleday, 1990, Vol. 1, p. 563).

Isaiah (in the 700s BCE) and Jeremiah (in the 600s BCE) both prophesied that Babylon would become desolate, and that is what it is today (see Isaiah 13:19–22 and Jeremiah 51:37). Babylon had always been a symbol of pride and ambition; thus it was destined to fall. (The mystic Babylon referred to in Revelation, however, was not the Tower of Babel). What was Babylon? According to the *Anchor Yale Bible Dictionary*, "As a symbol, Babylon embraces more than the empire, city, and culture of Rome. It is the sphere of idolatry and worldliness under the temporary control of Satan, a worldliness in opposition to the people of and work of God, a worldliness epitomized first by Babylon and then by Rome" (Vol. 1, p. 566).

Babylon and the Jews

Babylon conquered the kingdom of Judah in 598 BCE, and the city of Jerusalem was finally destroyed in 586 BCE. The temple was destroyed, and ten thousand Jews were taken captive to Babylon. When Cyrus, king of Persia, conquered Babylon in 538 BCE, he allowed the Jews to return to Israel. During this same period, Buddha was active in India, and Confucius in China. These men were contemporaries of Jeremiah and Isaiah. Babylon was conquered by Alexander the Great, and in 312 BCE it was dismantled by Seleucus for the building of another city farther north.

Babel/babble

The author of this story about the city and tower of Babel was also accounting for the origin of various languages. There were many myths about the origin of multiple languages. One myth about the confusion of languages was that it was the result of a rivalry between two gods. The Hebrew author derived the word *Babel* from a word meaning confuse, confound. This story, however, is not a scientific explanation of multiple languages. Many differences in languages develop because of the separation of individuals from other individuals.

Did the builders of Babel literally start speaking the languages they would use in the places to which they would be scattered? Or did the builders have various and conflicting motives and reasons, and therefore they simply couldn't understand or imagine what a fellow builder was talking about as he spoke his mind? The builders may have assumed unity and have had no expectation of being scattered. They apparently did not ask God to show them how to establish a city and become "a people." Their confused thoughts were a mixture, perhaps, of fear, ignorance, and the sin of selfishness.

The reverse image of Babel

The chaos that resulted from the attempt to build a tower at Babel is the reverse image of what would come after Christ Jesus fully explained the relationship between God and man. After Jesus' ascension on the day of Pentecost, multitudes were gathered with one accord to receive the blessing God has always intended for man. Peter reminded the apostles that God had said through the prophet Joel, "I will pour out my Spirit upon all flesh" (Acts 2:14–17). Still today, every man and woman must choose between the fruitless efforts to storm heaven and the fruitful effort to receive God's outpouring grace.

The builders at the Tower of Babel became unable to communicate. They were divided by language and scattered. Was this the first Diaspora? At Pentecost, on the other hand, the multitudes heard the message of the Holy Spirit as though it were in their "own tongue." The Lord confounded the languages at the Tower of Babel because the builders' motives and acts were self-centered rather than God-centered. At Pentecost, the apostles' pure motive was to come together to worship God. When multitudes then gathered, every man heard the apostles speak in his own native tongue.

Abram/Abraham

Babylonia was a land of pagan gods, but man, creation of the one all-knowing Mind, God, could think beyond the concept of many gods, and Abram did. Man-made gods cannot truly satisfy. Abram was ready for the higher concept of one God. He distinctly heard God tell him to leave pagan Babylonia and go to a yet unnamed land, the land of Canaan. Abram came into this land around 1800 BCE, ten generations after Noah's son Shem. "And Terah took Abram his son, and Lot the son of Haran his son's son, and Sarai his daughter in law, his son Abram's wife; and they went unto Haran, and dwelt there" (Genesis 11:31).

Some Bible readers may consider *Adam* to be "the first man," but how could that be? *Abram* is a much better candidate for the first man because he was ready to acknowledge that there is only one God. Abram enters the human drama about 1850 BCE, nine hundred years before the Genesis stories are compiled. The authors of the Genesis stories about Adam and Eve, and Noah and Enoch do not indicate any knowledge of Abraham. He was progenitor of the Hebrews, faithful to God and friend of God. Abraham, not Adam, was the principled example of man reflecting and obeying God. His grandson Jacob would achieve the next major breakthrough—his recognition that man is meant to be a prince, having "power with God and with men" (Genesis 32:28).

Abraham's nature was further defined in relation to his nephew Lot. Lot yearned for the man-made structures of a city. When Sodom and Gomorrah imploded from immorality, Lot and his daughters barely escaped. Lot's wife was not ready for a complete renunciation of materialism, and she turned into a pillar of salt. Salty tears, perhaps?

When Abram was ninety-nine years old, God appeared to him and changed his name to Abraham. God made a covenant with Abraham that he should be a father of many nations, giving him the land as an everlasting possession and promising him that He would be their God. A covenant is the opposite of a curse. Adam was cursed and dismissed from the garden, but God blessed Abraham and his seed (see Genesis 17:1–8). Abraham knew the value of rising up in thought and going with God's plan.

God's plan was not clearly known until it was revealed to Abraham. Before Abraham, the builders of the Tower of Babel appeared not to have any interest in God's plan, only in their own plan to reach heaven. The God as revealed in Genesis chapter 1 surely had nothing to do with the story of Babel. Perhaps Babel's later inhabitants made up this story because they wanted an explanation of the existence of so many languages or of the brick ruins they found.

The first chapter of Genesis was written years after the story that began in chapter 2. There are two distinct accounts of the creation of man. The anthropomorphic view of the Lord God that began in Genesis 2 could not prevent readers from learning a vital lesson from the story of Babel about how mankind is to see itself rising in thought toward a better understanding of its relationship to God.

The Babylonians attempted to build a tower. There are towers on today's landscape as well. Almost everywhere Islam has a presence, there is a minaret, a tall slender tower of a mosque with a balcony from which the people are called to prayer. Do these towers of Islam serve a good purpose, the purpose of good? Yes, their purpose is to get the people's attention and remind them to pray, whereas the intention of the builders of the Tower of Babel was to make a name for themselves.

Babel came to be called Babylon. People going forth from Babylon founded the nations of Assyria and Egypt. In later years, Babylon conquered Israel more than once and became a symbol for paganism. Israel also warred with Assyria and Egypt. It seems these three nations symbolize the kinds of obstacles that threaten ascending thought as exemplified by Enoch and the Abrahamic concept of one God. Self-promotion, as illustrated by Babel, is not thought rising in response to God's commands and promises. Self-promotion is doomed to divide mankind, not unite and protect it. The self-destruction of Babel ensued, but the seed of right motive and ascending consciousness (which cannot be killed) continued to grow in the dark to later break forth—or emerge gently—as human thought learned the grace of yielding to the uplifting will of God.

Nehemiah

More than a thousand years after Abram emerged from the land of many gods and learned fidelity to the ways of the one God, a man named Nehemiah (about 400 BCE) illustrated this grace. He answered the call to leave his important position in court as cupbearer and confidante to King Artaxerxes of Persia.

With the king's blessing, Nehemiah returned to Jerusalem. The city's walls and houses had been broken down. He quietly surveyed the situation and then called on the Jewish leaders and people to rise from the lethargy of defeat and rebuild the walls of the holy city of David. The citizens had not lost all hope and were stirred to build for God. There was no motive of self-promotion. The seeds of hope and faith just needed to be nurtured so they could emerge into visible action. The people "had a mind to work," and they finished the walls and gates in fifty-two days. I can imagine how the citizens of Jerusalem rose up by ones and hundreds to express gratitude for their liberated hopes!

The men who weren't part of the crew working on the walls, however, were influenced to fight against Jerusalem and to hinder the work. These enemies were listening to fear, jealousy, and other ungodlike suggestions. They spread lies about the motives and desires of the builders. Did the builders stop work to fight the liars? No. Every builder had "one of his hands wrought in the work, and with the other hand held a weapon" (Nehemiah 4:17). The workers knew that it was just as important to protect their rising mental states of hope and commitment as it was to place stones in the rising walls.

Babel/Babylon was a city full of self-indulgence and sin. The Tower of Babel could not rise, because it did not represent thought focused on God and therefore rising. The walls of Jerusalem could rise again under the leadership of Nehemiah because the people had held on to hope and their fidelity to God. Fidelity provided good soil in which hope could grow and blossom.

Christ Jesus

Human thought progressed through the Old Testament, and after millennia, Jesus the Christ appeared on the human scene. What instructions did Christ Jesus give about finding the presence and power of the Most High? He said, "Except ye be converted, and become as little children, ye shall not enter into the kingdom of heaven. Whosoever therefore shall humble himself as this little child, the same is greatest in the kingdom of heaven" (Matthew 18:3, 4). The qualities of thought required were humility and *childlikeness*.

The only "building" required was the building of a Godlike or *spiritual* sense of identity. Jesus went so far as to tell his listeners, "Be ye therefore perfect, even as your Father which is in heaven is perfect" (Matthew 5:48). When his disciples asked him why he spoke to the people in parables, he explained, "For this people's heart is waxed gross, and their ears are dull of hearing, and their eyes they have closed; lest at any time they should see with their eyes, and hear with their ears, and should understand with their heart, and should be converted, and I should heal them. But blessed are your eyes, for they see: and your ears, for they hear" (Matthew 13:15, 16). It seems that the people's hearts and ears and eyes had not risen above the self-focused ambition of those building Babel. They had become resigned to dullness and separated themselves from God. Conversely, the *disciples* had responded to the call of the Master with humility and childlikeness.

Man is meant to know God's law and to know it on God's terms, but a sense of mortal selfhood cannot know God. There is no indication that the builders of Babel were motivated by unselfed love. And that's what Christ Jesus required: strive to discern and not forget the needs of others. The builders of the Tower of Babel wanted to be noticed and not forgotten. Christ's perspective is that every individual should discern the needs of others and not forget to address them. That divine perspective would ring through in the words of the Old Testament prophets as well as in the words of the New Testament.

A Towering Explanation

The title of this chapter is, "The Tower of Babel, Abraham, Christ Jesus, John the Revelator, and the Towering Revelation Given to Mary Baker Eddy." Obviously the revelation given to St. John came before Mary Baker Eddy's revelation. But I am placing this discussion of Mary Baker Eddy's revelation right after the section about Christ Jesus because it reveals the truth about Jesus and the Christ.

Let us observe that St. John's revelation could be interpreted to hint at the revelation of God's law as a *divine Science*. God's law is meant to be known and applied. The same can be said about Christian Science: it is meant to be known and applied, as is, for example, the science of mathematics.

To John was revealed the prophecy of the woman "pained to be delivered" and the "little book open." To John was also revealed the holy city, New Jerusalem, and the temple.

What could the "little book open" refer to? Perhaps the opening of the spiritual sense of the Bible through the light provided by another book that was revealed to Mary Baker Eddy, called *Science and Health with Key to the Scriptures*—a book that unwraps the deeper spiritual significance of the Bible. This towering revelation came to Mary Baker Eddy about 1,800 years after St. John's revelation, which revealed to him the Christ, Truth practiced by Jesus (see Revelation 1:1).

As the message of *Science and Health* became more widely known, there was reaction from the pulpit, press, and public, some of it negative. Some people claimed to be "confused" by its language and message. Others countered that it was the "new language" of Spirit.

This book was not a visible tower that God condemned for venturing into unauthorized territory. Far from it. This book was a towering declaration that God is Life, Truth, and Love itself that explained the spiritual nature of reality and man's oneness with God. What a contrast with Babel! God was facilitating not the condemnation of man, but man's desire to reach a higher view. Mary Baker Eddy's discovery, which she named Christian Science, was to show seekers how to get a better glimpse of God—and themselves. This book and the religion that emerged from it were not built on material and false knowledge or selfish motives, as Babel had been, but on what she called "divine Science" and divine Love.

Mary Baker Eddy is known as the *Discoverer* of Christian Science, not its *creator*. She discovered and articulated the spiritual laws of man's relationship to God. The builders of Babel, on the other hand, had tried to *create*, not discover, a way to relate to God. Christian Science enables one to experience God's promise made in the book of Jeremiah:

> But this shall be the covenant that I will make with the house of Israel; After those days, saith the Lord, I will put my law in their inward parts, and write it in their hearts; and will be their God, and they shall be my people. And they shall teach no more every man his neighbour, and every man his brother, saying, Know the Lord: for they shall all know me, from the least of them unto the greatest of them, saith the Lord: for I will forgive their iniquity, and I will remember their sin no more (Jeremiah 31: 33, 34).

By the end of the nineteenth century, the teachings of Christian Science were towering over religions derived from merely human concepts of God and man. For centuries, theologians had sought to reach heaven by building with man-made bricks—personal convictions and opinions of human minds. Even when these convictions were offered with the best of intentions and out of selfless devotion, the foundation of their convictions was a material man. Human minds cannot build up matter to reach heaven.

Even after the publication of *Science and Health* in 1875, most theologians did not "leave off" from building on sand. Instead, they dug in. The very core of their mental construction was threatened, and this riled the baser elements of what St. Paul calls "the carnal mind" and Christian Science calls "mortal mind". This supposed "mind" attempts to build a tower meant to secure its opinion, and it usurps dominion. Its apparent purpose is to reach heaven and receive God's confirmation, but of course it had to fail—has to fail—because God does not serve human purposes.

Contrasting and conflicting states of mind—selfish purpose *versus* selfless sacrifice—are vividly illustrated by the prophets and saints in the Bible. These mental states can also be symbolized by two contrasting objects: a tower and a book—a tower of personal sense *versus* the exalted and exalting revelation that the senses of man are *spiritual*. This book, *Science and Health*, fully describes human states of thought, which cannot reach heaven or breach the spiritual state of thought committed to one God, one all-knowing Mind that is actually the Mind of man. Man needs to acknowledge this Mind, and like Abram, he too, can hear the call, leave the human concept of many minds, and go forth to find the promised land, "the land of Christian Science, where fetters fall and the rights of man are fully known and acknowledged" (*Science and Health*, p. 227:1).

In 1898, twenty-three years after the publication of *Science and Health*, Eddy wrote about the prosperity of Christian Science, warning its adherents:

> The growth of human inquiry and the increasing popularity of Christian Science, I regret to say, have called out of their hiding-places those poisonous reptiles and devouring beasts, superstition and jealousy. Towards the animal elements manifested in ignorance, persecution, and lean glory, and to their Babel of confusion worse confounded, let Christian Scientists be charitable. Let the voice of Truth and Love be heard above the dire din of mortal nothingness, and the majestic march of Christian Science go on *ad infinitum*, praising God, doing the works of primitive Christianity, and enlightening the world (*The First Church of Christ, Scientist and Miscellany*, by Mary Baker Eddy, p. 245:10).

Witnesses to this tower of explanation simply needed to keep on "doing the works of primitive Christianity, and enlightening the world."

What a faithful Abraham

When we are introduced to Abraham, God is promising him *land*, not cities. It's the "land of Canaan" (see Genesis 17:8). Abraham's first act was to acknowledge and thank the God that had brought him and his clan into a new land. Near Bethel, Abraham built "an altar unto the Lord, and called upon the name of the Lord" (Genesis 12:8). Abraham had no personal agenda to find out more about another god. Abraham was simply willing to find out more than he had learned from looking at the images he was offered in the pagan place called Ur.

We see in Abraham a different set of motives and acts than those exhibited by Adam and Eve or by those journeying east after the flood to settle in the plain of Shinar, where they proceeded to build a city and a tower. Abraham responded to a call, indicating he had been listening. We see in the unnamed builders of Babylon and its truncated tower the motive to be noticed and not forgotten. They had no apparent purpose to honor the Lord nor to "seek first his kingdom."

Thought had a long way to rise from this counterfeit building project in order to duplicate the ascending thought of Enoch and Noah. Enoch "walked with God: and was not; for God took him" (Genesis 5:24). Noah had also listened and had been receptive, and that enabled him to save family and animals for posterity.

After the flood, Shem, Ham, and Japheth, the sons of Noah, "journeyed from the east" and "found a plain in the land of Shinar; and they dwelt there" (Genesis 11:2–4). They decided to "build a city and a tower." Had they lost the memory of Enoch because of the flood, and forgotten the great possibilities of his kind of thinking and "walking"? Had they perhaps rejected the Lord who had caused such devastation as the flood, and yet still hoped to get the Lord to notice and preserve and respect them?

Honesty and humility, the banners of Abraham's journey, were providing true leadership. Adam and Eve had not identified with these moral and spiritual attributes, so they were unable and unready to receive the land and to value the garden and God, its rule maker. Abraham's ability and readiness ensured that he would stay focused on God's plan. God had called Abraham to leave the familiar and go to the unknown. He did so. God therefore made a covenant with Abraham, as was recorded in Genesis, and said to him,

> For all the land which thou seest, to thee will I give it, and to thy seed for ever. And I will make thy seed as the dust of the earth: so that if a man can number the dust of the earth, then shall thy seed also be numbered. Arise, walk through the land in the length of it and in the breadth of it; for I will give it unto thee (Genesis 13:15–17).

The covenant was finally fulfilled when his wife Sarah gave birth to Isaac.

What a sorry Lot: Genesis 13 and 19

When the land could not sustain the great flocks and families of Abraham and his nephew, Lot, they separated: "Then Lot chose him all the plain of Jordan; and Lot journeyed east: and they separated themselves the one from the other. Abram dwelled in the land of Canaan, and Lot dwelled in the cities of the plain, and pitched his tent toward Sodom" (Genesis 13:11, 12). We've already learned that one of these "cities of the plain" was Babylon. There was much evil in Sodom and Gomorrah. Abraham tried to save Sodom (see Genesis 18), and then Lot tried to save his in-laws, but only Lot, his wife, and their two daughters followed the angel out of the city as the Lord rained down fire and brimstone, destroying both cities (see Genesis 19:24). The Lord was credited—or blamed—for the destruction of the two cities, but perhaps it would be more accurate to say that natural law (the law of God) was expressed as the internal combustion of evil. The city burned with brimstone (sulfur), making it impossible to breathe.

The "cities" didn't work for Lot, but he was wise enough to realize this. He refused, at first, to let his thought and actions get carried away by greed or base sexuality. But his two daughters "made their father drink wine" (see Genesis 19:33–35), and then each lay with him, conceived, and bore children. The lines of Moab and Ammon evolved from these father/daughter encounters. Moab and Ammon would be the perpetual enemies of Israel. Was the theme of rising thought slowly being reversed and eviscerated through Lot, Abraham's nephew?

Their different purposes had separated them. Abraham offered Lot the first choice of direction—land or cities. Lot chose the city. Abraham understood the wider purpose of the land. It was not difficult to perceive that God was the creator of the earth, of *land*. It was a continuing challenge, however, to perceive that God was also the creator of the good represented by *cities*. The cities of Sodom and later Jerusalem were destroyed, Sodom in prehistory, and Jerusalem when the temple was destroyed by the Roman Emperor Vespasian in 70 CE. The city of Rome figured prominently in the lives of Jesus and Paul. Rome, like Sodom, disintegrated from within because of its pagan base and immoral practices, and it fell in 476 CE.

Early on, Christian Science and other Christian denominations came to a parting similar to that of Abraham and Lot. Christian Science placed more emphasis on following Jesus' command to "heal the sick."

In *Science and Health*, Eddy recommended following the actions of Abraham when he separated from Lot:

> If ecclesiastical sects or medical schools turn a deaf ear to the teachings of Christian Science, then part from these opponents as did Abraham when he parted from Lot, and say in thy heart: "Let there be no strife, I pray thee, between me and thee, and between my herdmen and thy herdmen; for we be brethren." Immortals, or God's children in divine Science, are one harmonious family; but mortals, or the "children of men" in material sense, are discordant and ofttimes false brethren (p. 444:22–27).

There are more details about the building of her church—this tower of revelation—in the foreword to *The First Church of Christ, Scientist and Miscellany*.

The stories of Babel and Sodom (where Lot settled) seem to illustrate the downward gravitational pull of trying to build on a foundation that excludes God. Both are stories of thought disintegrating instead of rising. It is unnatural for thought and life to recede and self-destruct. The continuing history of the children of Israel vividly illustrates that each person must resist and overcome every ungodlike temptation and tendency toward materiality. Through much tribulation, the people of God will fulfill the vision of John the Revelator and wear the white robes of purity as they lift up their voices in praise to God and the Lamb (see Revelation, chapter 7).

These seekers will reach heaven by looking up. In the place where God dwells with man, they will see visions of the Almighty God and the meek man modeling dominion, Christ Jesus. These seekers will see no need to build a staircase up a tower of brick to get closer to a God called "the Lord." The one God will show ownership of this title—*the Lord*. The Psalmist's and God's prophets will show the good and great works of *the Lord*.

Old Jerusalem

Many centuries after Abraham and Lot, David and his men captured Jerusalem, and as king he made it his seat of government. It became the capital city of the Jews' Promised Land and was the heart of the Jewish nation. The nation fell when the Babylonians captured that particular city. Six hundred years after David, Nehemiah returned to rebuild the city walls that had been broken down.

Four hundred years after Nehemiah, Jesus did much of his teaching in and around this city. In Jesus' time, the pagan Romans governed the city, and the Jewish leaders waited for a Messiah who would deliver the Jews from the Roman occupation. The Messiah they were given offered instead deliverance from ignorance, fear, and sin.

Jerusalem, as represented by the temple, fell for the last time in 70 CE, when Rome destroyed the recently completed temple, rebuilt by Herod to win the favor of the Jews. The Jews continued worshipping on the Temple Mount until Hadrian rebuilt the city and erected a temple honoring Jupiter Capitolinus (see *Anchor Bible Dictionary*, K. W. Clarke, 1960:273–274). A generation after Jesus departed, Paul tried to bring Christ Jesus' message to the people of Jerusalem, but with their same obtuseness, Jewish leaders resisted the message and tried to kill Paul. So Paul took Christ's message to Gentile cities far beyond Jerusalem. Christian churches throughout Asia (the Middle East) resulted from this sowing.

A new book and a new city

Toward the end of the first century, a cruel and aggressive emperor of Rome imprisoned the apostle John on the Isle of Patmos, off the coast of Asia Minor. There he had a vision of "one like unto the Son of man" (see Revelation 1:11–13), as Paul had seen a vision of Jesus a generation earlier. The vision instructed John, "I am Alpha and Omega, the first and the last: and, What thou seest, write in a book, and send it unto the seven churches which are in Asia."

In his vision, John saw the Lord God Almighty sitting on a throne and holding a sealed book. An angel called out, "Who is worthy to open the book and loose the seven seals?" (Revelation 5:2). Then John saw the Lamb of God take the book from the hand of the One on the throne. John asked about the multitudes in white robes praising God and the Lamb, and he received the answer, "These are they which came out of great tribulation, and have washed their robes, and made them white in the blood of the Lamb. Therefore are they before the throne of God, and serve him day and night in his temple: and he that sitteth on the throne shall dwell among them" (Revelation 7:14, 15).

Multitudes had sought "the throne of God," not by trying to build a material structure but by living a life of selfless service and sacrifice. They "came out of great tribulation." The survivors of the flood also wanted to "stand before the throne of God," but they had not learned (or remembered) that the ones who "wash others' feet" reach the throne of God, not the ones who "build with bricks" and seek to storm the heavenly gates or pay a bribe to get through, and they were denied and scattered.

Those in the heavenly kingdom "came out of … tribulation" by clinging ever more steadfastly to rising thought, the kind of thinking demanded of every seeker of spiritual reality. John was shown the City of God, in which there was no temple, because every *individual* was "the temple of the living God":

> And I John saw the holy city, new Jerusalem, coming down from God out
> of heaven, prepared as a bride adorned for her husband. And I heard a great
> voice out of heaven saying, Behold, the tabernacle of God is with men, and
> he will dwell with them, and they shall be his people, and God himself shall
> be with them, and be their God (Revelation 21:2, 3).

God dwells with His children, but the misguided materialists who sought to find "the Lord" up at the top of a tower, instead of in the heart and mind, would not be aware of His presence.

When John tried to worship the angel that had shown him such a vision, the angel stopped him and said, Don't do this. I'm just a fellow servant with you and the prophets and all those who keep the word of the book. John writes, "The Spirit and the bride say, Come. And let him that heareth say, Come. And let him that is athirst come. And whosoever will, let him take the water of life freely" (Revelation 22:17).

God was not saying, "I cannot be known, and I condemn and scatter those who presume to try." For many centuries after the first effort to storm heaven through a willful building project, individual prophets and saints looked up, beyond themselves, and helped others do likewise. Christ Jesus shared the clearest vision of the God-man relationship.

Paul carried this vision to other nations not so steeped in limited, personal, and materialistic interpretations of the law of Moses and the prophets. John received messages from God that he sent as letters to "the seven churches." These messages contained strong correctives as well as praise for the people's efforts. The Lamb of God also revealed to John more about the heavenly city and the new location of the temple—with man. In this revelation, there is no "Lord" or anthropomorphic God determined to condemn and scatter mankind.

The city of God, New Jerusalem, was a city in the new land of *spiritual consciousness.* Abraham had been promised *a land* that would include everything man needed, a grand-scale garden of Eden!

The "river of the water of life" flowed through this land and through the streets of the city. "The tree of life" grew on each side of the river, and the leaves of the tree were for "the healing of the nations."

In the first "land," Adam and Eve had seen this tree of life in the middle of the garden. They must also have seen the river that "went out of Eden to water the garden." The river divided into four heads: Pison, Gihon, Hiddekel, and Euphrates (see Genesis 2:10). *River* is defined in *Science and Health* as "channel of thought" (p. 593:14). The spiritual meaning of each river is given in the *Glossary* of *Science and Health.* Eddy interprets Euphrates as "metaphysics taking the place of physics" and "the reign of righteousness."

Each physical object we have been considering in the chapters from Genesis and Revelation appears to have more than one meaning: tree, tower, land, city, river, and temple. How important it is to recognize this as we study the Bible, especially since Jesus showed that physical objects—like bread and wine, for example—mean more than they appear to mean. It's as though the characters in the stories we read, and the transcribers of these stories, are inviting us to come forward and be willing—even eager—to reason together with the aim of hearing and accepting the most spiritually rewarding message.

Come, let us reason together

The people of Babel were trying to reach God by means of a material tower outside of themselves. Finally, after two thousand years of thought rising, falling, and rising again, Jesus Christ came and taught that the man of God's creating is pure and meek, and a peacemaker. The pure in heart see God. The meek inherit the earth. The peacemakers "shall be called the children of God" (Matthew 5:9). The people of Babel thought they could find God from outside themselves, in a physical place through physical means. Jesus taught, "The kingdom of God is within you" (Luke 17:21).

A generation later, Paul took Christ Jesus' message not only to the Jews but also to the Gentiles, by whom it was more widely received. St. John recorded the revelation that he described as "a great voice out of heaven, saying, Behold, the tabernacle of God is with men, and he will dwell with them, and they shall be his people, and God himself shall be with them, and be their God" (Revelation 21:3). This revelation is the apex of thought rising.

John wrote, "And they heard a great voice from heaven saying unto them, Come up hither" (Revelation 11:12). *Come up hither* has been the command and the invitation of rising thought to reason with God and be transformed through tribulation as well as through spiritual understanding, the cross and the crown. The Lord, as He requested in Isaiah (see Isaiah 1:18, 19), repeats His invitation to us, "Come now, and let us reason together."

5

BOOK OF SAINTS

Particular churches have designated certain persons as *saints* and continue to do so, and bookstores stock biographies of saints.

Many religious texts refer to Paul as *St. Paul*, but the Bible does not refer to Paul as a saint. The word *saints* appears ninety-five times in the Bible, but the word *saint* is used in only three verses:

- the people envied "Aaron the saint of the Lord" (Psalm 106:16)
- Daniel heard a saint speaking, and another saint talking to that saint (Daniel 8:13)
- Paul wrote, "Salute every saint in Christ Jesus" (Philippians 4:21)

What is a saint? Three definitions from Dictionary.com are as follows:

1. Any of certain persons of exceptional holiness of life, formally recognized as such by the Christian Church
2. A person of great holiness, virtue, or benevolence
3. A founder, sponsor, or patron, as of a movement or organization

Webster's Dictionary for Students, Third Edition, emphasizes these two points:

1. A good and holy person and especially one who is declared to be worthy of special honor
2. A person who is very good, especially about helping others

The moniker applies to all people claiming their natural, though seemingly extraordinary, identities as God's offspring: God's ever-children under the care of Father-Mother God, and growing into a fuller realization of the oneness of creator and creation, God and man.

Several books of the Bible are listed in the Bible as having been written by saints—Saints Matthew, Mark, Luke, and John, and *The Revelation of St. John the Divine.* Biblical writers relate the words and deeds of saints, such as Abraham, Jacob/Israel, Joseph, Elijah, Elisha, Isaiah, Paul, John, Sarah, Ruth, Hannah, Abigail, the Virgin Mary, Mary Magdalene, Lydia, and the ultimate saint, Christ Jesus.

In Bible study, we read stories of individuals who sought and found the truth, or who were called to move out of the dream of mortality and into conscious spiritual aims and acts.

Many people have led exemplary and selfless lives but are not referred to as saints—for example, Mahatma Gandhi; Nelson Mandela; Mother Teresa; and Clara Barton, founder of the American Red Cross. Did their lives illustrate these two descriptions of a saint?

On his weekly National Public Radio program, *A Prairie Home Companion*, Garrison Keillor, humorist and philosopher, tells stories about the people in the fictional town of Lake Wobegon. He lists one of the show's writers as "Sara Bellum." Garrison's stories reveal that he celebrates people who fit our two descriptions of a saint, and he tosses gentle jibes toward people who don't score on either criterion.

Two women, Betty Williams and Mairead Corrigan, could be considered saints because of their work to stop the fighting and bring peace to Ireland. Their efforts were widely recognized, and they were awarded the Nobel Peace Prize in 1977.

Several twentieth-century writers also come to mind. To me they illustrate our definition of saint: A. A. Milne, C. S. Lewis, E. B. White, Rachel Carson, Toni Morrison, and Pearl Buck. A present-day saint in China is Chai Ling. Her story appeared in *The Christian Science Monitor* on August 16 and 23, 2010:

> Chai Ling led the protesters at Tiananmen Square. She was later denounced by the Chinese government as the second most-wanted "culprit" of the political upheaval and forced to flee her native land. Now living in the United States, Ms. Chai is working to protect China's women and girls. More than 35,000 forced abortions were performed in China each day in 2009, Chai says—a death toll that far exceeds the estimated thousands of protesters who died in the 1989 massacre.

Another present-day saint is Malala Yousafzai, a fifteen-year-old Pakistani teenager who gained international attention in 2012 after being shot in the head by the Taliban for attending school. She survived, and one year later she addressed the United Nations about her experience and her beliefs. Her speech was covered by hundreds of the world's news media and is widely available online. In it, she said, "The extremists were, and they are, afraid of books and pens." Urging worldwide action against illiteracy, poverty, and terrorism, she urged, "Let us pick up our books and pens. They are our most powerful weapons … They thought that the bullets would silence us. But they failed."

I'm sure you can think of others "worthy of special honor," and we thank them all. You might even write some of them a letter!

A Bible concordance will list the names of many individuals who fit our definition of a saint, more names than just David and Paul, Sarah and Mary. In every age and place, saints serve to uplift thought and keep one focused on spiritual progress. This popular hymn is an ode to saints. It is based on the Swedish poem by Lina Sandell-Berg:

> O Father, Thy kingdom is come upon earth,
> Thou rulest in all Thy creation;
> Thou sendest Thy witnesses, telling Thy worth,
> To call and entreat every nation,
> With news of Thy mighty salvation.
>
> They lift up a light amid shadows of fear,
> And Love is Thy banner above them;
> No trouble shall touch them, no foes that appear
> Shall e'er from their loyalty move them;
> 'Tis Thou dost uphold and approve them.
>
> They go in Thy strength, and they speak in Thy name,
> With power of Thy promise forth faring,
> And during the battle the victory claim,
> Their trust in Thy truth is their daring,
> Salvation to all men declaring.

(Hymn No. 204, Lina Sandell-Berg, *Christian Science Hymnal*, © 1932, renewed 1960, The Christian Science Board of Directors. Used with permission.)

6

TRUE DISCIPLESHIP—THEN AND NOW

Jesus' twelve disciples "left all" and promised to follow him. One of them, Judas, forgot that promise and allowed himself to be bought by a religious sect that feared Jesus' popularity and hated his spirituality. Judas betrayed his Master by telling the Pharisees where they could find him and arrest him for the crime of "blasphemy." Jesus had called himself the Son of God and had presumed to "forgive sins," which they said only God could do. Jesus was demonstrating that *the Son of man hath power upon earth to forgive sins* (see Luke 5:24).

Daily, Jesus carried out his mission of proving that disease and sin were not inevitable aspects of the human condition and were not God's will. Jesus also knew that he must likewise prove that death is not an aspect of the human condition or God's will. He had already proved the temporal and unreal nature of "death" by calling Lazarus to come forth from his four-day experience in the tomb, and by restoring the son of the widow of Nain (see Luke 7:11–18). And he knew he would also prove the impermanence and unreality of death for himself. "Then said he unto the disciples, it is impossible but that offences will come: but woe unto him, through whom they come" (Luke 17:1).

After the crucifixion, Judas experienced that woe. He repented of his apostasy, but his path of self-destruction seemed set. The needed transformation, beyond repentance, would have to unfold on the other side of the line in the sand drawn by the human belief in death.

The other disciples huddled in fear after the crucifixion. They chose another disciple, Matthias, to bring their number back up to twelve, but still they didn't know how to proceed without their Master. Without employment as disciples, they returned to their former business as fishers—of fish. But Jesus had called them to be "fishers of *men*," and that calling had not been canceled by Jesus' apparent death on the cross.

After Jesus' resurrection, he talked with them. No doubt they were comforted but apparently clueless about how to continue as disciples when there was no Master to follow. Christ Jesus was teaching them another lesson in compassion. Instead of disdaining or rejecting them for their lack of spiritual insight, he patiently proceeded to show them how to find an abundance of this essential commodity of "fish" by casting their nets on the right side (see John 21:1–12). Through this analogy, he was showing them how to connect "material abundance" with obedience to the call from *the stranger*, the Master, calling to them from the shore of eternal life.

Jesus perceived and taught the true nature of man as created by God. As the Christ, the Son of God, and as Jesus, the son of man, he exemplified the man to whom God gave dominion over all the earth, the man entitled to the perfection offered by the Word (see John 1) and demanded by the creator, God (see Genesis 1: 26–27). Jesus came to prove once and for all that every man and woman reflects that same creator, God.

The disciples had toiled all night and caught nothing. Christ Jesus stood on the shore and called to them to "cast their nets on the right side" (John 21:6). When they did, their nets almost broke from the size of the catch. This must have awakened them from their waywardness. They bypassed the excitement of the catch and immediately saw that it symbolized their assured success as fishers of men. They hurried to shore, where their loving Master had breakfast waiting for them, a meal of cooked fish and warm bread. How patiently their Master must have reminded them again of their calling. They were to continue the Christly work of teaching, preaching, and healing. They did, and their story is told in the Acts of the Apostles.

While they were following Jesus during his three-year ministry, did the disciples have their own "followers," friends and family members eager to learn from them that Life, Truth, and Love were truly divine and demonstrable now in everyone's human experience of life and truth and love?

For a few years, the disciples were with their Master day and night, but after Christ Jesus' ascension, they might have been in more regular touch with family and friends. Doubtless they inspired multitudes to look to Jesus, not themselves, and to find the Christ, the true nature not only of Jesus but of themselves also, and of every man, woman, and child. They had experienced Jesus as the great teacher, healer, and savior.

Did they also regard Jesus as God? Not at all! They accepted Jesus' revelation that he was the *Son* of God, the Christ. They glimpsed something of their Master's main message that man is not a mortal but is a spiritual idea and consequently able to accept complete healing now. Many did. According to John, many more received healing than are recorded in the Scriptures. "And there are also many other things which Jesus did, the which, if they should be written every one, I suppose that even the world itself could not contain the books that should be written" (John 21:25).

Did the disciples have *disciples*? I think not. Surely they rejected and corrected any attempt by others to idolize them. They could not allow personal exaltation, because Jesus' way of perceiving the Christ consciousness had permanently liberated them from the dark, unenlightened perception that some persons had a closer relationship to God than others.

When Peter proclaimed, "thou art the Christ, the Son of the living God" (Matthew 16:16), Jesus did not praise Peter's *personal* discernment. Instead, Jesus focused immediately on *spiritual* insight, which is always individualized but never personal. Peter had progressed along the path of realization that spiritual progress relieves one of any sense of personal importance. Spiritual progress assures one of eternal importance as an individualized manifestation of God, of Life and Truth and Love. Spiritual progress is a practical Science, not a varying opinion and not subject to the spiritual attainments of other humans on the path of enlightenment.

Peter's prompt acknowledgment, "thou art the Christ," revealed the depth of his understanding. Such depth is an essential foundation for continued spiritual progress, and Jesus acknowledged this by giving Peter a new name. "And I say also unto thee, that thou art Peter, and upon this rock I will build my church; and the gates of hell shall not prevail against it" (Matthew 16:18).

The "rock" on which Jesus would build his church was not the shifting sand of human consciousness and not the current inspiration of any person. Jesus would and did build his church on solid spiritual ground, on "whatever rests upon and proceeds from divine Principle" (*Science and Health*, p. 583:12). His church would be and is immaterial, "the structure of Truth and Love." His church would be and is filled with individuals committed to the spiritual growth that enables them to obey the command of their Master: heal the sick.

> Christianity is the summons of divine Love for man to be Christlike—to emulate the words and the works of our great Master. To attain these works, men must know somewhat of the divine Principle of Jesus' life-work, and must prove their knowledge by doing as he bade: "Go, and do thou likewise" (*The First Church of Christ, Scientist and Miscellany*, p. 148:28, by Mary Baker Eddy).

Christians with this commitment reject mere personality and personal superiority in favor of Jesus' way. "Jesus beheld in Science the perfect man, who appeared to him where sinning mortal man appears to mortals. In this perfect man the Saviour saw God's own likeness, and this correct view of man healed the sick" (*Science and Health*, p. 476:32).

There are innumerable churches and groups throughout the world dedicated to worshipping and obeying God, honoring Christ Jesus, and following his example. They will effectively bless the world to the extent that they release Jesus from the notion that he was able to heal and save because he was God. These groups and individuals can search the Scriptures for what Jesus said about himself and his relation to God and to man. Jesus understood that he and the Father were one—exactly as Mind and idea are one, as sun and sunshine are one. Cause must have effect. Cause and effect are one.

In vain is any theological effort to praise God (cause) and damn man (effect). Such a stance will never forward the Master's holy order to teach, preach, heal, and be perfect. It does not please God (Mind) to condemn man (idea). It pleases God to express in man all there is to Life, Truth, Love, Soul, Spirit, Mind, and Principle—the seven Scripture-based synonyms for God given in *Science and Health* (see pp. 465:8-10; 587:5-8). Obviously, the aim of organized church groups is to help members emulate the compassion of Christ Jesus and reach out to all mankind with that same compassion of the Christ. It heals and transforms, condemning only the sense of personal knowledge (opinion) that would insert itself as a medium between God and man.

King Saul lost his throne and his life, and thus his special opportunity to bless his fellow man, because he sought help from a familiar spirit (a medium) rather than from God (see I Samuel 28, 31). Mortals get nowhere by bowing down to images and mediums, trusting *personal* understanding, which is always limited and sometimes severely skewed. Is there no here-and-now help for us seekers of the light who seem to see and fear obstacles, even death and destruction? Of course there is help.

If the Son of God practiced such compassion and power to lift up and help, the Father must have (does have) compassion beyond our imagining, as well as equal power and authority over all that would pull us down and victimize us.

As did Christ Jesus, so also does the Father detect and build up consciousness, spiritual receptivity. Scientific Christians, Christian Scientists, are taught to hear and obey what God said to Peter and the other disciples after they had witnessed the transfiguration (Matthew 17:1–8). In this event, Jesus (revelation) was talking with Moses (the law) and Elijah (prophecy). Peter wanted to build something, a tabernacle in honor of each one, but God audibly and decisively overruled such temporal thinking. Succinctly did God, Mind, say to the disciples, "Hear ye him." *Build your lives on the rock of spiritual understanding—Christ as the true nature of man. Don't build material buildings to honor Jesus or any of the saints.*

A disciple's duty is to hear and understand and practice the teachings of the Son of God. Numerous disciples did that. At Pentecost, fifty days after Jesus' ascension (see Acts 2:1–4), many were "filled with the Holy Ghost" and began to speak as inspired by the Spirit. Perhaps disciples "then" were as challenged as disciples "now" to constantly distinguish between human hope or opinion and divine direction precisely when it is needed.

For three hundred years after Jesus' ascension, disciples preached and healed "in his name." The healing work declined, however, as the newly established Christian Church in Rome, dedicated to Saint Peter, succumbed to hierarchical assumptions that limited interpretation of the Scriptures to the word of those higher in the hierarchy.

The more removed people became from the simple realm in which Jesus worked, the more personal opinion took on the disguise of having the authority of the Christ. This darkened, mortal thinking weighed heavily on Christians for hundreds of years during which time Christian healing was lost.

In the 1500s, Martin Luther broke free. In protesting the excesses of religious privilege, he launched the Protestant Church. Unfortunately, that church kept many of the false assumptions of the Roman Catholic Church, especially the non-biblical notion that Jesus was God. Oh, yes, Jesus said, "I and my Father are one" (John 10:30), but in dozens of other teachings, he described the distinct nature of God the Father, and the Christ, which was Jesus' understanding of the true Godlike nature of man. Jesus said, "My Father is greater than I" (John 14:28). He also asked, "Why callest thou me good? There is none good but one, that is, God" (Mark 10:18).

In due time came the completed revelation about this distinction. Mary Baker Eddy explained the distinctness and oneness of God and man in her book *Science and Health with Key to the Scriptures*, published in 1875. One of many explanations states, "Jesus is the name of the man who, more than all other men, has presented Christ, the true idea of God, healing the sick and the sinning and destroying the power of death. Jesus is the human man, and Christ is the divine idea; hence the duality of Jesus the Christ" (*Science and Health*, p. 473:12).

True disciples then and now devote themselves to pure (unselfed) worship of God and perception of God's works. They pray, and they learn more about prayer from the first chapter of *Science and Health* titled *Prayer*. Refusing to identify themselves as limited mortals, true disciples let the promise of Christ Jesus grow more prominent in their thinking. These two promises precede that chapter:

> For verily I say unto you, That whosoever shall say unto this mountain, Be thou removed, and be thou cast into the sea; and shall not doubt in his heart, but shall believe that those things which he saith shall come to pass; he shall have whatsoever he saith. Therefore I say unto you, What things soever ye desire, when ye pray, believe that ye receive them, and ye shall have them (Mark 11:23–24).

> Your Father knoweth what things ye have need of, before ye ask Him (Matthew 6:8).

7

WHICH WITNESS? WHICH TESTIMONY?

From our youngest years we were taught to obey our parents—and teachers—especially when there seemed to be other voices to obey, like the internal and external voices of selfishness and dishonesty. We chose rightly—except when we chose wrongly, and then we got into trouble. Do we adults continue to face choices every day about which influence (testimony) to accept and what action to take? Of course, and our children certainly do. Good and evil act out their alleged battle on this stage called *choosing which testimony to accept*.

False witness testimony is symbolized by a talking serpent in Genesis 2. True witness testimony is illustrated by the Old Testament prophets and by the New Testament revelators—Christ Jesus, Paul, and John. In the opening verses of Revelation, John refers to Jesus Christ as the "faithful witness" (Revelation 1:5).

The Bible reverberates with voices urging us to adopt specific doctrines and actions: Moses' Ten Commandments, for example, and Jesus' Beatitudes. Readers and students of the Bible are being called to be faithful witnesses to the one God. "A faithful witness will not lie: but a false witness will utter lies" (Proverbs 14:5).

According to the dictionary, a witness is "an individual who, being present, personally sees or perceives a thing; a person or thing that affords evidence; a person who gives testimony" (Dictionary.com). Who was present at the creation of the world? Indeed, who is present as the spiritual nature of creation unfolds in the heart hungering after righteousness, right thinking?

The operative word in the title of this section is *which*, a word that implies choosing. Which one? Which testimony is from the *truth-teller* (spiritual sense) and which is from the mere *storyteller* (material sense). True witnessing is a challenge, especially for one who has been taught, or allowed, to believe that both evil and good are real.

Traditional theology often acknowledges that both are real: the testimony of evil is as real as the testimony of good. Poor mortals can only hope that with God's help the *good testimony* (words of deliverance and healing) will win out over *evil testimony* (words of resignation to sin, disease, and death). In religion, witnesses tend to group around a particular doctrine or leader, a cynosure.

As a result, mankind has come to be divided into thousands of religious sects. Ironically, many of these incompatible groups preach the supremacy of Christ Jesus, who came to fulfill prophecy and prove "man's unity with God" (John 10:30; *Science and Health*, p. 18:1–3; *Science and Health*, p. 497:13). Separation and division seem to characterize religion and politics, two phenomena that characterize a nation.

But *no*. Inspired thought says *no* to separation and division. We know from the faithful witnessing of prophets, poets, Christ Jesus, the disciples, and Paul that the testimony of material sense, which witnesses to sin, disease, and death, is not just as true as the testimony of spiritual sense, which witnesses to one good God or creator, still and ever in charge of one good whole and holy creation. This is not an abstract description. This creation is you and me. We have met the "enemy," the belief of man separated from God, but it is not us! It is false belief imposed on us, and we can shake off this imposition just as Paul shook off the viper and felt no harm (see Acts 28:5).

How true and compelling is Joshua's command to the children of Israel as they entered the Promised Land: "Choose you this day whom ye will serve" (Joshua 24:15). The Bible is alive with guidance on how to do this, how to choose and serve God. It offers vivid illustrations of groups and individuals who chose between the testimony of good and the testimony of evil—at the Red Sea, for example, or when Peter and Paul were ordered to stop preaching the gospel of Jesus Christ and they continued anyway.

The careful teacher of the Bible to teens helps them grasp and verbalize the transforming importance of dismissing material sense testimony and choosing spiritual sense testimony. The prophet Elijah's demonstrations provide a great context for this discussion.

At one point, Elijah and his servant were fleeing the death threats of Queen Jezebel. Elijah had just publicly humiliated Baal, the Queen's god, in a contest over which god could send fire and burn the sacrifice. Baal, of course, sent no fire. The one God sent a fire that burned not only the sacrifice but also the stones of the altar.

Early one morning, Elijah's servant saw armies descending upon their hiding place. "Alas, my master! how shall we do?" (II Kings 6:15).

Elijah answered, "Fear not: for they that be with us are more than they that be with them." The material sense threat of certain death was meaningless when compared to the spiritual sense testimony that omnipotent God is equal to every occasion. After his triumph in this instance, this faithful witness of the one God continued to prove that spiritual sense testimony is the only real and legitimate testimony. He never wasted time wondering *which* report was *more* true.

Christ Jesus is the great study for learning about true witnessing. His disciples learned and practiced this same true witnessing. Among numerous examples would be Paul and Silas singing in prison (see Acts 16, especially verse 25). They were witnessing truly, looking "not at the things which [were] seen, but at the things which [were] not seen" at the moment when they were singing (II Corinthians 4:18).

Do all of us faithfully adapt such stories to our own lives so that we are ready to help students do the same?

We don't stop to analyze it in so many words, but we are dealing with witnesses and testimony every day—actually, all the time. Sometimes the witnesses seeking to influence us are alleged to be experts, even superior beings, such as theologians who study and preach the nature of God and creation. Are these experts our religious *superiors*? We've "come a long way," but society is still hierarchical—sometimes mildly, sometimes aggressively. Does submission to such experts necessarily include submission to the Master Christian? No.

In Jesus' day, Pharisees presented themselves as the experts on "the law and the prophets." The Pharisees and Sadducees were sure that this loose cannonball named Jesus should submit to them, the acknowledged (and superior) interpreters of scripture. When the paralyzed man was lowered "into the midst before Jesus," he said to him, "Man, thy sins are forgiven thee." The Pharisees unknowingly exposed a paradigm shift when they challenged Jesus, "Who can forgive sins, but God alone?" (Luke 5:18–21). The great paradigm shift was from matter-based *apparent reality* to a God-based Science, the provability of God's will being done "on earth as it is in heaven."

The Pharisees believed sin was real, so they could not "forgive sins." As a result, they were bearing false witness and rehearsing false testimony about the purpose of Jesus.

Furthermore, they were showing no compassion toward the man "taken with a palsy." Jesus knew that the Pharisees objected to his claim that he was the Son of God, but he proceeded with the lesson that had to be taught and learned: "But that ye may know that the Son of man hath power upon earth to forgive sins, [he said unto the sick of the palsy,] I say unto thee, Arise, and take up thy couch, and go into thine house" (Luke 5:18–21). In other words, "Get up and go home!"

The man had been brought in by his friends, so he may or may not have been seeking forgiveness—or even healing. But Jesus knew the man's thought and perhaps detected that it had been *immobilized* by some particular "sin" or just by a general belief in mortality. The disabled man must have been very distraught about "sin."

Jesus *forgave* the man before healing him. Whether the human consciousness is seeking forgiveness or not, forgiveness is one of the essential things that humans do need to seek, accept, and come to understand. In the prayer Jesus gave to his disciples, and to us, he stipulated, "Forgive us our debts, as we forgive our debtors" (Matthew 6:12). The Bible shows that forgiveness happens within the covenant between God and man (as characterized in the Old Testament through the story of David). Forgiveness also happens because of the oneness of God and man (as illustrated in the New Testament through the story of Paul).

Do you seek forgiveness when you ask God for healing? Now that I have brought up the subject, I am aware that when I seek spiritual healing I am seldom thinking of *forgiveness*. I seek help, guidance, and confirmation from God and from others whose witness is strong and pure. I receive what I ask for, and I sometimes receive correction, too (at no extra charge). These true witnesses turn me (again) to the Master Shepherd who leads me, feeds me, protects me, and "restores my soul" (see Psalm 23).

No one offering spiritual inspiration, no knowing friend or Christian witness, tries to stand in the Master's stead. Instead, such a one shines the light afresh on the goal. Surely one of the goals in every healing is one's acknowledgment of his or her pure spiritual identity, described in I John 3:1–3:

> Behold, what manner of love the Father hath bestowed upon us, that we should be called the sons of God: therefore the world knoweth us not, because it knew him not. Beloved, now are we the sons of God, and it doth not yet appear what we shall be: but we know that, when he shall appear, we shall be like him; for we shall see him as he is. And every man that hath this hope in him purifieth himself, even as he is pure.

My best efforts to be a true witness to my oneness with God reassures me and simultaneously stirs up my confidence that I am indeed "the son (daughter) of God" and realizing it in increased measure. This acknowledgment is basic to my healing and spiritual growth.

In summary, the true witness identifies with *the* true witness, Christ Jesus. Jesus accepted the testimony of the one Almighty God in regard to creation. His life and words show us all how to turn to God for every solution and explanation.

It's not just people, however, that are true or false witnesses. Our five physical senses (seeing, hearing, feeling, smelling, and tasting) are on the scene all the time, giving their own testimony. Appropriating the pronoun *I*, they say *I see* smiling faces. *I hear* the murmur of voices. *I feel* a gentle breeze. *I smell* something baking in the oven. *I tasted* the pie.

The material senses may seem harmless enough. But then they presume to take over one's body and one's business. They project a battleground where uncertainty or false certainty fire up the big *which*: Which is true—spirituality or materiality? My consciousness, like a camera, has to decide which picture to snap and which to reject. If I'm not feeling well, do I record the discouraging prognosis of a "professional" or the encouraging words of a spiritually minded friend, practicing the reasoning and divine authority of Christ Jesus? The words of the latter reflect the divine prognosis: Thou art whole.

The irony is that what the physical senses perceive as real—as flesh and bone—have no "mind of their own." They are illustrations of *effect*, not cause. The material senses are not cause, but they seem to be the effect (and expression) of false belief.

To all appearances, these ever-active material senses defy God and defile man, God's idea. These senses assume absolute authority. In their ignorance and arrogance, they are, of course, hoisted on their own petard—done in by their own devices. The absolute one God has not been absent from the scene or silenced by universal assumptions that the material senses are natural and essential to man, whether their testimony is terrifying or tentative. *True* authority, however, says this to the prophet _____ (put your name here): "You are my shining: you can never be vulnerable to evil. I am Mind, expressing liberating ideas in and as you. It is natural for you to choose the one unerring sense, spiritual sense. Cherish the fact that I AM omnipotent, omnipresent, and omniscient. Follow my directives. Bear witness to my testimony on your behalf. I am with you to help you."

Whether we are dealing with personal sense testimony or material sense testimony, let us know and teach that every traveler to the Promised Land (spiritual consciousness) chooses, moment by moment, between threatening or promising images of the past, present, future, and especially the *now*. No traveler is locked in a "fate capsule" traveling through time and space.

Because creation reflects God, Spirit, spiritual sense testimony is the only real and present testimony. Spiritual sense maximizes every student's readiness to witness truly, to choose and know the Truth that makes us free (see John 8:32).

8

SIN/SIN-ER: "WHAT'S IT TO YA!" WHAT IS IT TO *YOU?*

Am I a sinner? How readily I answer, *No.* For one thing, I endeavor to avoid doing any of the things named on a typical list of sins: lie, cheat, hate, steal, defy God, ignore God, ignore the needs of my fellow man, indulge selfish wants, or avoid personal and civic responsibilities. I hope I am likewise innocent of other sins you might name.

For another thing, my religion, Christian Science, does not tell me I am a sinner. Instead, it teaches me that I am the child, the reflection, of the all-good God, who created only good, as we're told in Genesis: "And God saw everything that he had made, and behold it was very good (Genesis 1:31). Because God is all good, He could not and did not create evil or sin, nor a mortal, sinful man; to believe otherwise is illogical, as Mary Baker Eddy points out in the Christian Science textbook:

> God is as incapable of producing sin, sickness, and death as He is of experiencing these errors. How then is it possible for Him to create man subject to this triad of errors, — man who is made in the divine likeness? ... Does God create a material man out of Himself, Spirit? Does evil proceed from good? Does divine Love commit a fraud on humanity by making man inclined to sin, and then punishing him for it? ... In common justice, we must admit that God will not punish man for doing what He created man capable of doing, and knew from the outset that man would do. God is "of purer eyes than to behold evil" (*Science and Health*, p. 356:19–26).

So I can and must refuse, refute, and destroy every suggestion (or seeming evidence) to the contrary. My religion reveals that accusations of guilt, though appearing as my own thinking, are conceived and brought forth by Satan (evil, devil) and its hatred of God, good, and man as His perfect spiritual idea. My Master Teacher did not say, "Be ye therefore guilty." Christ Jesus' command to every would-be follower is, "Be ye therefore perfect, even as your Father which is in heaven is perfect" (Matthew 5:48).

The more I focus on this perfect model, with all its attributes and implications, the quicker I am to detect the counterfeit—sinning, mortal man—and to refuse it. Every time I claim and fight for my true identity as one of the wonderful works of God, I am "working out my salvation" and to this end, God is working with me. That's what the apostle Paul tells me in Philippians:

> Wherefore, my beloved, as ye have always obeyed, not as in my presence only, but now much more in my absence, work out your own salvation with fear and trembling. For it is God which worketh in you both to will and to do of his good pleasure. Do all things without murmurings and disputings: That ye may be blameless and harmless, the sons of God, without rebuke, in the midst of a crooked and perverse nation, among whom ye shine as lights in the world ... (Philippians 2:12–15).

Conversely, every time I seem to lose sight of the perfect model and my consciousness agrees to devilish mortal mind's accusations that I lack, I fear, or I hate, my self-concept wanders from the way. Even then, my creator and faithful friend, God, stays with me, holds me, and leads me. Perhaps the Psalmist experienced these attacks of self-doubt, but he was inspired to affirm God's presence and care in this psalm:

> O Lord, thou hast searched me, and known me. Thou knowest my down-sitting and mine uprising, thou understandest my thought afar off. Thou compassest my path and my lying down, and art acquainted with all my ways. Whither shall I go from thy spirit? or whither shall I flee from thy presence? If I ascend up into heaven, thou art there: if I make my bed in hell, behold, thou art there. If I take the wings of the morning, and dwell in the uttermost parts of the sea; Even there shall thy hand lead me, and thy right hand shall hold me (Psalm 139:1–3, 7–10).

The Lord does indeed encompass my way and teach my tongue to talk. The Shepherd, divine Love, persistently brings me back into the fold of attending only to Love's assurances, not sin's accusations. Divine Love meets our every need by being an insistent voice in consciousness that says, You have been, are now, and ever will be my image and likeness.

There are many kinds of sins, but they all come down to a belief in a power apart from God, a belief that breaks the First Commandment in Exodus 20. Christian Science requires this deeper and higher awareness of sin as stated in the following:

> It is a sin to believe that aught can overpower omnipotent and eternal Life, and this Life must be brought to light by the understanding that there is no death, as well as by other graces of Spirit. We must begin, however, with the

more simple demonstrations of control, and the sooner we begin the better. The final demonstration takes time for its accomplishment. When walking, we are guided by the eye. We look before our feet, and if we are wise, we look beyond a single step in the line of spiritual advancement (*Science and Health*, p. 428:32).

Human experience seems to be an unending tug-of-war between the influences of good and of evil. That same mental conflict undoubtedly hounded the people of Jesus' day, too, but Christ Jesus preached and proved that one could and should choose God as the only Father, Teacher, Judge, Protector, and Deliverer. Delay in choosing God results in choosing mortality—and sin.

So, am I a sinner? How obediently and gratefully I answer, No! I have agreed to the continuous rebirth of righteousness—the knowledge that God alone creates and unfolds all that is me, tenderly correcting me and crowning the human endeavor to have only one God, one source of being, doing, and learning.

As the spiritual image and likeness of God, I can demonstrate my sinless nature and *stop* sinning. I need not and will not agree that a power called sin could ever displace the sovereignty, the absolute reign and rule of divine Mind, of divine Life, Truth, and Love. Because I reflect sinless being, I am alert to detect and reject the claim that sin is a power opposed to God, separating man from God. Because of my sinless nature, I accept the constant challenge to have only one God, one Mind, one Life, and my reliance on God increases. Divine Life, the only creator, enlarges my commitment to have but one God, and it arms me for the fight. It's not a fight against actual evil. It is a fight to accept and act out the dominion that is native to me, as it is to all, as established in Genesis 1:

> And God said, Let us make man in our image, after our likeness: and let them have dominion over the fish of the sea, and over the fowl of the air, and over the cattle, and over all the earth, and over every creeping thing that creepeth upon the earth. So God created man in his own image, in the image of God created he him; male and female created he them. And God blessed them, and God said unto them, Be fruitful, and multiply, and replenish the earth, and subdue it: and have dominion over the fish of the sea, and over the fowl of the air, and over every living thing that moveth upon the earth (Genesis 1:26–28).

Because God creates me in his image and likeness, I am willing to "fight the good fight with all my might." What a privilege. What a blessing. What a singular way to worship

God and honor His creation. I heed this message by John S. B. Monsell, which is sung as a hymn in many churches:

> Fight the good fight with all thy might,
> Christ is thy strength, and Christ thy right;
> Lay hold on Life, and it shall be
> Thy joy and crown eternally.
>
> Run the straight race through God's good grace,
> Lift up thine eyes, and seek His face;
> Life with its way before us lies,
> Christ is the path, and Christ the prize.
>
> Faint not nor fear, His arms are near;
> He changeth not, and thou art dear;
> On Him rely and thou shalt see
> That Christ is all in all to thee.
>
> (Hymn No. 59, John S. B. Monsell, *Christian Science Hymnal.* Used courtesy of The Mary Baker Eddy Collection.)

So what about sin? Jesus said, "Whosoever committeth sin is the servant of sin" (John 8:34). It's encouraging to ponder what Mary Baker Eddy reveals about sin. She doesn't try to define it as a frightening reality, nor does she agonize over its meaning. She does make it clear just how I am to detect sin, and think and pray about it. In *Science and Health* she writes,

> There are many species of insanity. All sin is insanity in different degrees. Sin is spared from this classification, only because its method of madness is in consonance with common mortal belief (p. 407:29–32).
>
> Sin has the elements of self-destruction. It cannot sustain itself. If sin is supported, God must uphold it, and this is impossible, since Truth cannot support error (p. 481:24–27).

And in her book *Miscellaneous Writings 1883–1896*, she writes,

> We have no enemies. Whatever envy, hatred, revenge—the most remorseless motives that govern mortal mind—whatever these try to do, shall "work together for good to them that love God." Why? Because He has called His own, armed them, equipped them, and furnished them defenses

impregnable. Their God will not let them be lost; and if they fall they shall rise again, stronger than before the stumble (p. 10:4–12).

And finally, Eddy explains how sin is forgiven:

> We acknowledge God's forgiveness of sin in the destruction of sin and the spiritual understanding that casts out evil as unreal. But the belief in sin is punished so long as the belief lasts (*Science and Health*, p. 497:9).

Sin claims to have a history, commencing in Genesis 2 with the story of Adam and Eve and the serpent. Genesis also tells the story of Joseph, who kept rising like a cork in the sea of sin, which repeatedly tried to drown him in adversity. He persisted in trusting God and disdaining the serpents of hatred, revenge, and self-pity. His trust in God's perfect purpose kept lifting him, even during episodes of imprisonment, toward the kingly position from which he would save Egypt, Canaan, and his brothers, the children of Israel, from famine.

While imprisoned on the Isle of Patmos, John the Revelator had two visions that, when realized, would permanently reassert God's government of the universe and His power over the devouring dragon.

Chapter 10 of the book of Revelation tells of a mighty angel who strode uncontested upon the sea and the earth, the very image of one empowered by divine purpose. This angel of revelation delivered to John "a little book open," along with the command to "Go and take the little book which is open in the hand of the angel which standeth upon the sea and upon the earth. And I went unto the angel, and said unto him, Give me the little book. And he said unto me, Take it, and eat it up; and it shall make thy belly bitter, but it shall be in thy mouth sweet as honey" (verses 8, 9).

Chapter 12 describes a woman wearing the sun, moon, and stars, and who was "pained to be delivered." There also was "the great red dragon" ready to "devour her child as soon as it was born." She brought forth a spiritual sense of man destined to rule all mankind, and "her child was caught up unto God, and to his throne." This cosmic woman was declaring, "Time for deliverance," heedless of a long shadow cast by a small serpent swollen with self-destruction.

Michael and his angels defeated the dragon, and "the great dragon was cast out, that old serpent, called the Devil, and Satan, which deceiveth the whole world" (Revelation 12:9).

The Revelator "takes away mitre and sceptre. He enthrones pure and undefiled religion, and lifts on high only those who have washed their robes white in obedience and suffering. Thus we see, in both the first and last books of the Bible, —in Genesis and in the Apocalypse—that sin is to be Christianly and scientifically reduced to its native nothingness" (*Science and Health*, p. 571:31–36).

Christian Science explains it this way: God is omnipotent; sin is impotent. In every awakening, some aspect of the sinner is consumed; his sins are destroyed, and the individual is freed from sin—saved. So what about sin? Here are some things you find out when you get right inside of S-I-N:

S-I-N: **So** it's **n**ecessary, something I necessarily believe and do? **S**ay it's **n**ot!
S-I-N: **S**cience it's **n**ot. Science is knowledge and understanding, which everyone wants.
S-I-N: **S**uccessful it's **n**ot because **s**atisfying it's **n**ot.
S-I-N: **S**in **is n**egative. Some would say **s**in **is n**othing until you buy its goods, which are "beds", which are sins.
S-I-N: **S**ee it **n**ot, **s**ay it **n**ot, **s**ow it **n**ot.

There's an alphabet soup of sins: avarice, bigotry, callousness, dishonesty, indifference, jealousy, lust, manipulation, pride, racism, sexism, treachery, violence, and warring. No doubt you can add other sins that you hate or fear or feel victimized by.

You may try to ignore sin, but sin is a mild or raging concern to countless people in all cultures. Does progress for mankind—and you—hinge on controlling, even conquering, the blatant as well as hidden influences of this debilitating belief? **(Discuss.)**

But, "Why bother?" you may say. "Sin has been around since the beginning of human history. We just have to cope with its eruptions in our lives and keep moving forward." Indeed, we must keep moving on, but we owe it to God, ourselves, and our neighbors to destroy this pestilence. Destroy sin? Wouldn't that require the power and will of God? Yes, indeed, and God's will and power are focused on demonstrating the perfection of being, which excludes sin. If God's allness excludes it, then as His image and likeness I can exclude sin. I can purify my worship of God and my concept of God's creation, as I am encouraged to do in this passage from I John:

> Behold, what manner of love the Father hath bestowed upon us, that we should be called the sons of God: therefore the world knoweth us not, because it knew him not. Beloved, now are we the sons of God, and it doth not yet appear what we shall be: but we know that, when he shall appear, we shall be like him; for we shall see him as he is. And every man that hath this hope in him purifieth himself, even as he is pure (I John 3:1–3).

9

IMAGE AND IMAGES

According to the record of creation in the first chapter of Genesis, God created man, male and female, in his own image, and God gave them dominion.

According to the counterfeit creation story in the second and third chapters of Genesis, the Lord God created man and woman out of matter, not giving them dominion, but instead, a tree representing the knowledge of good and evil. Along with the tree came tempting fruit and a serpent tempting Eve and Adam to eat the fruit.

Was it nutritious fruit—or a temptation that could have been resisted? The penalty for disobedience was expulsion from the garden of Eden and a life of sorrowful effort. What a sad image (picture) that story paints. More accurately, the story in Genesis 2 and 3 presents *images* of disobedience that contradict the *image* of dominion presented in Genesis 1. Man cannot gain dominion through disobedience but expresses dominion by agreeing with the oneness of God and His image and likeness.

How could the first "human" be so unlike the man created by God and given dominion over all the earth? It is much more believable that an *obedient* man would represent the first "human," and the first human for whom we have an extended record in the Bible is Abraham. He must have been seeking the truth about God, because when God called him to leave the gods of his family and his country, he obeyed. Abraham was guided to the Promised Land. Like the mythical garden of Eden, the Promised Land contained challenges, but Abraham was faithful in his obedience to the one God—and therefore he and his offspring succeeded in establishing a people, the Jews, who tried to turn away from gods and images, and to worship the one God.

Later, when the Jews in the Promised Land were experiencing extended drought and famine, they accepted Joseph's invitation to come to Egypt, where there would be plenty of food. The Egyptians worshipped images, and while the Jews were in Egypt, many began to worship the same visible images rather than worship an invisible God.

After the Jews' four hundred years in Egypt, Moses was called to lead them away from Egypt, back to the Promised Land. En route, Moses received from God Ten Commandments, which he gave to the people. As you probably remember, God commanded them to have only one God and to stop making and bowing down to images.

The Bible traces the history of the Jews over a period of almost two thousand years, from the appearance of Abraham around 1850 BCE to Paul's and Peter's letters to the churches. Does this sweep of history show that *images* of gods won out over image, man as the image of God? No. It shows Father-Mother God sending prophets, Christ Jesus, Paul, John the great Revelator, and others to educate and inspire creation to know itself, to be Godlike.

When did this distinction emerge between *bowing down* to an image and *being* an image of God? Abraham looked and listened for the truth and then acted in accord with Truth. Doesn't that pretty well describe a reflection, acting as its original acts? When the one God commanded him to leave the land of many gods and travel "to a new land he knew not where," he did. Abraham obeyed. In this new land, his descendants would grow in their understanding of the one God and expel multitudes that clung to multiple gods.

Eventually in this new land, the Jews got carried away by attraction to the old images, and they literally got carried away into captivity. Around 721 BCE, the pagan nation of Assyria "carried Israel away into Assyria" because "the children of Israel did secretly those things that were not right against the Lord their God, and they built them high places in all their cities, from the tower of the watchmen to the fenced city" (II Kings 17:6, 9). They served idols.

The story of Adam, in contrast to the account of the obedient Abraham, described a man who seemed unwilling or unable to rise above the mist of uncertain commitment. Instead of attending to the one creator, God, Adam deferred to a human, Eve. She was created as a helper intended to make Adam complete. A little rising and lifting up of her head—of their heads—would have revealed that the layer of mist was thin and low-lying. Above it was the light of clarity, of one God and God's divine image and likeness, male and female.

In the low-lying mist, Eve saw the distorted image of a serpent talking. Instead of dismissing the serpent as an illusion, she listened to the serpent's argument, excited that she was being offered the promise that she, too, would be a god and know it all, know good and evil. She bought the goods of the self-serving false advertiser and shared the illegal harvest with Adam.

Would Abraham have accepted the fruit so readily? No. Surely he would have responded, "Throw it away!" Remember? We left that place of many gods, having seen for ourselves the emptiness of its promise. We heard the voice of the one God saying, Come out from among them and be separate. It was the clear and original light of "in the beginning God" ensuring that we would detect and reject the false promise of the serpent, which appealed to pride and greed.

Abraham and Sarah … now there's a pair of worthies perfectly linked (as by reflection) to the one God! The various enticements to doubt or to revert to graven images that seemed more *at hand* could not long darken their light and joy. The one God was showing them that fidelity was the path to safety and progress. They could walk in this path with confidence and peace of mind, and they did. They would not have been fooled by the illusive serpent's offer, "I can make you as gods, knowing good and evil." Their words, as ours, would have been, "We don't want to know evil. We want to know God, good."

Abraham and Sarah understood something of man as the image and likeness of Father-Mother God. This understanding enabled Abraham and Sarah to have a child in old age (see Genesis 18). The seed of monotheism was to prosper throughout the world because of their fidelity.

The novel writer who invented Adam and Eve assumed the role of creator. This *greatest wrong* was not an actual *wrong*, but only an assumed power opposed to the one Almighty God and His great truth: one perfect creator of perfect images unfolding as creation.

Adam and Eve understood nothing of man as the image and likeness of Father-Mother God. Their seed of "wrong notions" about God is "fading out" (see *Science and Health*, p. 357:19). The story of Adam and Eve dramatized the destructive results of disobedience. They broke the law, and they were expelled from its protection but not from its demands.

The demand of God is light and life, so I believe Adam and Eve gradually learned during their next several hundred years of life to yield to God's law and love it. Their reward was a third son, Seth, whose descendants "turned again to the Lord" and prospered. Brilliant lights, such as Enoch and Noah "walked with God," lifting up all mankind by their example. They became images of success—not images to be worshipped, but examples of obedience to inspire future generations. The descendants of Noah's son Shem cherished God's promise to them: "God shall enlarge Japheth, and he shall dwell in the tents of Shem" (Genesis 9:27).

Enoch, Noah, Shem, and Abraham revealed the possibility of choice, the necessity to choose. Choose God. It's a continuous and decisive mental action. It's an expectant and grateful mental state abiding in light that forever excludes the dark and distorted image of a separation, of wanting to be separate, or of fearing separation.

The great continuing question for everyone, whose answer seems to ebb and flow, is, What image do we accept as true, the image of Adam or the image of man as created in God's own likeness? I believe that through all the shifting scenes of human existence, I must continue to choose man/me as the image and likeness of God, knowing, seeing, hearing, feeling, only as a reflection, the expression of God. With equal ardor I must continue to refuse and reject the misty image of man/me as separate and distinct from God, and proud of it! I am a distinct and distinguished expression of God, or I am in a dream from which I must awaken. Which is it?

Thank God, I cannot *sleep* in peace. Rather do I sing for joy that thought continuously awakens me and gives me rest. In the garden of eternal good and infinite variety, I am content to enjoy God and His creation forever. My continuing education course is to ask, as *image*, What is God knowing and doing? What is He imaging forth? This asking will mean continuing and expanding deliverance from the separatist's question, What do the images of personal sense presume to be knowing and doing—about matter?

But wait! Why should Eve have considered the talking serpent *an illusion*? Couldn't she logically have concluded that the Lord God was using a new means of communicating? After all, the serpent was one of the "beasts of the field which the Lord God had made" (Genesis 3:1). Why wouldn't she perceive the serpent as the Lord God's way of offering more blessings? "Opened" eyes that would enable her to know good and evil might have seemed very logical. But note! Eve did not detect the subtle requirement that she would have to doubt the finality of God's direct command (to Adam) not to eat of "the fruit of the tree which is in the midst of the garden" (verse 3) and disobey that command. We could and do fault her (in a way that we don't fault ourselves) for accepting a spokesperson instead of demanding to learn about this change in instructions directly from the Lord, or through Adam, who originally told her about the command from God.

Joshua urged the Israelites, "Choose you this day whom ye will serve" (Joshua 24:15), implying that the people should not choose false images. He concluded, "As for me and my house, we will serve the Lord."

We all must choose between material sense and spiritual sense, or Soul, God. Mary Baker Eddy writes, "Science has inaugurated the irrepressible conflict between sense and Soul. Mortal thought wars with this sense as one that beateth the air, but Science outmasters it, and ends the warfare. This proves daily that 'one on God's side is a majority'" (*Miscellaneous Writings 1883–1896*, p.102:27).

What can we conclude about *image* and *images*? *Required* (according to God's law): Thou shalt serve the Lord thy God, and him only shalt thou serve. In other words, be God's image and likeness. *Forbidden* (according to God's law): Thou shalt not make unto thee any graven image. One who acknowledges himself/herself as God's *image* sees endless possibilities. One who is looking for or making "graven" or false images faces only dead-end disappointments.

I am—and you are—the image and likeness of God, "the compound idea of God, including all right ideas" (*Science and Health*, p. 475:14).

10

THE IMAGE GOD MADE DID NOT DISINTEGRATE INTO IMAGES

Image. When you think of something, what's the first association that comes to mind? A matter thing or a mental thing? An image can be a mental picture, an ideal. *What do you imagine life is going to be like when you move to London?*

The mortal body appears to be a matter thing that can be healthy or diseased, an image visible in the mirror and known through five material senses. And disease appears to be a condition of the mortal body, entirely apart from thought. Christian Science, however, describes disease as "an image of thought externalized" (*Science and Health*, p. 411:23).

Was the Almighty God the first to use the word *image*? The first chapter of Genesis records that God created man to be like God: "And God said, Let us make man in our image, after our likeness: So God created man in his own image, in the image of God created he him; male and female created he them" (Genesis 1:26, 27).

Images. This word brings to mind photographs as well as pictorial and sculptural representations of God made by pagans. Such images are counterfeit gods that would be forbidden once the people received the Ten Commandments through Moses. Centuries earlier, Abraham had obeyed God's call to leave images behind and travel to an undisclosed land.

Maybe events prior to the emergence of Abram (later called Abraham) on the world scene never happened! Maybe there never were an Adam and Eve, or a Noah or an Enoch, or a Tower of Babel! Maybe folks just sat around making up stories about how it all came to be, and the best stories survived and got written down.

Still, I think we would want to ask the question, Why did they tell and repeat the stories until they became mythology, oral history? Simply put, people want to know their history, or lacking access to that knowledge, they make up their own story. These images of thought become externalized and immortalized as oral history.

Monotheism describes that shift from belief in many images called "gods" to the one God that called Abraham to adopt this elevated mental image. Today we might take monotheism for granted, but it was centuries in the making.

It was first Enoch and then Noah who "walked with God" (Genesis 5:22; 6:9)—the one God. And because of his allegiance and obedience to God, Noah was led to build an ark to save himself, his family, and his animals from the flood. Afterward, God made a covenant with Noah, and what Noah heard was that never again would God destroy the earth. Actually, God had not destroyed His creation; the story shows that sin had *self*-destructed, as it always must, but Noah's obedience provided his protection (see Genesis 6:9).

A sculptor's hands may carve or mold material images of God. Hands also represent man's ability to do good, as when Jesus laid his hands on the crippled woman (Luke 13:13–14) and immediately she was the very image of normality and health. She was no longer bent over and unable to *lift up herself.*

Sometimes an image is a model used by a sculptor or painter, and Mary Baker Eddy utilized this meaning when she wrote, "We must form perfect models in thought and look at them continually, or we shall never carve them out in grand and noble lives" (*Science and Health*, p. 248:27). Mortals mentally register images (mental pictures), and if they don't like the image, they can edit or delete it. *Science and Health* is right on target when it says, "Blot out the images of mortal thought and its beliefs in sickness and sin" (p. 391:3–4). A bad image can be replaced by a good image, a material image by a spiritually mental image, an image of sickness with an image of health.

The human or mortal mind seeks to be acknowledged and feared by projecting images of matter onto consciousness, but man is neither a roll of unexposed film nor a book of history with no words or pictures on its pages. As Genesis tells us, man is the image and likeness of God (Genesis 1:26).

Religion provides an approach to God. Religion makes statements about God and God's creation—man and the universe. It also makes statements about evil. Is religion a human institution, or is it divine? Did Jesus believe in an "evil one" that dogged his preaching and practice and finally managed to crucify him? The more this "evil one" sought acceptability as cause and effect, the more Jesus insisted instead on God's presence and power, and his own perfect being and safety. He did not agree with matter images or with mental images of evil and hopelessness. He adhered absolutely to God and the images God created in his own likeness, which God described as being "very good" (Genesis 1:31).

What about the image or symbol of a *talking serpent*? We know that snakes can't talk; so perhaps what Eve really heard were her own thoughts tempting her to believe in another creator besides the one God, good, that would allow her to know good *and* evil.

On the other hand, Jesus listened only to the one God, his Father, and spoke and did only what God told him to do and say. Even though he did not write down God's words or appoint a biographer, the words of truth he heard could not be lost. They were shared orally for a generation, and then the apostle Paul and the disciple Mark began to write down Jesus' story in order to "tell the old, old story of Jesus and his love," as the traditional hymn says (No. 414, A. Katherine Hankey, *Christian Science Hymnal*. Used courtesy of The Mary Baker Eddy Collection).

Paul described the way of renewal in Romans this way: "Be not conformed to this world: but be ye transformed by the renewing of your mind …" (Romans 12:2). From that perspective, rise to a more spiritual concept of yourself and find increasing strength, health, usefulness, beauty, freedom, dominion, and productivity.

That's a good idea, but how? By using material building blocks? The troubling thing about material strength, material health, material usefulness, material anything is that each material thing deteriorates and "man" is left "without hope" (Job 7:5). But by being "transformed by the renewing of your mind" (Romans 12:2), you can use the spiritual building blocks that Christ Jesus did and Paul described—building blocks of spiritualized thoughts—and the body is proved to be the temple of God. "What? know ye not that your body is the temple of the Holy Ghost which is in you, which ye have of God, and ye are not your own?" (I Corinthians 6:19).

After the flood (Genesis 11) Noah's sons went forth to populate the earth. Some settled in Ur and began to build a tower toward heaven, that they might be remembered and protected. God exposed this Tower of Babel as selfish human ambition and rejected the use of material building blocks to reach spiritual understanding. These builders were scattered far and wide, but they picked up the pieces of their lives and moved on because progress, not defeat, is the law of Life, God.

The sun is never defeated but is always rising, always present, in this world. So also is the *son*, God's idea or image and likeness. Man—male and female—was given dominion, and that mental quality ensures that we humans will rise again and again. *Dominion* drives us onward and upward. As we gradually perceive that all we want is spiritual, not material, of Spirit and not of matter, we become more alive—closer to life, not closer to death (see *Science and Health*, p. 214:19).

As Christian Science describes it, "Mortals are inclined to fear and to obey what they consider a material body more than they do a spiritual God. All material knowledge, like the original 'tree of knowledge,' multiplies their pains, for mortal illusions would rob God, slay man, and meanwhile would spread their table with cannibal tidbits and give thanks" (*Science and Health*, p. 214:19). Socrates sought and found some understanding of the immortality of man; thus he was unafraid of the poison he swallowed or the poison (hatred and jealousy) of his enemies (see *Science and Health*, p. 215:28).

Thought that is naturally rising spiritually is fiercely opposed by the lingering belief that evil is as real as good. Isn't this the very belief for which we fault Eve? Thus the choice we must constantly make: "Error bites the heel of truth, but cannot kill truth. Truth bruises the head of error—destroys error. Spirituality lays open siege to materialism. On which side are we fighting?" (*Science and Health*, p. 216:7).

Because of God's law, it is natural for the human mind and body to rise above sin, disease, and death. It is not natural for the human mind and body to submit to sin, disease, and death. "I shall not die, but live and declare the works of the Lord" (Psalm 18:1). Now that's a declaration of risen thought!

If there is indeed one God, which there is, then God's creation, His image and likeness, did not disintegrate into a maze of images, some frightening, some attractive. There is/was no other god creating counterfeit or false images. More and more of us must go deeper and deeper into the implications of this fact—the fact that the image God made did not, could not, disintegrate into images.

11

RISING THOUGHT ENCOUNTERS
AND CONQUERS ILLUSION

Can thought rise from *babble* to *clarity*—from the fear and uncertainty at the Tower of Babel to the clarity and harmony of New Jerusalem? Please say yes. Jesus showed that thought could rise from babble to clarity when he healed a man of deafness and impaired speech:

> And they bring unto him one that was deaf, and had an impediment in his speech; and they beseech him to put his hand upon him. And he took him aside from the multitude, and put his fingers into his ears, and he spit, and touched his tongue; And looking up to heaven, he sighed, and saith unto him, Ephphatha, that is, Be opened. And straightway his ears were opened, and the string of his tongue was loosed, and he spake plain (Mark 7:32–35).

Jesus expected his disciples to exhibit clarity of thought and demonstrate the harmony of being, and not to be "blind guides," as he called the Pharisees in Matthew 23. Jesus said to Philip, "Have I been so long time with you, and yet hast thou not known me, Philip? he that hath seen me hath seen the Father; and how sayest thou then, Shew us the Father?" (John 14:9). If Philip had exhibited more clarity of thought, he would have known who Jesus was and what his relationship with the Father was.

Jesus also expected clarity of thought of his other followers: "Verily, verily, I say unto you, If a man keep my saying, he shall never see death" (John 8:51). He expected them to "keep [his] saying." He told them, "I am the door: by me if any man enter in, he shall be saved, and shall go in and out, and find pasture" (John 10:9). Jesus expected his disciples to rise to his level of thought and go through the door to the understanding of God—the reality that he had demonstrated for them.

Can thought rise from the babble of collective confusion to the brilliance of revelation? Jesus didn't doubt it for a moment!

Jesus taketh with him Peter, and James, and John, and leadeth them up into an high mountain apart by themselves: and he was transfigured before them. And his raiment became shining, exceeding white as snow; so as no fuller on earth can white them. And there appeared unto them Elias with Moses: and they were talking with Jesus (Mark 9:2–4).

And Peter, James, and John witnessed the event. They had gone with him physically to the site, and they witnessed the transfiguration, no doubt terrified. Peter suggested that they "make three tabernacles," and Mark explained that "he wist not what to say." A voice out of the cloud interrupted Peter and instructed the disciples, "This is my beloved Son, hear him." If Jesus had not thought that they could rise to the brilliance of revelation, would he have brought them with him up on the mountain?

John the Revelator elected to be "in the Spirit on the Lord's day" (Revelation 1:10). John was willing and able to transcend material sense, rise from material to spiritual sense, and thus see what the angel was showing him. He described where he was, and why, and what the voice told him:

I John, who also am your brother, and companion in tribulation, and in the kingdom and patience of Jesus Christ, was in the isle that is called Patmos, for the word of God, and for the testimony of Jesus Christ. I was in the Spirit on the Lord's day, and heard behind me a great voice, as of a trumpet, Saying, I am Alpha and Omega, the first and the last: and, What thou seest, write in a book ..." (Revelation 1:9–11).

Thought rises when the human mind yields to Truth. Jesus did not condemn the adulterous woman brought to him by the scribes and the Pharisees. When one by one her accusers departed without stoning her, Jesus admonished her, "Go, and sin no more" (John 8:11). I feel quite sure that she "went and sinned no more"—she couldn't have! When Jesus healed you, you were healed! Your thought was purified and transformed—as hers no doubt was.

For most people, there is not a sudden huge leap from error into truth or from ignorance into light. It is a step-by-step process, but consciousness does have to be challenged and wakened. Throughout the Bible, there is a rising of thought from the merely physical to the spiritual. Jesus demonstrated the Mind of God, the divine Mind. Paul later made the statement, "Let this mind be in you which was also in Christ Jesus" (Philippians 2:5).

How do we explain the disturbed, downcast, or distorted thought that seems to challenge and sometimes negate risen thought? In the same way we account for six as the sum of two plus two, or the musical note *A* having the sound of *B* or *C*. We don't *explain* such impossibilities, we *correct* them. Such impossibilities are simply errors, *illusions*—notions that seem to be true but are not. If a mind or man separate from God were a possibility or a reality, Jesus would not have reversed God's will in order to restore health and harmony.

Much earlier in the history of rising thought Moses doubted his ability to lead the children of Israel out of slavery in Egypt. God told him to cast his rod on the ground. It became a serpent. God then told him to pick up the serpent, at which point it again became a rod (see Exodus 4:4).

The more divine wisdom compels thought to rise, the more quickly thought rejects phases of arrogant *mortal belief* that confuse the learner and stultify progress.

Thought is rising, must rise, to correct illusions of every sort. Man is meant to dwell in the light of Truth, not in the darkness of lies and chaos. God's first creation was light (see Genesis 1:3). We must agree to this correct sense of identity and mentally reverse the notion of "2 + 2 = 6" even if 6 is written very large right before our eyes. It is the will of God that I know myself truly and correct each notion or suggestion that limited matter is created by unlimited Spirit, even if matter is written large right before my eyes.

The five bodily senses do not aid rising thought. Mortal mind (the illusion that matter has a mind) tries to focus thought on matter but calls it something else. Mortal mind calls escaping from sin, disease, and death an illusion. But no. Rising thought requires reasoning, and reasoning requires thought. Jesus' obedience to God required that he always let his thought rise to a spiritual perspective.

Paul wrote in his letter to the Romans, "To be carnally minded is death; but to be spiritually minded is life and peace" (Romans 8:6). As our thought rises, we become more spiritually minded, and as we become more spiritually minded, thought rises.

What if I accepted the fact that evil really can't be true if God is Truth? Then I would always and instantly expose evil and master it. Once evil has been exposed as a lie, I cannot be affected by it.

Jesus proved that neither person, place, nor thing could determine his life or his demonstration of true manhood. He lived a higher sense of manhood than had ever been lived before. He showed his followers how to keep his sayings and go through the door he had opened, and he promised them, "Lo, I am with you alway" (Matthew 28:20).

Is there thought that does not rise and conquer illusion? The Bible appears to be full of examples, like the example below from the final days and hours before the crucifixion. Jesus' thought kept on rising throughout this tortuous time and his days in the sepulcher, but what about the thought of all the others involved in this travesty of justice?

All the chief priests and elders of the people delivered Jesus to Pontius Pilate, the governor, without whose consent there could be no crucifixion. Pilate knew their motive was envy. His wife urged him, "Have thou nothing to do with that just man" (Matthew 27:19), but the Pharisees whipped up the crowd to demand the crucifixion of Jesus and the release of the criminal Barabbas.

Pilate's thought and courage rose up and stood tall, and he asked, "Why, what evil hath he done?" (Matthew 27:23). However, "When Pilate saw that he could prevail nothing, but that rather a tumult was made, he took water, and washed his hands before the multitude, saying, I am innocent of the blood of this just person: see ye to it" (Matthew 27:24).

In our last snapshot of Pilate, he is washing his hands in ritual purification of collaboration, but what about his thinking? He had let his thought sink to the level of self-preservation at the expense of an innocent man, a man who had brought only unselfish blessings to the people of Jerusalem. Can a thought so dashed down ever rise? Jesus answered yes when he said from the cross, "Father, forgive them; for they know not what they do" (Luke 23:34). I like to think of Pilate, ashamed and terrified, as ready to hear these words of forgiveness and to grow worthy of them.

What Paul and Jesus knew about evil that Pilate did not know is that evil has a hypnotic effect, making us sometimes think it is real. Can hypnotism convince someone that evil is real—as Moses was tempted to believe when his rod became a serpent? Not if that individual is alert to its hypnotic suggestions and deliberately rejects them as unreasonable and thus untrue. Why would God allow hypnotism to confuse man? God could not allow something He did not create to affect His creation. *Illusion* is not *something; it is illusion!* It is nothing and is proved to *be* nothing by one who finds his or her identity in God, divine Mind.

Like Moses and other Biblical prophets, we can always acknowledge what God's ideas and infinite manifestation are doing in and as each of us. Rising thought does encounter and conquer illusion. For example, when Moses and the children of Israel arrived at the Red Sea with the Egyptian army in pursuit, Moses rose to the occasion, lifted his rod above his head signifying his God-given authority, and heard God's command to move forward. He obeyed, and God parted the waters so that the children of Israel could cross over.

PART III
GETTING TO KNOW THE BIBLE—SPIRITUALLY

12

SOME MAJOR SCRIPTURAL EVENTS

Abraham heard God's call to move to another land.

When they were old, Abraham and Sarah had a son, Isaac.

Isaac and Rebekah gave birth to twins, Jacob and Esau.

Jacob pretended to be Esau in order to get the blessing from his father, Isaac.

Jacob had to run away from his angry brother, Esau.

Many years later, God told Jacob to go back home.

Jacob wrestled with an angel, overcame his fear, and received a new name, Israel.

Israel's twelve sons and their descendants became the twelve tribes of Israel, the "children of Israel."

Israel's son Joseph forgave his brothers for selling him into captivity.

Joseph invited his brothers and father to come live in Egypt.

Four hundred years later, Pharaoh enslaved the children of Israel.

God called to Moses from the burning bush and told him to lead the children of Israel back to their own land of Canaan.

During the forty-year journey, God gave Moses the Ten Commandments that would help and protect the children of Israel. God said, Do not ever believe that a statue or a person is a god or has any power to hurt you or to help you. Wisdom warns *us*, Do not believe in an anthropomorphic god that acts like a human.

Christ Jesus said that the two great commandments are to love God with all your heart, soul, mind, and strength, and your neighbor as yourself (see Matthew 22:37; Mark 12:30; Luke 10:27).

13

QUESTIONS AND COMMENTS TO HELP YOU GET TO KNOW THE BIBLE—SPIRITUALLY

Bible study and Sunday School are full of purpose. In brief, they help us get to know God and ourselves. Questions and "discussion sheets" help facilitate this purpose. All the following items draw on the Bible and the Christian Science textbook, *Science and Health with Key to the Scriptures*, by Mary Baker Eddy. Each discussion sheet ideally contains at least one example like the items listed in this chapter. Students should consider the questions and statements and you will find answers in **(boldface words or citations in the parenthesis).** What students answer is determined through looking things up, discussion, and teacher input. This process will help us get to know more about the Bible.

About the Bible

Do you know who wrote the Bible? More than fifty people wrote poems, prophecies, histories, letters, and prayers. These sixty-six books were finally collected into one book, the Bible.

Do you know how long it took for the Bible to be written? **(About twelve hundred years.)** Proverbs were being collected from as early as about 1050 BCE, and the last book—II Peter—was probably finished about 150 CE. That's about twelve hundred years, isn't it? Some of these Biblical authors were just writing about human and material events and people. Others had a great desire to know God and to have a sense of Spirit, or spiritual sense, which is the opposite of material sense.

(Note: The date for every person and event before Jesus was BC, now called BCE—before the Common Era. Everything after Jesus became AD, now called CE—the Common Era.)

Do Christian Scientists use the whole Bible? **(Yes.)** Christian Science weekly Bible Lessons include stories from every book of the Bible. Their words and stories help thinkers and seekers know what to do and what not to do, how to behave and how not to behave. They help me. Do they help you? **(Answer.)**

Why do we read the Bible in Sunday School? One reason, according to the Christian Science textbook, is that "the Bible contains the recipe for all healing" (*Science and Health*, p. 406:1). And, we need to know the Bible because it, along with *Science and Health with Key to the Scriptures*, is our **(Pastor)**. These books deal with the spiritual relationship between **(God)** and **(man)**.

Can you name twelve books of the Bible? **(Write them down; don't be concerned about spelling.)**

What is the first tenet of Christian Science? (See *Science and Health*, p. 497:3.) Paraphrasing here, as students of the Bible, we let the **(inspired)** Word of the Bible guide us. How do you find the inspired Word among so many words? The inspired Word usually leads us to a spiritual or moral lesson; it leads us to light and not darkness; to life, not death; to good, not evil.

How many books are there in the Bible? **(Sixty-six.)** The Bible is about **(fifteen hundred)** pages long!

Can you find the "inspired Word" in *any* book of the Bible? **(Yes, with the "key" to the Scriptures, you can find the inspired Word in virtually any book of the Bible.)** The inspired Word is any story or passage that teaches the truth about God, man, and the universe. The Bible can help us understand every concept in the Lord's Prayer, which is further explained by its spiritual interpretation, given in the Christian Science textbook (see *Science and Health*, p. 16:24-15).

Every time we read a Bible story, we should ask, what are the **(facts)** of the story?

It is so important to be accurate, isn't it, and sometimes we can get an incomplete, wrong impression from reading a story. As we review the story, the thing we want to ask is, What is it about the story that I want to understand better? Let's review what some faithful and courageous thinkers did as they brought to light the great differences between God and gods, Spirit and spirits. Underline their names.

About 1800 BCE, God led **(Abraham)** to the land of Canaan, where he could learn more about the new idea of the "one God." In Canaan, Abraham found paganism, belief in spirits and idols or "matter gods," but he stayed true to the one God and brought up his son **(Isaac)** and his grandson Jacob to worship the one God.

Did God change His mind about having Abraham sacrifice his son Isaac? No. Isn't it more likely that God wanted Abraham to understand that there must be no more child or human sacrifice? Sacrifice was a *human* notion that their various gods must be appeased like people; but it never was a law of the one God, whose intent was to make of Abraham a great nation.

About 1700 BCE, there was a famine in Canaan, and **(Jacob/Israel)** led his family, the children of Israel, to Egypt, where there was food and where his son Joseph was in charge of distributing the food. During their four hundred years in Egypt, the early Egyptian pharaohs permitted the children of Israel to worship the one God. Eventually, an unfriendly pharaoh made the Jews his slaves. As slaves, the Jews worked to build the pyramids.

About 1200 BCE, **(Moses)** led them out of slavery, out of Egypt, but they found the same paganism when they arrived in Canaan, the Promised Land. What pagan beliefs and practices did Moses tell the people to avoid? (**"There shall not be found among you any one that maketh his son or his daughter to pass through the fire, or that useth divination, or an observer of times, or an enchanter, or a witch, Or a charmer, or a consulter with familiar spirits, or a wizard, or a necromancer ... Thou shalt be perfect with the Lord thy God."**) (See Deuteronomy 18:10–11, 13.)

A few years later, **(Joshua)** conquered the pagan Canaanites in the Promised Land.

About 700 BCE, the prophet **(Isaiah)** was again warning the Jews, also known as **(the children of Israel),** about pagan practices and urged them to hear God's call: "Look unto me, and be ye saved, all the ends of the earth: for I am God, and there is none else" (Isaiah 45:22).

Over a period of one thousand years, these servants of the one God—Abraham, Jacob-Israel, Moses, Joshua, and Isaiah—warned God's chosen people to reject and destroy pagan beliefs and practices. It seems the people just kept going back to the worship of many gods. Their beliefs in spirits and spiritualism prevented many of the people from finding and worshipping the one God, one Spirit.

Any belief and practice is "pagan" if it ignores God, Spirit, or makes other powers equal to God. Paganism tries to set up matter as the source and cause of everything. What would a pagan belief and practice look like in our world of today? **(Answer.)**

Could the prolonged *darkness* of belief in matter forever resist the *brightness* of God's plan for His people? About 550 BCE, the prophet Ezekiel saw visions of true God and true man. He said Babylon had destroyed Jerusalem and the temple because the Jews had stopped worshipping God, and that the people would learn from this experience and return to God.

The Promised One, the Messiah, finally came and told the full truth about God and man. His message changed thought, and it even changed the measurement of time to "before Christ" and "after Christ."

About eighteen hundred years after Jesus walked the earth and healed extensively, another inspired thinker, Mary Baker Eddy, discovered the Science or spiritual laws of the one God, and in 1875 she published a book that explains this Science. In it, she describes the continuous good the one Almighty God gives to all mankind through His ideas, including you and me and everyone. She wrote, "Spirit blesses man, but man cannot 'tell whence it cometh.' By it the sick are healed, the sorrowing are comforted, and the sinning are reformed. These are the effects of one universal God, the invisible good dwelling in eternal Science" (*Science and Health*, p. 78:28).

Is it important to your future to honor Spirit and discard spirits? (**Yes.**) Will you continue to look for and find "the one God, the invisible good dwelling in eternal Science"? (*Science and Health*, p. 78:12). How will you do this? How will you find something that is invisible? (**Discuss.**)

The following items are taken from a number of different Sunday School lessons and are not meant to be read consecutively, nor is there a sequential flow. They are just examples of Biblical figures, Biblical teachings, and Biblical events illustrating how students can learn more about the Bible.

Who taught Abraham? Abraham learned from (**God**) that there are not many gods, as everyone believed. There is only (**one God**). Let's see what you remember about the history of "listening man," which began with the man named (**Abraham**).

Abraham had two sons: Ishmael by wife (**Hagar**), and Isaac by wife (**Sarah**).

Isaac had twin sons: Esau and Jacob.

Jacob had twelve sons, and he gave his favorite son, Joseph, (**a coat of many colors.**)

The descendants of Abraham, living in the land of Canaan, went to Egypt to buy "bread" or food and finally settled in Egypt because of the long famine. What great-grandson of Abraham was a prince in Egypt and invited the Hebrews to come live in Egypt? (**Joseph.**)

The son of Isaac named (**Judah**) helped to convince Joseph that his brothers, the sons of Jacob-Israel, were coming in peace to ask for food. The word *Jews* came from "Judah," the spokesperson for his brothers.

What descendant of Abraham led the Hebrews out of Egypt after an "unfriendly" pharaoh made them slaves? (**Moses.**) The daughter of Pharaoh found the baby Moses in a basket, floating in the river. She raised Moses to be an Egyptian prince. Who taught Moses about the history of the Hebrew people? (**His mother.**)

Isaiah was a great prophet who was living in the Promised Land of Canaan, which the Hebrews came to under the leadership of (**Moses**) and (**Joshua**) around 1387 BCE. In 587 BCE, the Babylonians destroyed the Jews' temple in Jerusalem and took the Jews as prisoners or captives to Babylon. After the Jews had been in captivity in Babylon for about fifty years, King Cyrus of Persia allowed the Jews to return to their homeland. Isaiah knew that the Jews, the children of Israel, had been taken captive not just because Babylon was a very strong and conquering country, but also because the Jews had stopped putting God first, had stopped obeying the First Commandment, and had stopped trusting God for their protection.

The prophet Isaiah urged the Jews to improve, spiritualize, their concept of God, to see God as the Holy One, the one "all-mighty" God. Was this Almighty God powerless to prevent the Jews from being taken into captivity? God was never powerless and unable to protect His people, but the Jews broke the covenant God had made with them. They needed to gain a better understanding of their God and a more sincere desire to have only one God, to love God, and to obey God. What did Isaiah say about this to the people? (See Isaiah 40:25-26, 28.)

What was God's covenant with Abraham? "And when Abram was ninety years old and nine, the Lord appeared to Abram, and said unto him, I am the Almighty God; walk before me, and be thou perfect. And I will make my covenant between me and thee, and will multiply thee exceedingly" (Genesis 17:1, 2).

Isaiah told the people that a Messiah, or Savior, would come. Did Isaiah's prophecy come true? (**Yes.**) What is your proof? (**The history and works of Jesus.**)

Queen Jezebel (wife of King Ahab) sent a death threat to the prophet Elijah because Elijah had proved that the prophets of (**Baal**) had no power at all (I Kings 18). Elijah had proved that there is only one Almighty God, and yet he was afraid when he received the death threat, and he ran away. How could a person who had proved his knowledge of the allness of God run away in fear from a human who worshipped a man-made god? (**A good question for class discussion.**)

How did God heal Elijah's fear? Remember? It had something to do with wind, earthquake, and fire (see I Kings 19:11–12).

According to many Bible scholars, the Adam and Eve story was probably written about 1000 BCE. At that time, the Hebrews were a strong nation and **(David)** was their king. Over the next nine hundred years, prophets faithful to the one God gave the Hebrew people a better understanding of God. Can you name some of these prophets? **(Elijah, Elisha, Isaiah, and Jeremiah.)**

Looking at the chronology at the back of this book on page 205, what do you notice about the book of Proverbs? **(It was written in part *before* Genesis!)**

A spiritual account of creation, Genesis 1, was written in late 500 BCE. In this true history, Spirit, God reveals a spiritual expression of itself, a spiritual creation where man and woman have **(dominion)** and are declared to be **(good)**, not fallen.

In the Old Testament, Abraham, Moses, and many prophets obeyed God's call to teach the people the truth about the one God. Who was the great teacher of this great truth in the New Testament? **(Jesus.)** He received and held on to the truth. Now, Christians, including Christian Scientists, receive and hold on to this truth by learning about God from the **(Bible)** and from **(*Science and Health*)**.

The apostle Paul explained what it means to "hold on." He wrote, "If we **(live)** in the Spirit, let us also **(walk)** in the Spirit" (Galatians 5:25). This book is called Galatians because it was **(Paul's)** letter to the church in **(Galatia)**.

What son of Jacob-Israel was a servant to Potiphar? **(Joseph; see Genesis 39:7–23.)** Joseph refused to have sexual relations with Potiphar's wife when she tried to seduce him. Our textbook says that "**(Chastity)** is the cement of civilization and progress" (*Science and Health*, p. 57:1). What does "chastity" mean? (Have students look up the definition in the dictionary.) This declaration about progress is in the chapter titled (*Marriage*) in *Science and Health*. Does chastity apply to everyone? In what way?

The Romans arrested the apostle Paul because Paul was stirring up public thought by talking about Christ Jesus and saying that even though Caesar claimed to be God, he was not God. They sent Paul by ship to Rome, where he would be tried, but they had no intention of giving Paul a "fair trial." Was Paul angry and resentful about this injustice? **(No.)**

We know Paul kept his thought focused on the fact that God governs man and the universe, because when the ship was about to sink, he was ready to fearlessly demonstrate God's control, God's plan of good for every man on the ship, and not just for himself. The story of this shipwreck is in Acts 27.

Do you remember the story of Naaman? He was a captain in the Syrian army, and he had a skin disease called leprosy. See how much of this story you can tell in your own words; then read the story in II Kings 5:1–4, 9–14.

Was Naaman healed by "dipping himself seven times" in the Jordan River? (**No, not really.**) What, then, did heal him? (**Humility and willingness to follow Elijah's directive.**) Who are the main characters in this story? (**Naaman**); the (**prophet Elijah**); a little (**maid**); and Naaman's (**servants**), who said "(**wash**) and be clean" (verse 13). It looked like Naaman had fallen into a bad habit of pride and belief in another god called disease. Did God still love Naaman? (**Yes.**) How do you know? (**He healed Naaman.**)

The wise people writing the book of Proverbs, such as King Solomon and others, listed seven things the Lord hates (see Proverbs 6:16–19): a proud (**look**); a lying (**tongue**); hands that shed innocent blood; a heart (or mind) that devises (**wicked**) imaginations (plans); feet that make haste to run to (**mischief**), a (**false witness**) that speaketh lies; and a man who soweth (**discord**) among brothers.

What was the name of the man who betrayed Jesus with a kiss? (**Judas.**) Have you ever heard of the "seven deadly sins"? Do you know what they are? (**Wrath, greed, sloth, pride, lust, envy, and gluttony.**) Which of the "deadly sins" do you think influenced Judas? (**Discuss.**) Had he fallen into some bad habits, like greed and envy? Maybe he was envious that he wasn't as pure as his Master. He did not overcome these ungodlike habits with spiritual convictions, such as gen(**erosity**), gra(**titude**), and unself(**ed love**). Was Judas a "fallen man"? (**Discuss.**) Everyone must "wake to the (**truth of being**)" so that what will cease? (**The mortal dream.**) (See *Science and Health*, p. 218:32).

How did the wise men know to go to Bethlehem? (See Matthew 2:1–2.) Wise people had been looking for a "king" because the prophet Isaiah had told them that "the gov(**ernment**) shall be upon his shoulder" (Isaiah 9:6).

Was the Lord already their King? (**Yes.**) Isaiah 43:15 says, "I am the Lord, your Holy One, the creator of Israel, (**your King**)." Why were the children of Israel looking for a king? (**Discuss.**)

Do you and I pray for a King to come? (**Yes.**) What prayer is used in all Christian churches that prays for God's kingdom to come? (**The Lord's Prayer.**) There is another prayer that is prayed by Christian Scientists that uses words such as *kingdom, reign, rule,* and *govern.* What is it called? (**The Daily Prayer.**)

When God told Moses to lead the children of Israel out of slavery, did Moses say, "Great idea! Let's go!"? (**No!**) (See Exodus 3:10–12.) What did Moses say to God? (**"Who am I, that**

I should go unto Pharaoh ..."). But God reassured Moses that he could do it. What did He say to Moses? **("Certainly I will be with thee.")** How long did it take for the children of Israel to reach the Promised Land? **(Forty years.)**

Let's say you and your family were among the thousands of Hebrew slaves in Egypt. Would you have believed this man named **(Moses)** who said, "Let's get out of here. We are God's people, and we cannot be enslaved"? **(Maybe not.)**

When we look at a map, we see that to walk from Egypt to the Promised Land, you have to get across the Red **(Sea)** and then get across miles and miles of **(desert—see Exodus 13:17–18)**. The people were afraid, but Moses said "fear not, stand still, see the salvation of the Lord" (Exodus 14:13), and the people followed their leader.

Moses led the people out of Egypt, but it was **(God)** that provided a pillar of **(fire)** by night and a cloud by day to **(guide)** them and p**(rotect)** them.

Were the children of Israel satisfied travelers as they walked their way to freedom with signs of God's presence and evidence of Moses's faithful leadership? **(No.)** Why, oh why, did they murmur (grumble)? (See Exodus 16:2, 3, 11–15; Numbers 20:2, 7, 8, 11.)

Does it sometimes seem easier to suffer from wrong and complain, than to claim and demonstrate what's right? **(Discuss.)** *Science and Health* points out, "Whatever enslaves man is opposed to the divine government. Truth makes man free" (p. 225:2–4). Are there any children of Israel around today? **(Yes.)** Check the g**(lossary)** of *Science and Health* for the definition of children of Israel (p. 583:5).

Do you think Moses wanted to experience God as the only reality? **(Yes.)** Moses was raised in a palace as an Egyptian prince. Egypt was a pagan country; people believed in many gods. But Moses' mother had taught him very well about the one God, so he was a faithful Hebrew but lived as an Egyptian.

Because Moses was seeking a fuller understanding of God, "the Lord appeared unto him in a flame of fire." What was burning? **(A bush.)** Let's read that account in Exodus 3:1–5. What did God want Moses to do? **(Go unto Pharaoh and lead the children of Israel out of Egypt—see verse 10.)** Did Moses obey God? **(He took some convincing, but yes, he obeyed.)**

To accomplish his task, Moses needed to be sure that God, Spirit, was the only power, even in the present reality. Perhaps he prayed using words like these: "Nothing is real and eternal—nothing is Spirit—but God and His idea" (*Science and Health*, p. 71:1–2). Let's make this into a positive statement. Instead of beginning with "Nothing," we'll begin with

"Everything." Could we say it like this: Everything real is of Spirit; Mother-Father God is All-in-all, and I am Her idea?

Moses was a great deliverer. Elijah was a great prophet. There are many stories about Elijah in I Kings. Elijah proved to the priests that there is only one God, and Baal is not his name! Queen Jezebel worshipped Baal, so she tried to kill Elijah for insulting Baal. Would you be frightened if someone were trying to kill you? (**Of course.**) Elijah was frightened. He ran away and hid in a cave. But the Lord was with him and asked, "What doest thou here, Elijah?" (I Kings 19:9). Or we might describe it this way: Elijah knew he was cared for by God, so he asked himself, "What am I doing here? Who am I afraid of?" What did God, divine Mind tell Elijah to do, and what did Elijah learn? (See I Kings 19:11–12.)

Perhaps Elijah spoke words like these from *Science and Health*: "Spiritual facts are not inverted; the opposite (**discord**), which bears no resemblance to spirituality, is (**not real**)" (p. 207:30–31).

Which Biblical thinker could have said these words: "Be strong and of a good courage; be not afraid, neither be thou dismayed: for the Lord thy God is with thee whithersoever thou goest" (Joshua 1:9). Moses? (**Yes.**) Joshua? (**Yes.**) Isaiah? (**Yes.**) Jesus? (**Yes.**) Mary Baker Eddy? (**Yes.**) Who else?

The Psalmist (David) was aware of a dark shadow on his path, "the valley of the shadow of death" (Psalm 23:4). He decided not to be afraid. Because of that decision, he became even more aware of help at hand: *a rod and a staff.* Every shepherd used his rod to defend the sheep against (**wolves/bears**). He used his staff to guide and control the (**flock/sheep**). In what ways is God a rod and a staff for us? (**Discuss.**)

Let's always be sure to know God (**protects**) me, and God (**guides**) me. The Psalmist put it this way: "The steps of a good man are ordered by the Lord" (Psalm 37:23).

Because the Psalmist knew that he was being protected and guided, he saw a much brighter path. Instead of a dark shadow, he saw God as the great Shepherd (a defender and guide), and he could see that kindness and love (goodness and mercy) would be with him every day (all the days of his life) and that he actually lived in God's "house" with an abundance of food, drink, and safety. Is that where you live? (**Yes.**) No matter where you live now, or may live twenty years from now, you always *live* in your (**"house"**), and your "house" is your (**consciousness or thinking**).

Who is speaking in Psalm 23? (**David.**) Did this same person write many psalms? (**Yes.**) How do you know? (**Look at the subheadings for the psalms.**)

People started writing down their prayers and songs (psalms) about **(three thousand)** years ago, from about 1000 BCE to about 165 BCE. Let's look at our chronology at the back of this book on page 205 and note when the book of Psalms was written. The psalms were still being written after all the other books in the O**(ld)** T**(estament)** had been finished.

There are **(150)** psalms in our Bible. Some tell the history of the Hebrews, a history that began with what man? **(Abraham.)** (See Genesis 17:1, 2, 4, 5.)

There are 365 **(days)** in a year, and Enoch lived 365 **(years)** on earth. Then did Enoch die? **(No.)** What happened? (See Genesis 5:23–24.) Enoch did not die; he did not believe in the "evidence before his material senses," so instead, Enoch **(walked with God)** and demonstrated eternal life (*Science and Health*, p. 214:5).

Would this statement also be true: Jesus walked with God, and he was not, for God took him? **(Yes.)** (See Mark 16:19.)

What is a "contract"? **(Look up in a dictionary, or discuss.)** Do God and man have a contract? **(Yes.)** In the Bible, a contract is called a *covenant*. The first covenant was between God and the man **(Noah)**. After the flood, which destroyed much of the world known to the Hebrews, Noah thanked God that he and his family and his animals had not drowned. Then God made a covenant with Noah. What was the covenant? (See Genesis 9:11, 13.)

Did Jesus make a covenant with his disciples and with us? What was it? In the following examples, what is the responsibility of each party to the covenant? Jesus said, "[W]hosoever believeth in me shall never die" (John 11:25–26).

- He also said, "*[A]sk*, and it shall be given you; *seek*, and ye shall find; *knock*, and it shall be opened unto you" (Matthew 7:7).
- He also said, "[H]e that *followeth me* shall not walk in darkness, but shall have the light of life" (John 8:12).

The name of the man that Jesus raised from the dead was **(Lazarus)**. As Jesus prayed at the tomb, the first thing he said was "Father, **(I thank thee)** that thou hast heard me" (John 11:41). Christian Science explains that "Jesus restored **(Lazarus)** by the understanding that Lazarus had never died, not by an admission that his body had died and then lived again" (*Science and Health*, p. 75:12–20).

Zacchaeus was a rich Jew who helped the "enemy"—the Roman government—collect taxes from the Jews. The Jews did not like Zacchaeus or trust him, but this man wanted to see Jesus. How did Zacchaeus manage to see this famous Jesus, who was surrounded by a crowd of people? (See Luke 19:2–10.) Did Jesus criticize Zacchaeus? **(No.)** What did Jesus do? **(Called to him, talked to him, and healed him.)** Do you know anyone who seems to be selfish and not loving and not generous? What difference would it make if you saw this person in the same way, in the same light, in which Jesus saw Zacchaeus?

Look up the term *doctrine* in a dictionary. What is it? In Jewish and Christian history (before Christian Science), "atonement" was a way of describing how Jesus, the innocent, let himself be crucified so that mortal man, the guilty, would be spared, not killed, for his evil thoughts and actions. Does this definition of "atonement" describe God's control of His Son—His sons and daughters? **(A good question for discussion.)**

God and Christ Jesus give us a true meaning. Atonement must mean the "at-one-ment" planned by the perfect creator, God, for His/Her perfect creation, man. Are you and I "perfect creation, man"? **(Yes.)** Every Sunday, we hear the fact again: "All is i**(nfinite Mind)** and its i**(nfinite manifestation)**" (*Science and Health*, p. 468:10).

Who provides your food and clothes? **(Your parents.)** Yes, your parents, but not mortals. We need to remember that **"(Spirit)** duly feeds and clothes every object, as it appears in the line of spiritual creation, thus tenderly expressing the **(fatherhood)** and **(motherhood)** of God" (*Science and Health*, p. 507:3–6).

Where in the Bible do we find the Beatitudes that Jesus gave us? **(In Matthew 5:1–12.)** Jesus is teaching us the thoughts and actions and the "be-attitudes" that make us useful, happy, and satisfied. Jesus blesses those people who "grieve," who are sorry for their mistakes, and who are **(humble)** and willing to o**(bey)**. Whom do you look up to as an example of honesty, humility, and right thinking? **(List them and discuss.)**

The Gospel of Mark tells how Jesus came preaching and saying, "**([R]epent ye),** and believe the gospel" (Mark 1:15). To "repent" means to be sorry for insisting on mistaken beliefs. To "repent" means to change your thinking. Do you ever *repent*? **(Discuss.)**

Here are three important ideas: be humble, obey, and repent. These attitudes and actions help us discover who we are. With respect to Christ Jesus, who are we? **(Jesus' humble followers.)**

Mark 3:1–5 tells about Jesus healing a man with a withered (or useless) hand. Religious leaders were watching but not rejoicing. They just wanted to accuse Jesus of breaking one of Moses' Commandments because Jesus "healed" (or "worked") on the **(Sabbath)** day. These religious leaders refused to repent, to change their thinking. Jesus was "grieved" for the "hardness of their hearts," but he went ahead and did what God wanted. What was it? **(Jesus healed the man.)** These religious leaders believed in error—the mistaken thinking that God causes suffering. Because they were not willing to question their thinking and change it, they let error, which is wrong, sink into evil, which is bad and seems to cause or allow suffering. What did Jesus know that enabled him to prove that error/evil is unreal, powerless? **(That man is the son of God, the image and likeness of God, and therefore God-like or perfect.)**

Here's one way to say it: everything real is of Spirit; Mother-Father God is All-in-all, and I am Her idea.

Two prophets in the Old Testament wrote long books. That's one reason they are called major prophets. Who are they? I**(saiah)** and J**(eremiah)**. One of these prophets said, "And ye shall seek me, and find me, when ye shall search for me **(with all your heart)**." That prophet was J**(eremiah)**. (See Jeremiah 29:13.)

In his Sermon on the Mount, Jesus didn't just say to the people, "Do better." Jesus said, "Be ye therefore **(perfect)**" (Matthew 5:48). Jesus was able to heal because he did what he said. He saw the **(perfect man)** (*Science and Health*, p. 476:32–34).

One time, the disciples saw Jesus talking to Moses (who was born about 1,200 years before Jesus) and Elijah (who was born about 600 years before Jesus—see Mark 9:2–9). This was possible because man is spiritual and i**(mmortal)** and has no a**(ge)**, and therefore never dies. Like Jesus, we are acknowledging only our i**(mmortal)**, deathless c**(onsciousness)**. In this consciousness, ideas can be touched; they are tan**(gible)** and real (*Science and Health*, p. 279:11–12).

The spiritual facts of being, or reality, appear as we divest (get rid of) false t**(rusts)** and **(material)** evidence. By doing this, we "sweep away the **(false)** and give place to the **(true)**" as it say in *Science and Health*, p. 428:8–14.

The Psalmist said to God, "Open thou mine eyes, that I may behold wondrous things out of thy law" (Psalm 119:18). Theology is the study of G**(od)**. I expect most students of theology and physics have expressed the same sincere desire as the Psalmist expressed. Does God "open their eyes"? **(To a point—according to their degree of receptivity.)** And yet these seekers still view matter as part of God's law. Is matter part of God's law? **(No!)** Why? Because "law" deals with unchanging facts, whereas "matter" is always changing.

As our textbook on Science tells us, "matter is the f**(alsity)**, not the f**(act)**, of existence" (p. 127:16–22). It states further, "There is **(nothing)** in Spirit out of which **(matter)** could be made ..." (p. 335:8). A chapter in *Science and Health* called *Science, Theology, and Medicine* states, "This theology of Jesus healed the sick" (p. 138:30) and "The theology of Christian Science includes healing the sick" (p.145:31).

Theology and physics teach that matter is real and good (*Science and Health*, p. viii:9–12). What is "theology"? What is "physics"? (Look up both terms in a dictionary.) It seems like what we can *see* is matter and what we *can't see* is idea, but a spiritual thinker *can* see idea. Jesus looked at matter, saw God's perfect idea, and healed the body.

One time a ruler asked Jesus, "What shall I do to inherit eternal life?" (Luke 18:18–24). Maybe he wanted to have a good life here and a continuing life instead of death. What would you tell the ruler to do? (**Discuss.**)

Jesus said, "Keep the commandments."

The ruler said, "I do that already."

Well, then, Jesus said, the next thing you need to do is "sell everything you have and give the money to the poor. Have treasure in heaven. Come follow me." Did Jesus want the man to be poor? (**No.**) Jesus wanted the man to desire and accept heavenly r(**iches**) first so that he could then have human r(**iches**) to share with others. Did the man follow Jesus? (**No.**)

The apostle Paul said (II Corinthians 4:18),

- Don't keep looking at matter: it is t(**emporal**) (a word like "temporary").
- Do keep looking at idea: ideas are e(**ternal**) (they are forever).

All the good and useful things God is giving us do not come in big brown trucks called the (**UPS truck**). They come by way of GTS: gratitude—thought—Spirit.

How about "heaven and earth"? Theology and physics say that matter is where we live now and heaven is where we go when we die. What does the Lord's Prayer say about heaven and earth? (See *Science and Health*, p. 16-17.)

What are some of your favorite Bible stories? (**List them.**) Let me give you some hints about a few stories, and you can probably tell the whole story.

A good story about "matter" is told by Luke in Acts 3:1–9. It seemed like a man was suffering from sick matter (he was lame) and he was hoping to receive good matter (alms or money), and Peter and John went around the belief called matter and healed the man through their understanding of the Christ, the Christ-man: "In the name of Jesus Christ of Nazareth rise up and walk … and the man leaped up and stood and walked with them into the temple" (Acts 3:1–9).

Did Peter, John, and the man prove that matter is not man's condition? (**Yes!**)

Where is the Sermon on the Mount? **(In Matthew 5–7.)** In that collection of teachings, Jesus talked about treasures. In Matthew 6:20–21, he said we should lay up (put) our treasures in **(heaven)**. Why? **(Because what you "treasure" is what you love with your heart, your thought.) (Discuss.)**

There are material riches and heavenly riches. What's the difference? **(Discuss.)**

Jesus gave some good guidance. He said, "Seek ye the **(kingdom of God)** [heavenly riches] and all these things [material riches] shall be added unto you" (Luke 12:31). And don't worry, he said. "It is your Father's good pleasure to give you **(the kingdom)**" (Luke 12:32). God loves us so much that He gives us every thought and idea and thing we need, *and* God helps us want what He gives!

I'm thinking of a time when Jesus was talking to thousands of people outside of town. The people were hungry for the love of God that Jesus was talking about. When the people got hungry for food, what did Jesus do? (See Matthew 14:17–21). Is this Bible story about "substance"? **(Yes.)** What kind of substance? **(Spiritual substance.)**

In Exodus, what did the "Promised Land" represent? **(Consciousness of "eternal, harmonious existence")** (see *The First Church of Christ, Scientist and Miscellany* by Mary Baker Eddy, p. 44:1–6). Who is in the Promised Land right now? **(We are.)** What are some words or phrases in the Lord's Prayer that could be examples of the Promised Land?

Many key people in the Bible accepted and acted on the idea that there is only one God taking care of man, not many gods. We call them mono**(theists)**, and the worship of one God is called "monotheism." Among them are Abraham, Isaac, Jacob, Joseph, Judah, Moses, Joshua, Isaiah, Jesus, and Paul. Are there more? **(Yes.)** All these people were men. There were also many women who witnessed to the truth of being: Hagar, Sarah, Miriam, Ruth, Hannah, Anna, Mary the mother of Jesus, Martha and Mary (the sisters of Lazarus), and Dorcas.

Why did this early group of monotheists come to be called the children of Israel? **(Because they were descendants of Jacob/Israel.)** Who was "Israel"? **(Jacob.)** What is a monotheist? **(One who worships only the one God.)**

Biblical law and prophecy have always declared God's promises. **(Moses)** is the Old Testament leader who represents law. What law? **(God's law, the Ten Commandments.)**

Moses also prophesied the coming of a great prophet when he said, "The Lord thy God will raise up unto thee a Prophet from the midst of thee, of thy brethren, like unto me; unto him ye shall hearken" (Deuteronomy 18:15). Who did this prophet turn out to be? (**The Messiah, Christ Jesus.**)

(**Elijah**) is the Old Testament leader who represents the great (**prophets**). Isaiah also prophesied the coming of the Messiah, who would "feed his flock like a shepherd: he shall gather the lambs with his arm, and carry them in his bosom, and shall gently lead those that are with young" (Isaiah 40:10–11).

Moses gave the children of Israel a way out of being slaves to the Egyptians, and Jesus gives us a way out of being slaves to what? (**Sin, disease, and death.**) Do you remember what Jesus said? It's around the cross and crown logo on the cover of *Science and Health* (**find it on the cover**).

Who were the first man and woman we learn about in the Bible? Some think they were Adam and Eve because of the story beginning in Genesis 2:6. However, most Bible scholars recognize the Adam and Eve story simply as an allegory, not as a historical chronology of creation.

I like to think of Abraham as the first man, illustrating that creation consciously, intentionally reflects God, the creator. Abraham chose to look for and obey the one God. Listen to what God said to His creation in Genesis 17:1: "I am the Almighty God; walk before me, and be thou perfect." Isn't this what Abraham did?

Adam, on the other hand, was focused on himself and Eve. They listened to the "serpent's" suggestions. Did Abraham do better? (**Yes.**) One example of Abraham deliberately "walking before God" rather than focusing on himself was when he still trusted God's direction—even though God told him to sacrifice his son Isaac. But God did not intend that Abraham kill Isaac. God wanted Abraham to learn that there was to be no more child sacrifice, which had been a pagan practice at that time, and that fidelity or obedience to God could mean only good for man, woman, and child. We cannot lean in two directions at the same time! Who leaned on God, Adam or Abraham? (**Abraham.**)

What are some examples of Abraham deliberately "walking before God" rather than focusing on himself?

- Abraham was called by God to leave his homeland in Haran and go to an unknown land that God would show him—the land of Canaan (Genesis 11:30–31; 17:15; 13:6–9).
- For many years after he married Sarai, Abraham had no children, yet he kept on believing God's promise that he would be the father of "many nations" and would have as many descendants as there are stars in the sky (Genesis 15:5).

- Abraham sent his son Ishmael and his mother away into the desert, at Sarah's request. after Sarah bore Isaac. That couldn't have been easy for Abraham to do (Genesis 21:1–7).
- Abraham obeyed the Lord's command to sacrifice his son Isaac. One wonders how any father could accept or obey such a command! Of course, the Lord intervened, perhaps teaching Abraham that child sacrifice was not a demand of the one God, but was to be prohibited in the culture Abraham would represent (Genesis 22:1–13).

Do you suppose we could summarize the main events of the Bible in fifty words? Someone did. Read this, and let's see what details we can recall for each couplet:

God made, Adam bit, Noah arked, Abraham split, Joseph ruled, Jacob fooled, Bush talked, Moses balked, Pharaoh plagued, People walked, Sea divided, Tablets guided, Promise landed, Saul freaked, David peeked, Prophets warned, Jesus born, Christ-man walked, Love talked, Anger crucified, Hope died, Love rose, Spirit flamed, Word spread, God rules, Man reflects(urbandictionary.com).

And for a more serious summary, see the following:

Some Major Biblical Events, People, and Instructions
(that can be better understood through Christian Science)

1. A few generations after the allegory of Adam and Eve, Enoch "walked with God," ascended.

2. Noah built an ark though he couldn't see a sea.

3. Abraham heard God's call to move from a pagan land to another land.

4. When they were old, Abraham and Sarah had a son, Isaac.

5. Isaac and Rebekah gave birth to twins, Jacob and Esau.

6. Jacob pretended to be Esau in order to trick his father, Isaac, into giving him Esau's blessing.

7. Jacob had to run away from his angry brother, Esau.

8. Many years later, God told Jacob to go back home.

9. Jacob wrestled with an angel who removed Jacob's fear and gave him a new name, Israel.

10. Jacob-Israel's twelve sons started the twelve tribes of Israel, the children of Israel.

11. Jacob-Israel's son Joseph forgave his brothers for selling him into captivity.

12. During a great famine at that time, Joseph, now a prince of Egypt, invited his brothers and father to come live in Egypt, where food was plentiful.

13. Four hundred years later, Pharaoh had enslaved the children of Israel.

14. God called to Moses from the burning bush and told him to lead the children of Israel back to their own land of Canaan, the Promised Land.

15. During the forty-year journey, God gave Moses the Ten Commandments that would help and protect the children of Israel when they reached the Promised Land.

16. David united the tribes of Israel and wrote many psalms. His son Solomon built the great temple and wrote many proverbs.

17. Through His prophets, God told us never to believe that a statue or a person is a god or has any power to hurt us or to help us.

18. Prophets like Isaiah and Jeremiah urged the people to reject false gods and return to the one God.

19. Nehemiah rebuilt the walls of Jerusalem after the people's long captivity in Babylon, and Ezra renewed the people's knowledge of God.

20. Christ Jesus said the great commandments are to love God with all your heart and your neighbor as yourself.

21. Christ Jesus' teachings and healings proved that sin, disease, and death are not man's lot.

22. The apostle Paul established Christianity in many Gentile cities, even in Rome, the center of paganism and power.

23. John the Revelator saw an angel who had in his hand "a little book open."

24. Mary Baker Eddy, discerning the Bible's spiritual message, explained that we can keep all the commandments and we can also follow Jesus' instructions to heal because God, good, the only creator, is all-powerful (omnipotent), all-present (omnipresent), and all-knowing (omniscient). Man is not *self*-created; man is God's image and likeness.

25. Wisdom warns us, do not believe in an anthropomorphic god, a capricious god who acts like a human and has human limitations.

These Individuals Trusted God and Refused to Fear
(Can you add more names and stories?)

Abraham. In Abraham's day, there was no Christianity, only paganism. The one God said, "Leave that pagan land (pagan thought), and I will establish you in a Promised Land where there will be abundance and safety for all." God established a covenant with Abraham. Later, when Abraham thought God had told him to sacrifice his son Isaac, Abraham heard the one God say to him, "Do not kill your son. All nations of the earth will be blessed because you trusted your son to Me."

Joseph. When Pharaoh, king of Egypt, could not understand his dreams, Joseph (a prisoner) offered to interpret them. Joseph said, "I cannot explain them, but God will explain them, and we will all be saved." Joseph trusted God, and Egypt was saved from seven years of famine.

Moses. When Moses and a million descendants of Jacob-Israel needed to get across the Red Sea in order to reach the Promised Land, Moses asked God, "What shall we do?" Moses trusted God's instruction to "go forth" and step into the water and walk across the sea on dry land.

David. He played music for the king, but King Saul was jealous of David, who expressed the spirit of God. King Saul chased David around the country trying to kill him. But David was always listening for Mind's guidance and refused to fear. He was protected and eventually became king of Israel.

Elijah. When this prophet had no food because of a famine in the land, he did not panic. He trusted God, divine Mind, which told him to go to the home of a poor widow. She was able to feed him because Elijah helped her prove the law of God—that there is always enough. Later, when her son suddenly died, Elijah did not panic. He prayed with confidence and expectation of good. The boy was restored to life.

Jesus. When Jesus' enemies were trying to push him off a cliff, he just walked calmly through the crowd and returned to his disciples.

Peter. The disciple Peter was put in prison because he taught the people about Christ Jesus. Peter was not afraid, because he prayed. The church members also prayed constantly for Peter. One day, Peter's chains fell off, and he walked out of the prison.

Pick a few statements that helped you the most in *getting to know the Bible*.

14

GETTING TO KNOW THE COMMANDMENTS: THE RULES OF THE GAME

A game is an organized activity with a purpose. And in order to play a game, the players need to know the rules.

Think of your favorite sport; players have to play by the rules, don't they? There are also rules that govern your daily activities and conduct, whether you are interacting with your family members, friends, or work associates. Life lived by the rules is more pleasant and more of a blessing to others.

Are there rules about how we relate to God and to our fellow man? Yes. God gave Moses these rules, and they are known as the Ten Commandments. Moses received them during the Exodus when he was leading the children of Israel out of bondage in Egypt to the promised land of Canaan. According to the Bible, the journey took forty years, during which time the children of Israel learned how to obey these rules, or laws, and how to free themselves from the worship of idols. You can read the whole story in the book of Exodus, which means, of course, "going out of."

The Ten Commandments are rules, or laws, that God gave to Moses almost three thousand years ago. Being that old, are they still relevant to you and me today? Yes, they are! And were they relevant to Christ Jesus? Yes, indeed. He taught these laws to his followers. He taught them how to have no other gods but the one Almighty God and how to love their neighbor as themselves.

Here is a summary of the Ten Commandments that God gave to Moses (see Exodus 20:3):

1. Thou shalt have no other gods before me.

2. Thou shalt not make unto thee any graven image, or any likeness of any thing that is in heaven above, or that is in the earth beneath, or that is in the water under the earth: thou shalt not bow down thyself to them, nor serve them.

3. Thou shalt not take the name of the Lord thy God in vain; for the Lord will not hold him guiltless that taketh his name in vain.

4. Remember the sabbath day, to keep it holy.

5. Honour thy father and thy mother: that thy days may be long upon the land which the Lord thy God giveth thee.

6. Thou shalt not kill.

7. Thou shalt not commit adultery.

8. Thou shalt not steal.

9. Thou shalt not bear false witness against thy neighbour.

10. Thou shalt not covet thy neighbour's house, thou shalt not covet thy neighbour's wife, nor his manservant, nor his maidservant, nor his ox, nor his ass, nor any thing that is thy neighbour's.

Commandments 1 through 4 deal with man's relationship to God, while Commandments 6 through 10 deal with man's relationship to man. The Fifth Commandment, "Honour thy father and thy mother," can be seen as dealing with both God as Father-Mother and our human parents.

Jesus knew this very well. In fact, that's why when one of the scribes tried to trick him into singling out just one commandment as "the great commandment in the law," Jesus' answer was to summarize all Ten Commandments this way: "And Jesus answered him, The first of all the commandments is, Hear, O Israel; The Lord our God is one Lord: And thou shalt love the Lord thy God with all thy heart, and with all thy soul, and with all thy mind, and with all thy strength: this is the first commandment. And the second is like, namely this, Thou shalt love thy neighbour as thyself. There is none other commandment greater than these" (Mark 12:29–31).

Furthermore, Jesus said, "If ye love me, *keep* my commandments" (John 14:15).

Everything in our life pertains to these two important relationships: Man's relationship to God, the creator, and man's relationship to God's creation. The Bible has countless illustrations of these two grand relationships. Familiarity with these biblical relationships is a must if we're going to enjoy the game called life and bless others in the process. As Jesus also said, "if thou wilt enter into life, keep the commandments" (Matthew 19:17).

However, to keep the commandments, we need to know what they mean—what their spiritual meaning is—because only by understanding them in this way will we know how we're supposed to think and act. So let's take a look at each of them from a spiritual standpoint.

1. **Thou shalt have no other gods before me.** This is the commandment that says you must serve and love only one God. But who or what *is* God? Many religions talk of God as if He was a person, with humanlike qualities, capable of creating good and evil, a mortal man and a spiritual man. But the Bible tells us that God is Spirit or spiritual (John 4:24, NRSV); that He is love (I John 4:8); that He is life (Romans 8:10); and that He is truth (I John 5:6). So wouldn't that suggest that we're supposed to "worship" things that are spiritual and not material—such things as love, life, and truth—and not material things like clothes, friends, movie or sports stars, cars, money, exercise, food, and other such things? Can you name something or someone, perhaps, that's become a "god" to you and your friends?

2. **Thou shalt not make unto thee any graven image, or any likeness of any thing that is in heaven above, or that is in the earth beneath, or that is in the water under the earth: thou shalt not bow down thyself to them, nor serve them.**

   This commandment prohibits our making God into something limited or physical. It also means the reverse—we shouldn't make something limited and material into a god.

   In the Bible, people created "graven images," or idols, made from wood or stone and decorated them with gold and precious gems, thinking these would have power to control the weather; their crops; whether their babies were boys or girls; or whether they would be happy, successful, or protected. Yes, it sounds a bit foolish today, but don't we do the same thing? Just watch thirty minutes of TV, and you'll see commercials for weight-loss pills and wrinkle removers; exercise programs and body-shaping devices; potions and pills to make you happy or restore your energy; and clothes or electronic devices we just "have to have" because without them we won't be happy or feel complete. Are we bowing down and "idolizing" these material things? Are we "serving" certain friends by letting them run our lives and maybe encourage us to act in ways that we're not comfortable with or very proud of? Are we fearing certain foods or diseases or health laws—and in this way serving *them*? Or are we serving God, Life, Truth, and Love, and in this way finding true happiness, health, and wholeness? Is there anything in your life right now that you might be "idolizing"—giving it the power to make you feel happy or complete, or unhappy or incomplete?

3. **Thou shalt not take the name of the Lord thy God in vain; for the Lord will not hold him guiltless that taketh his name in vain.** This commandment is often thought of as prohibiting swearing. And while it does do that, it goes much farther. Taking God's name in vain has much to do with being hypocritical or asking God for help but believing that it's really a useless request. For instance, if we say we

believe that God is Love, and then don't live up to that statement in our conversation or actions, that's taking God's name in vain. This Third Commandment is about "walking the talk"—striving to live up to being Godlike, being truthful, honest, loving, and meek. (See the discussion on "meekness" in chapter 15, "Getting to Know the Beatitudes.") Can you give any other examples of one's taking God's name in vain?

4. **Remember the sabbath day, to keep it holy.** Yes, this commandment means that we should remember to go to church on Sunday, even though the material demands on our time today do everything they can to pull us away from church. Many young people are committed to playing sports or other activities on Sunday mornings, while others feel they need to catch up on sleep, rather than attend church or Sunday School. But submitting to material beliefs and demands seldom gives us anything in return that's of real value or that truly satisfies. The Sabbath day is more than a single day of the week, as Christ Jesus pointed out. We need not only attend church or Sunday School but also keep the holiness that the Sabbath day represents in our thought throughout the week; in other words, to live pure and spiritual lives 24/7—not simply on Sunday mornings. How do you remember the Sabbath to keep it holy throughout the week?

5. **Honour thy father and thy mother: that thy days may be long upon the land which the Lord thy God giveth thee.** This commandment does, indeed, mean honoring, helping, and respecting our parents. But it goes well beyond that. The book of Genesis states, Let "us" make man in "our" image and likeness. Who is this "us"? Do you suppose this refers to both God's Fatherhood and Motherhood? (See also chapter 16, "Getting to Know God," for further discussion of this point.) Christ Jesus said, "Call no man your father upon the earth; for one is your father which is in heaven" (Matthew 23:9). He recognized his true Father and true Mother as being God. And he honored God in everything he did. Remember his "two great commandments"? He told us to love God with all our heart, soul, and mind, and to love our neighbor as ourselves. Being obedient to this command—and living it—is truly honoring our father and mother. How do you honor your father and mother?

6. **Thou shalt not kill.** The meaning of this commandment is obvious, but with continuing high crime rates and school shootings, it doesn't seem like everyone is aware of this commandment at all. If they were aware of and obedient to this commandment, the killing would stop. Christ Jesus said, "The thief cometh not, but for to steal, and to kill, and to destroy: I am come that they might have life, and that they might have it more abundantly" (John 10:10). And he also said, "For the bread of God is he which cometh down from heaven, and giveth life unto the world" (John 6:33). We need to honor and to cherish God, Life, by expressing life

and love in everything we do. "Killing" isn't limited to taking one's physical life. Have you ever heard the term *killjoy*? It means someone who takes away the joy of another person. Similarly, we can also kill someone's self-respect by things we say or do – or tempt them into doing. We can also kill someone's confidence by making them fearful and full of self-doubt. What other good qualities in a person might someone be tempted to "kill"?

7. **Thou shalt not commit adultery.** Everyone knows this commandment, and they think it means you should not have sexual relations with someone other than your spouse. And that is true because marriage is a relationship built on trust and it must be kept that way. But "adultery" also has a much broader meaning. According to Dictionary.com, to "adulterate" something means "to debase or make impure," and some synonyms include to cheapen, contaminate, corrupt, degrade, falsify, pollute, and weaken, to name a few. So you can see how adultery can apply to many everyday activities—like companies that pollute the environment, people who corrupt government, students who cheat on tests, and more. Can you think of any other examples of "adultery"?

8. **Thou shalt not steal.** To steal something means "to take the property of another without permission or right, especially secretly; to appropriate ideas without right or acknowledgment; to take, get, or win surreptitiously" (Dictionary.com). This commandment has a lot to do with honesty versus dishonesty. Obviously, stealing would include plagiarizing someone's writings without giving him or her credit; cheating in school; stealing someone's friend away from him or her; or finding someone's lost item and keeping it for yourself, rather than trying to find its rightful owner. It can also mean depriving people of their joy and honesty or of their good reputation, making them unhappy by your comments or actions. Can you think of some other examples of stealing, other than taking someone's property? Is bullying a form of stealing? How?

9. **Thou shalt not bear false witness against thy neighbour.** Bearing false witness is telling lies and spreading rumors about another individual or group—whether in person or via Facebook or in any other way. It includes condemning, criticizing, and gossiping, none of which is attractive to the person doing it—and all of which can be very harmful to the person receiving it. It also includes bullying another person. It is a direct violation of the Golden Rule, "Do unto others as you would have them do unto you," and many of the other commandments. And it certainly runs counter to the teachings of Christ Jesus. Can you give some examples of what the opposite of bearing false witness would be?

10. **Thou shalt not covet thy neighbour's house, thou shalt not covet thy neighbour's wife, nor his manservant, nor his maidservant, nor his ox, nor his ass, nor any thing that is thy neighbour's.** The Tenth Commandment prohibits the coveting, desiring, or lusting after other people's property, family, home, good fortune—or even their looks or figure! In other words, desiring material possessions to make us happy or satisfied, because such desire inevitably leads to continual dissatisfaction—and even to war! But not all "coveting" is prohibited. Elsewhere in the Bible, the apostle Paul called upon the people of Corinth to "covet earnestly the best gifts" (I Corinthians 12:31), which are not material things but are spiritual ideas and qualities that are always lasting and fully satisfying. These would include love, unselfishness, generosity, sharing, rejoicing in others' success, and much more. Can you share some ideas of how individuals or corporations have gotten into trouble because they "coveted," or desired, to have something someone else had?

The health of society and its physical, mental, and spiritual progress depend upon our obedience to the Ten Commandments. Human history portrays the disasters that occur when humans presume to create their own laws or codes of conduct, based on serving self instead of serving the one God. Mary Baker Eddy, a great spiritual thinker, wrote these comments on the commandments in her book *Miscellaneous Writings* 1883–1896 (p. 37:2–17):

> Above physical wants, lie the higher claims of the law and gospel of healing. First is the law, which saith: — "Thou shalt not commit adultery"; in other words, thou shalt not adulterate Life, Truth, or Love, — mentally, morally, or physically. "Thou shalt not steal"; that is, thou shalt not rob man of money, which is but trash, compared with his rights of mind and character. "Thou shalt not kill"; that is, thou shalt not strike at the eternal sense of Life with a malicious aim, but shalt know that by doing thus thine own sense of Life shall be forfeited. "Thou shalt not bear false witness"; that is, thou shalt not utter a lie, either mentally or audibly, nor cause it to be thought. Obedience to these commandments is indispensable to health, happiness, and length of days.

15

GETTING TO KNOW THE
BEATITUDES, OR "BE-ATTITUDES"

What does the word *beatitude* mean? According to Dictionary.com, beatitude means supreme blessedness; exalted happiness. As you may know, the eight Beatitudes were given to us by Christ Jesus as part of his Sermon on the Mount (Matthew 5–7). And the Beatitudes (Matthew 5:3-11) all begin with the word *blessed*, which means to be made holy or consecrated; and in the New Testament, "blessed" means "happy."

But this happiness isn't a happiness that comes and goes with material things or special friends. This is a deep spiritual happiness that stays with us even when we lose material things and special friends, because it is based on God and His permanent goodness. So the Beatitudes, or the "be-attitudes," tell us the spiritual values and "attitudes" that help us live happy, good lives by living in accord with God.

An "attitude" reveals one's values and aims and ambitions. Attitudes are important because one's attitudes toward people and situations are reflected in one's thinking and behavior and therefore affect our "be-ing."

The Beatitudes given to us by Christ Jesus complement the commandments given to us by Moses. The Ten Commandments *promote* right thinking and action, and the Beatitudes, or "be-attitudes," *celebrate* right thinking and right action.

Through the eight Beatitudes, Christ Jesus wanted people to know what would make them successful, happy, and blessed. He also wanted them to know the qualities that are essential to having a right relationship with God. Let's see what qualities Jesus specified in the Beatitudes below and whether we can think of any additional essential qualities:

1. Blessed are the poor in spirit: for theirs is the kingdom of heaven.
2. Blessed are they that mourn: for they shall be comforted.
3. Blessed are the meek: for they shall inherit the earth.

4. Blessed are they which do hunger and thirst after righteousness: for they shall be filled.

5. Blessed are the merciful: for they shall obtain mercy.

6. Blessed are the pure in heart: for they shall see God.

7. Blessed are the peacemakers: for they shall be called the children of God.

8. Blessed are they which are persecuted for righteousness' sake: for theirs is the kingdom of heaven. Blessed are ye, when men shall revile you, and persecute you, and shall say all manner of evil against you falsely, for my sake. Rejoice, and be exceeding glad: for great is your reward in heaven: for so persecuted they the prophets which were before you.

Now let's take a look at each of the Beatitudes in a little more depth.

1. **Blessed are the poor in spirit: for theirs is the kingdom of heaven.** The first Beatitude is not asking us to be poor in the sense of poverty or lacking things. "Poor in spirit" implies having a humble or modest approach to God, or Life; not being "vainly puffed up" as it says in the Bible (Colossians 2:18) but rather having a willingness to learn and change, to be willing to ask God for help. Can you think of how being "poor in spirit" or humble might help resolve a problem that you're facing right now?

2. **Blessed are they that mourn: for they shall be comforted.** To mourn means more than simply "to grieve." In this context, it also means to regret one's mistakes and to have a deep desire for repentance—and only *then* are we comforted, truly comforted, by God. And this applies not just to a wrong done to another person, but also to how we treat ourselves. How often we "mourn" over our own perceived shortcomings or inadequacies, or a sense of being incomplete. How wonderful to know that even then we can be "comforted" by God, Love, by forsaking the regrettable and receiving the blessing of the unforgettable—or our true nature as God's image and likeness! Can you describe a time when you "mourned" or regretted a mistake and then felt God's comfort and forgiveness?

3. **Blessed are the meek: for they shall inherit the earth.** Meekness does not mean weakness. Christ Jesus was a very meek man, but he was also described as being "mighty." How can those two terms be reconciled? In the New Testament, "meek" is from the Greek term *praus*. It does not suggest weakness; rather, it denotes strength brought under control. The ancient Greeks employed the term to describe a wild horse tamed to the bridle. Therefore, couldn't meekness mean having the humility to ask God for help and having the strength to serve Him?

Meekness means being unselfed, and it enables one to "inherit the earth" and enjoy all the blessings of heaven—to feel God's presence and power—right here and now. Mary

Baker Eddy gave "earth" a spiritual definition that includes in part "a type of eternity and immortality." Meekness, then, does more than help us feel close to God, "in whom we live, and move, and have our being" (Acts 17:28)—through meekness we experience eternity and immortality. Has meekness ever helped you solve a problem and feel close to God?

4. **Blessed are they which do hunger and thirst after righteousness: for they shall be filled**. To "hunger and thirst" means to have a strong desire, a deep yearning or craving for righteousness in order to experience it. That desire is well described as hungering and thirsting, for, like food and drink, "righteousness," or right thinking and right acting, is essential to life and essential to knowing God. Righteousness is being motivated only by love and truth; and those who are righteous are "filled"—and satisfied. What is your heart hungering for?

5. **Blessed are the merciful: for they shall obtain mercy.** Mercy means "compassionate and kindly forbearance shown toward an offender, an enemy, or other person" (Dictionary.com). Synonyms include forgiveness, grace, humanity, kindliness, tenderness, and charity or love. As we take an honest look at our ways of thinking and living, we may realize our own need of mercy and compassion, especially when we've made a mistake where mercy and compassion may seem to be undeserved. If I hope to feel such compassion from God, I must feel equal compassion for all of my fellow human beings. How have you been merciful?

6. **Blessed are the pure in heart: for they shall see God.** One who is "pure in heart," or "pure-hearted," is "without malice, treachery, or evil intent," and "pure in heart" means untainted with evil, innocent, and free of guilt. Some synonyms are honest, sincere, and guileless (Dictionary.com). Could "pure in heart" also mean being our very best self—striving to be the very image and likeness of God, good, in thought and deed?

Christ Jesus, of course, is the master example of someone who was pure in heart. He understood that God was his Father who directed all of his thoughts and enabled him to bring about God's will of goodness for everyone he came into contact with. He claimed no selfhood apart from God. Christ Jesus' pure thought enabled him to know that his goodness was God's goodness—expressed humanly. How does innocence make you feel closer to God? Does guilt make you feel separated from God?

7. **Blessed are the peacemakers: for they shall be called the children of God.** Peacemakers carry out the will of God and prove themselves to be the sons of God. Peacemakers do not paint a layer of peace over evil that is simply trying to hide. Peacemakers expose and destroy evil and replace it with good, with peace—God's peace manifested. How have you been a "peacemaker"?

8. **Blessed are they which are persecuted for righteousness' sake: for theirs is the kingdom of heaven.** The kingdom of heaven belonged to Christ Jesus and belongs to us—but sometimes it requires us to stand up to being ridiculed by friends for our beliefs, and maybe even rejected by friends for obeying the commandment to love God, good, supremely and one's neighbor as one's self. Has anyone ever made you feel ashamed of your values?

Our "neighbor," of course, is everyone we know, everyone we've heard of, and everyone we haven't even met yet. Christ Jesus made it clear that we are to rejoice that there is a right way, and that right way is accessible to all who seek it. The prophets in the Old and New Testaments of the Bible were persecuted for declaring the truth, but this did not dissuade them or dim their achievements. It shouldn't dissuade us, either. We all need to stand up and "be"—to stand for what is right and good. That is the value of the "Be-attitudes"—they tell us how to "be" the man (the men and women) that God created.

16

GETTING TO KNOW GOD

Bible study and Sunday School are full of purpose. In brief, they help us get to know God and ourselves. Questions and "discussion sheets" help facilitate this purpose. All the following items draw on the Bible and the Christian Science textbook, *Science and Health with Key to the Scriptures*, by Mary Baker Eddy. Each discussion sheet ideally contains at least one example like the items listed in this chapter. Students should consider the questions and statements and you will find answers in **(boldface words or citations in the parenthesis)**. What students answer is determined through looking things up, discussion, and teacher input. This process will help us get to know more about God.

The Fatherhood *and* Motherhood of God

For hundreds of years, Christians referred to God only as Father, but there are many, many Bible verses that suggest God is both Father *and Mother*, expressing the strong and protective role of a father, along with the gentle, nurturing love of a mother.

The first suggestion of this dual role of God comes at the very beginning of the Bible in Genesis 1:26, 27: "And God said, Let us make man in our image, after our likeness: ... So God created man in his own image, in the image of God created he him; male and female created he them."

Have you ever wondered who "us" is? Could this be the Father-Mother God—who created both "male and female"?

The Bible is full of verses that clearly suggest the tender, nurturing, mothering nature of God. For instance, consider the following:

As one whom his mother comforteth, so will I comfort you; (Isaiah 66:13).

At the same time, saith the Lord, will I be the God of all the families of Israel, and they shall be my people. The Lord hath appeared of old unto me, saying,

Yea, I have loved thee with an everlasting love: therefore with lovingkindness have I drawn thee (Jeremiah 31:1, 3).

I will betroth thee unto me for ever; yea, I will betroth thee unto me in righteousness, and in judgment, and in lovingkindness, and in mercies (Hosea 2:19, 20).

The Lord is my shepherd; I shall not want. He maketh me to lie down in green pastures: he leadeth me beside the still waters. Thou preparest a table before me in the presence of mine enemies: thou anointest my head with oil; (Psalm 23:1, 2, 5).

And of course, Jesus lamented to the scribes and Pharisees,

O Jerusalem, Jerusalem ... how often would I have gathered thy children together, even as a hen gathereth her chickens under her wings, and ye would not! (Matthew 23:37).

Through these verses—and many more—we can practically feel God's mothering love for his creation.

Try to imagine the ideal mother. Try to feel the mother hug of God. Mary Baker Eddy helps us discover the one God through the synonyms she gave us that help define God (see *Science and Health*, p. 465).

God's mothering love, of course, is expressed by our human mothers—many of whom we're familiar with in the Bible. Who are some mothers in the Bible we have learned about and can learn from?

- Mary, the mother of Jesus
- Elisabeth, the mother of John the Baptist
- Sarah, the mother of Joseph
- Eve, the mother of Seth
- Hagar, the mother of Ishmael

Can you think of any others?

We're told a great story about motherhood in the twelfth chapter of Revelation.

And there appeared a great wonder in heaven; a woman clothed with the sun, and the moon under her feet, and upon her head a crown of twelve stars: And she being with child cried, travailing in birth, and pained to be delivered … And she brought forth a man child, who was to rule all nations with a rod of iron: and her child was caught up unto God, and to his throne (verses 1, 2, 5).

This was not to be a woman, a mother, who was to raise a child on her own. She was to represent the ideal of womanhood and motherhood, and her child was her spiritual idea of man who was to rule *all* nations—not just Jews and Christians—with a rod of iron. Iron was the strongest metal known in Bible times, suggesting that her rule was to be unbreakable, like a rod of iron.

The man child that she brought forth was the ideal man, parented by the one Father-Mother God. Perhaps this man-child is you(th).

The mother was given "wings," perhaps implying that she was to continue developing her own unlimited potential. She and the angel Michael were to cast the dragon out of heaven. I think the dragon was the serpent's bloated sense of self-importance, and this bloated sense of self-importance cannot exist in the allness of God, good.

In the story in Revelation 12, the last we see of the woman is the earth (human consciousness) helping the woman? The chapter ends with a seeming threat that man is to be pursued by the dragon; but no, remember the child (you) was caught up unto God and His throne. That is the kingdom of heaven where man lives, where you live. Christ Jesus, in the Lord's Prayer, said, "Thy kingdom come, thy will be done in earth as it is in heaven." God's will is the only will, and it means good for all of us. When we accept God's will, then we experience it.

Can you identify with this spiritual concept of motherhood, fatherhood, and youth? How could these images of bringing forth or "giving birth" to a new idea relate to your creativity and experiences in school? What would it mean for your experience to be caught up unto God and His throne? Could it mean the protection of your idea from a personal sense of creativity and understanding that man expresses creativity because it is God's law? Would it help to apply this sentence from the Scientific Statement of Being: "All is infinite Mind and its infinite manifestation …" (*Science and Health*, p. 468:8). After all, Christian Science teaches that God and man are one—you and your idea are one with God.

We've all been inspired with a good idea—perhaps it was when writing a paper for school or painting a picture, or composing a song or helping a friend. Or maybe it was trying something new and different—perhaps collecting food to help homeless people. But then thoughts of fear and doubt crept in suggesting that we'd fail, or our friends would question why we were doing something, and we were tempted to forget the idea. Isn't this the "dragon" trying to kill our "child-idea"? Don't let evil limit your life goals.

Mary Baker Eddy's poem Mother's Evening Prayer is a prayer to God, divine Love, to protect her "child"—her church and Christian Science. In the first verse she writes, "Keep thou my child on upward wing tonight." Read what Mary Baker Eddy has to say to you in her *Miscellaneous Writings, 1883–1896*:

> Beloved children, the world has need of you, — and more as children than as men and women: it needs your innocence, unselfishness, faithful affection, uncontaminated lives. You need also to watch, and pray that you preserve these virtues unstained, and lose them not through contact with the world (p. 110:4–9).

Now, before we explore some more about God and His creation, let's consider an important new word I've created: *wis.*

It is not "wiz" as in Cheez Whiz or math whiz. Wis is a combination of *was* and *is.* "In the beginning wis the Word, and the Word wis with God, and the Word wis God" (see John 1:1). Let me explain.

When I'm praying, there is the thought of the past and the present, as well as the future. God was, God is; hence, God wis. I've been using this word in my prayers occasionally, and it usually brings a smile to my face, but it also reinforces the sense of God as eternal—always was, always is, always will be. Maybe it would be *wise* of many of us to think of God, man, and the universe as wis. I like to be fresh in my approach to God, and God says to me, "I like it when you get fresh—when you think fresh inspired thoughts."

Where in the Bible is the first description of God's creation of heaven and earth? (**Genesis 1.**) God called His heaven and earth g(**ood**) (Genesis 1:31).

And what about man? "And God said, Let us make man in (**our**) image, after (**our**) likeness (Genesis 1:26). If we are made in the image and likeness of God, Spirit, we are spiritual and good.

The highest and best description of God is (**good**); while the lowest and saddest description of God is (**good and evil**). (**Discuss why.**)

There is a definition of God in *Science and Health* in the chapter that is all questions and answers. What chapter is that? (*Recapitulation.*)

The first question in *Recapitulation* is "What is God?" and the answer is what? (See *Science and Health*, p. 465:8–9.) If someone asks you *"Who is God?"* what will you answer? God is not a person, nor is Jesus God, as Jesus himself stated in John 14:28: "I go unto the Father: for my Father is greater than I." So, if someone asks, "Who is God?" couldn't you say with Jesus, God is my Father-Mother? Yes, of course.

What is the Christian Science definition of "sun"? "The symbol of Soul governing man,—of Truth, Life, and Love" (*Science and Health*, p. 595:1). Sun and sunshine can remind us of creator and creation. God is the sun; man and creation are the sunshine; and individual man is like a single ray of sunshine (see *The First Church of Christ, Scientist, and Miscellany*, by Mary Baker Eddy, p. 344:3–5).

A spiritual account of creation, Genesis 1, was written about 600 BCE. In this true history, Spirit, God, reveals a spiritual expression of itself, a spiritual creation where man and woman have d(**ominion**) and are declared to be (**good**), not evil or fallen (see Genesis 1:26–27, 31). Would our good parent, God, let His or Her children become "bad" or "fallen"? (**No!**) (**Discuss.**)

God, our creator, divine Love, does not accuse or punish its loved creation. Truth, God, is always correcting and comforting but never punishing!

Christ Jesus felt so at-one with God that he wasted no time thinking he was separate. He meant it when he said, "I and my Father are one" (John 10:30)—as in inseparable. (Some religions believe Jesus was God on earth, even though he said—directly and indirectly— that he was *not* God. See especially the book of John.)

Because we reflect or express God (just like a ray of sun includes all that the sun is), it is natural to receive from God everything we need, such as the spiritual qualities of strength, intelligence, and compassion.

In order to receive good from God, we may have to refuse the *belief* that we are separate from God, good, and limited. What did the apostle Peter tell us was required? "(**Humble**) yourselves therefore under the mighty hand of God, that he may (**exalt**) you in due time: casting all your care upon him; for he careth for you" (I Peter 5:6–7).

How do you know God cares for you? (**Discuss.**) Can you say with Biblical authority, "I am safe at all times if I am remembering that God, or good, is all p(**ower**), all p(**resence**), all action"? *Science and Health* gives us a definition of good. What is it? (See p. 587:19–20.)

Here's a wonderful thought: You were created because God had a wonderful idea and expressed it (manifested it) as you! So, shouldn't we all say, "Thank you Father-Mother

God!" (See John 1:12, 13.) Father-Mother God places every young person in the family of Man and in a family of people, relatives perhaps, who provide care and safety, opportunity and support.

You are the son (or daughter) of God—immortal—if you are led (governed) by the spirit of God. And the Spirit says, *Yes*, that's right! Because "as many as are led by the Spirit of God, they are the sons of God. The Spirit itself beareth witness with our spirit, that we are the children of God: And if children, then heirs; heirs of God ..." (Romans 8:14, 16, 17).

Where did Christ Jesus say the kingdom of God is? **(Within you—see Luke 17:21: "Neither shall they say, Lo here! or, lo there! for, behold, the kingdom of God is within you.")**

Does the kingdom of God, this perfect place of perfect order and peace, include sin? **(No.)** Or punishment? **(No.)** "Divine Love is infinite. Therefore all that really exists is **(in)** and **(of)** God, and manifests His **(love)**" (*Science and Health*, p. 340:12).

Something is called "a god" if people f**(ear)** it or w**(orship)** it. Why does Mrs. Eddy call sin, sickness, and death "popular gods"? (See *Science and Health*, p. 347:23.) Many television ads encourage us to trust d**(rugs)**. What's the danger? **(They don't really heal, and often their use will escalate and have unforeseen side effects.)**

Someone checking your homework might say, "You made an error." Dictionary.com tells us an error is "a mistake; a belief in something untrue." So another way of saying this would be, "You made a m**(istake)**." Is the error you made an "evil"? No, it is only a mistake. For example, it is error, a mistake, to say that God causes human suffering. But it is evil, wrong, to *keep* saying this after learning that God, good, causes only good. According to Dictionary.com, *evil is not just a mistake*; evil is morally wrong and harmful, and it is often accompanied by suffering.

Where do we learn that God causes only good? **(In the Bible; see Genesis 1:31 "And God saw every thing that he had made, and, behold, it was very good.")** Religious leaders in Jesus' time saw his proofs that God, good, causes only good, and yet they continued to insist that evil is real. Do people in our time believe that evil is real? **(Give some examples and discuss.)**

The Psalmist said, "The Lord gave the word: great was the company of those that published it" (Psalm 68:11). This verse is engraved in stone on the Christian Science Publishing House, which publishes Christian Science periodicals in Boston, Massachusetts. To "publish" means to issue or distribute—like printed material, for instance. It also means "to announce formally; to proclaim; to make publically or generally known," according to Dictionary.com. Can you name the Christian Science periodicals? **(*The Christian Science Monitor; The***

Christian Science Journal; *Christian Science Sentinel*; *Herald of Christian Science*; **and the** *Christian Science Quarterly Bible Lesson.*) These periodicals help readers know God better and trust God for healing.

How many thoughts or works of God are there? (**They're unlimited.**) The Psalmist wondered about that and then used the metaphor of sand to explain that they can't be numbered (see Psalm 139:18). How did the apostle Paul state it in the book of Romans: "For **(of)** him, and **(through)** him, and **(to)** him, are all things: to whom be **(glory for ever)**. Amen" (11:36).

Abraham was the first person we know of who realized that the many statue-gods all around him were powerless and worthless because they could not really *do* anything. They couldn't harm; and they couldn't do good.

And Isaiah described God in several ways (Isaiah 9:6, 7) when he wrote,

> [H]is name shall be called Wonderful, Counsellor, The mighty God, The ever-lasting Father, The Prince of Peace. Of the increase of his government and peace there shall be no end, upon the throne of David, and upon his kingdom, to order it, and to establish it with judgment and with justice from henceforth even for ever.

Jesus knew this to be true and proved it in healing, walking on the water, stilling the storm, and many other of his demonstrations of God's absolute power. In the final verse of the Lord's Prayer, he acknowledged this power this way: "For thine is the kingdom, and the power, and the glory, for ever" (Matthew 6:13).

Where in the Christian Science textbook is the Lord's Prayer and its spiritual interpretation? (**In the chapter,** *Prayer*, **pp. 16–17.**)

Mary Baker Eddy gave mankind seven specific words that help us get to know God and better understand His nature. These are often called the seven s**(ynonyms)** and include the following terms: M**(ind)**, Sp**(irit)**, So**(ul)**, Pr**(inciple)**, L**(ife)**, T**(ruth)**, and Lo**(ve)**.

See if the following citations from the Bible help you understand these synonyms and the nature of God (note that in this listing of citations "SH" is used as an abbreviation for *Science and Health*):

Mind: When you hear "Mind" or "divine Mind" used for God, think of God's unlimited intelligence, wisdom, creative power, spiritual consciousness, expansive thought. What other attributes of Mind can you name?

Philippians 2:5	Let this mind be in you, which was also in Christ Jesus:
Isaiah 55:8	[M]y thoughts are not your thoughts, neither are your ways my ways, saith the Lord.
Jeremiah 29:11	I know the thoughts that I think toward you, saith the Lord, thoughts of peace, and not of evil, to give you an expected end.
Psalm 139:17	How precious also are thy thoughts unto me, O God! how great is the sum of them!

What does "precious" mean? **(Of great value; highly esteemed for some spiritual or moral quality; dear; beloved; cherished.)** (Dictionary.com.)

Spirit: When you hear the word "Spirit" used for God, do you think about the spiritual "substance" of God, His omnipresence and indestructibility, His creative spirit or energy?

John 4:24	God is a Spirit: and they that worship him must worship him in spirit and in truth.
Psalm 139:7	Whither shall I go from thy spirit? or whither shall I flee from thy presence?
Job 33:4	The spirit of God hath made me, and the breath of the Almighty hath given me life.
Romans 8:1	There is therefore now no condemnation to them which are in Christ Jesus, who walk not after the flesh, but after the Spirit.

Soul: When you hear God described as Soul, what spiritual qualities do you think of? **(The one Ego; spiritual identity and individuality; radiant beauty; purity; joy; health; holiness; what else?)**

Job 23:13	But he (God) is in one mind, and who can turn him? and what his soul desireth, even that he doeth.
Psalm 90:17	And let the beauty of the Lord our God be upon us:
Psalm 51:10, 12	Create in me a clean heart, O God; and renew a right spirit within me. Restore unto me the joy of thy salvation; and uphold me with thy free spirit.
Psalm 42:11	Why art thou cast down, O my soul? and why art thou disquieted within me? hope thou in God: for I shall yet praise him, who is the health of my countenance, and my God.
SH, p. 60:29–31	Soul has infinite **(resources)** with which to **(bless)** mankind.

Principle: Look up *principle* in the dictionary; what does it mean? **("A rule or law exemplified in natural phenomena; a fundamental, primary, or general law or truth from**

which others are derived; an originating or actuating agency or force.") (Dictionary. com.) Thinking of God in terms of the above definition, what attributes come to mind? **(Law, universal cause, harmony, constancy … what else?)**

Genesis 1:1	In the beginning, God created the heaven and the earth.
James 1:17	Every good gift and every perfect gift is from above, and cometh down from the Father of lights, with whom is no variableness, neither shadow of turning.
Jeremiah 31:33	After those days, saith the Lord, I will put my law in their inward parts, and write it in their hearts; and will be their God, and they shall be my people.
SH, p. 112:32	God is the Principle of divine m**(etaphysics)**, not matter. "Meta" means a**(bove)**, so metaphysics means **(above)** physics. If something is based on Principle—the principle of mathematics, for instance—it has strict rules or laws, and these have no limitation.

Life: Think of all the qualities of Life and name some of them. **(Existence; being; vitality; immortality; agelessness; youthfulness; energy; what else?)** If someone says of a friend, "He really has a lot of life!" what are they saying about that person? **(Discuss.)**

Deuteronomy 30:20	[L]ove the Lord thy God … for he is thy life, and the length of thy days:
Job 33:4	The spirit of God hath made me, and the breath of the Almighty hath given me life.
I John 5:11	And this is the record, that God hath given to us eternal life.
Acts 17:28	For in him we live, and move, and have our being; … For we are also his offspring.
SH, p. 381:17	The Scripture says we live and move in the i**(nfinite God).**

What does "infinite" mean? If Life is God, does life end? **(Discuss.)**

Truth: What is the effect of truth? Does truth correct an error or lie? **(Yes!)** Jesus said, "And ye shall know the truth, and the truth shall make you free." When Jesus healed people, what "truth" about them do you think he was knowing? **(Discuss.)**

Deuteronomy 32:4	He is the Rock, his work is perfect: for all his ways are judgment: a God of truth and without iniquity, just and right is he.
Psalm 31:5	[T]hou hast redeemed me, O Lord God of truth.

Zechariah 8:8   And I will bring them, and they shall dwell in the midst of Jerusalem: and they shall be my people, and I will be their God, in truth and in righteousness.

On the walls of many churches and courthouses is a statement about truth. What is it? (**"And ye shall know the truth, and the truth shall make you free."**) (John 8:32:) What do the "rays of infinite Truth" do? (**Bring light instantaneously.**) (See *Science and Health*, p. 504:23.)

Love: Love is wonderful; and everyone wants to be loved. Where does the Bible tell us that love comes from? (See verses below.)

I John 4:8   God is love.

Jeremiah 31:3   The Lord hath appeared of old unto me, saying, Yea, I have loved thee with an everlasting love:

Zephaniah 3:17   The Lord thy God in the midst of thee is mighty; he will save, he will rejoice over thee with joy; he will rest in his love, he will joy over thee with singing.

I John 3:1   Behold, what manner of love the Father hath bestowed upon us, that we should be called the sons of God:

How does the Bible tell us to find love? (See verses below.)

I John 4:12   If we love one another, God dwelleth in us, and his love is perfected in us.

I John 4:7   Why does John urge us to "love one another"? (**Because "love is of God; and every one that loveth is born of God, and knoweth God."**)

In *Science and Health*, Mary Baker Eddy tells us that "Love giveth to the least spiritual idea (**might**), (**immortality**), and goodness, which shine through all ..." (see p. 518:19–23). Therefore, you have might, immortality, and goodness, right now.

Applying the synonyms for God

1. Do you know of a situation that is not completely harmonious? Which synonym for God will help you see harmony instead of discord? (**Principle, Mind, Love ... which others?**) Why?

2. What synonym for God protects you from lies about God's good and perfect creation? (**Truth, Love, Mind ... which others?**) How do these protect us?

3. Which synonym for God would help you resolve hurt feelings from an argument with a friend? (**Love, Mind ... which others?**) How?

There's a sign: PREPARE TO MEET THY GOD. The tone is ominous, quite unlike the goodness and blessing of omnipotent God, good. Here's a truer sign for each day of the week. READY NOW, GOD IS HERE NOW, MEETING EVERY NEED:

- ✓ Life is living you.
- ✓ Love is loving you.
- ✓ Truth is protecting, correcting, and comforting you.
- ✓ Spirit is constituting your substance.
- ✓ Soul is unfolding your spiritual identity.
- ✓ Mind is providing all your knowing.
- ✓ Principle is expressing all reality and opportunity.

What would you say each of these manifestations of God is doing for you each day? (**Discuss.**)

A word about popular music:

Do preteens and teens need to be alert about the underlying message of popular songs—and even a few Christmas carols that promote Santa Claus? Put the words "The one God" in place of "Santa Claus," and what's the message?

> You better watch out, you better not cry, you better not pout,
> I'm tellin' you why, Santa Claus is coming to town.
> He's making a list and checkin' it twice, he's gonna find out
> who's naughty or nice.
> Santa Claus is coming to town.
>
> ("Santa Claus is Coming to Town." Words by Haven Gillespie, Music by J. Fred
> Coots, © 1934 (Renewed) EMI Feist Catalog, Inc., and Haven Gillespie Music.)

We need to listen for and quietly contradict lyrics that often seem to discredit God and His loving care for His noble, beautiful, and pure creation. Do you sometimes hear popular music lyrics that are degrading? That make physicality and broken hearts seem acceptable and normal? How do you respond to them?

A thinking person like you is alert, like a detective. You arrest these suggestions that God may cause or allow this kind of behavior, and you declare the truth that God never created that kind of man. In Ecclesiastes we read, "Lo, this only have I found, that God hath made man upright; but they have sought out many inventions" (Ecclesiastes 7:29). What do you think these "inventions" mean?

And in Philippians, the apostle Paul counsels us: "Finally, brethren, whatsoever things are true, whatsoever things are honest, whatsoever things are just, whatsoever things are pure, whatsoever things are lovely, whatsoever things are of good report; if there be any virtue, and if there be any praise, think on these things" (Philippians 4:8).

You will know how to think and behave in tough situations, because the Bible tells us that God talks to us. For instance, in Isaiah we read, "And thine ears shall hear a word behind thee, saying, This is the way, walk ye in it …" (Isaiah 30:21).

Does God have a voice? **(Yes.)** Have you ever heard it? **(Tell us about it.)** What does it sound like? Here is how different authors of biblical books describe the voice of God:

1. The voice of the Lord is powerful (Psalm 29:4).
2. It shakes the wilderness (Psalm 29:8).
3. It is mightier than the pounding waves of the sea (Psalm 93:4).
4. It flashes like lightning, it thunders with authority (Psalm 29:3).
5. It proclaims the kingdom of heaven on earth (*Science and Health*, p. 174:17).
6. It says, "I have called thee by thy name; thou art mine" (Isaiah 43:1).
7. It comforts, saying, "Be still, and know that I am God" (Psalm 46:10); "Fear not: I am with thee" (Isaiah 41:10).
8. It said to Abraham: take your family away from the land of idols to a new place I will show you (Genesis 12:1, 4).
9. It said to Moses: I AM THAT I AM; so lead the Children of Israel out of slavery (Exodus 3:14–17).
10. It said to Elijah: get out of that cave where you are hiding in fear, and learn that the mighty voice of God is heard by man as a still small voice within (I Kings 19).
11. It told Jesus to notice a woman who had been unable to stand up for eighteen years and to heal her (Luke 13:11–13).
12. It told the apostle Paul to assure the ship's captain that no life would be lost even while the storm was destroying the ship (Acts 27:20–25).
13. It sounded like a trumpet to John the Revelator, telling him, "I am Alpha and Omega, the first and the last" (Revelation 1:10–11). There is only one God, as Abraham, Moses, Elijah, Jesus, and Paul told you and proved to you.
14. It told Mary Baker Eddy that in Science, in reality, there is "no power opposed to God and the physical senses must give up their false testimony" (*Science and Health*, p. 192:19–21).
15. It instills the courage to keep speaking the truth even while error screams louder, because error's "suggestions" and "threats" will always cease.
16. It says through Christian Science that there is no beginning and ending; there is only the All-in-all that is always here and now.

Pick a few statements that helped you the most in *getting to know God*.

17

GETTING TO KNOW THE
IMPLICATIONS OF JESUS' HEALINGS

Bible study and Sunday School are full of purpose. In brief, they help us get to know God and ourselves. Questions and "discussion sheets" help facilitate this purpose. All the following items draw on the Bible and the Christian Science textbook, *Science and Health with Key to the Scriptures*, by Mary Baker Eddy. Each discussion sheet ideally contains at least one example like the items listed in this chapter. Students should consider the questions and statements and you will find answers in **(boldface words or citations in the parenthesis).** What students answer is determined through looking things up, discussion, and teacher input. This process will help us get to know more about the implications of Jesus' healings.

Jesus' mission was "to prove what **(God is)** and what **(He does)** for man" (*Science and Health*, p. 26:14). Jesus' approach to healing every problem was to see and acknowledge "per**(fect)** God and per**(fect)** man" (p. 259:11). This was the basis of his "thought and demonstration." "Christ is the true idea voicing good, the divine message from God to men speaking to the human consciousness" (p. 332:9). Jesus was the man who lived and taught us about the Christ-man, the man with dominion mentioned in Genesis 1:26–27.

Christ Jesus felt so at-one with his Father-Mother God that he wasted no time thinking he was separate. He meant it when he said, "I and my Father are one" (John 10:30) and "[T]he father is in me, and I in him" (verse 38).

And he really meant it when he said (John 8:51), "If a man keep my saying, he shall never see death." That's like saying, he shall never be mortal. He shall never die. (See also *Science and Health*, p. 429:31–33.)

When is man mortal? **(Man is never mortal.)**

When is man immortal? **(Man is always immortal because there is no dualism, no "dual" creation of a mortal man and an immortal man.)**

Would you like to live an unselfish life that blesses everyone as Christ Jesus did? (**Discuss.**) Christ Jesus is the highest and truest model, but Mary Baker Eddy tells us that "mortals must change their (**ideals**) in order to improve their models" (see *Science and Health*, p. 260:19–20). What is your ideal, your model?

It seems that people today do not believe in "immortals." Most people believe that every man will die because mortals die. Mary Baker Eddy heard God telling her something very different: man is God's reflection; therefore, man cannot die. Is this like what Christ Jesus heard God telling him to say: "Be ye therefore perfect, even as your Father which is in heaven is perfect"? (**Yes!**) (See Matthew 5:48.) Man, creation, cannot die. Man is as alive as his creator, divine Life!

What are some main examples of Jesus turning away from the mortal view and yielding to God's view? He did that big-time when he, the innocent, was called guilty and put on the cross. While he was on the cross, what did he ask God to do to the Jews and Romans who were trying to kill him? (**To forgive them, "for they know not what they do." See Luke 23:34.**)

Maybe Mary Baker Eddy was thinking of that when she wrote her poem "Christ My Refuge." Jesus was not afraid of the cross. He might have said words like these: "I kiss the cross and wake to know a world more bright" (see Hymn No. 253, Mary Baker Eddy, *Christian Science Hymnal*. Used courtesy of The Mary Baker Eddy Collection).

Was health important to Christ Jesus? (**Yes.**) How do you know? (**Because he healed people.**) Did Christ Jesus expect his followers to do something about health? (**Yes, definitely.**) What did he tell us to do? (See Mark 16:12–20.)

In his Sermon on the Mount, Jesus didn't just say to the people, "Do better." Jesus said (**be perfect**) (Matthew 5:48). Jesus was able to heal because he did what he said. He saw the p(**erfect**) m(**an**). (*Science and Health*, p. 476:32–34).

The Psalmist said, "What time I am afraid, I will trust in thee. I will (**not fear**) what (**flesh**) can do unto me" (Psalm 56:3–4). And "The Lord shall (**preserve**) thee from all evil: He shall preserve (**thy soul**)" (Psalm 121:7).

Christ Jesus said to a woman who could not stand up straight, "Woman, thou art loosed from thine infirmity." Then what happened? (See Luke 13:11–17.) Even though the woman had not asked for a healing, she was willing to go to Jesus when he called her.

In Luke 7:36–39, 44–48, Jesus explained to the P(**harisees**) that a sinner can indeed put off sinful mortality and put on sinless immortality or perfect being. But *how* can a sinner put on the perfect man? The religious leaders in Jesus' day, the P**(harisees)**, said a sinner is a sinner and should be treated like a sinner.

But Jesus said, "Her sins, which are many, are forgiven; for she **(loved much)**" (Luke 7:47–48). Love is im**(mortal)**.

What does this story in Luke 13:11–17 mean for you and me? Perhaps it means this: I can do what Jesus did. But how? What does *Science and Health* tell us? **("Jesus beheld in Science the perfect man, who appeared to him where sinning mortal man appears to mortals")** (*Science and Health*, p. 476:32). What is "Science"? **(Discuss.)**

Science and Health tells us, "The way to extract error from mortal mind is to pour in truth through flood-tides of **(love)**" (*Science and Health*, p. 201:17). Did God send His Son into the world to punish sinners? **(No.)** Christ Jesus did not come to **(condemn the world)** but to save it, as he himself said (see John 3:17).

Jesus met a lot of people who were guilty of these things. What did he do when the Pharisees showed him a woman who had been "caught in the act" of doing wrong?

Let's read John 8:1–11. Did Jesus punish her? No. He wanted her and her accusers to understand that sin punishes itself, and he healed because she was willing to change and *be* healed, whereas the Pharisees were not.

Jesus comforted many by healing sickness and sin, and teaching them that God did not send sickness or sin. What Comforter did he promise to send that is always present, always restoring and multiplying peace and joy and power? **(The spirit of truth.)** (See John 14:16–17.) What book helps us know and trust this Comforter? (*Science and Health.*)

What is a rumor? **(An unconfirmed story; gossip; hearsay.)** There are two lines in the Lord's Prayer where Jesus warns his followers not to be led astray by rumors of temptation and evil. Read these two lines.

There are other ways to describe rumor; for example, Hebrews 13:9: "Be not carried about with divers and strange doctrines." Also, *Science and Health* (p. 316:3): "[L]ose sight of **(mortal selfhood)**" and (p. 286:1) "belief in a **(human doctrine)**."

Do you remember what happened in Jerusalem at the pool called Bethesda? (See John 5:2–14.) The man went to the temple after he was healed, perhaps to thank God. Then Jesus found him in the temple. What did Jesus tell him? He said, "Go and sin no more, lest a worse thing come unto thee" (verse 14.) Did he mean "give up the sin of believing you are a limited man, separate from God"? **(Discuss.)**

Jesus and the man knew the meaning of that command "sin no more." I think maybe Jesus wanted that man to claim his **(true sonship and dominion)**, his "at-one-ment" with God. What do you think Jesus wanted that man to start doing and stop doing? **(Discuss.)**

Maybe Jesus said to that man (and Christ Jesus definitely tells us), there are four things each of us must do to show that we are children of our Father-Mother God. What are they? **(love your enemies; bless them that curse you; do good to them that hate you; and pray for them which despitefully use you, and persecute you.)** (See Matthew 5:44–45.)

Did everyone appreciate what Jesus did, his power to heal? **(No.)** Why? **(Discuss.)** Did his work threaten established concepts of "science, theology, and medicine" of his time? How? **(Discuss.)**

Is it your duty and purpose in life to receive healing and to offer healing truths to others? Can you tell us about a healing you have witnessed?

Then and now, it takes certain qualities of thought to experience Christ-healing. These are qualities that bless and bring blessing; for example, humility, o**(bedience)**, mercy, p**(atience)**, and peacemaking. Jesus talked about these qualities in Matthew 5 when he gave us the B**(eatitudes)** during his Sermon on **(the Mount)**.

One time, the disciples saw Jesus talking to Moses (who was born about 1,200 years before Jesus) and Elijah (who was born about 600 years before Jesus) (see Mark 9:2–9). This was possible because man is immortal and has no a**(ge)**, no d**(eath)**. Like Jesus, we are agreeing only with immortal **(consciousness)** (*Science and Health*, p. 279:11–12).

Peter and John healed a lame man. They told him, "In the name of Jesus Christ of Nazareth rise up and walk ... and the man leaped up and stood and walked with them into the temple" (Acts 3:1–9). Do Christian Scientists heal "in the name of Jesus Christ"? **(Yes.)**

What are some things you appreciate about Christ Jesus? **(Discuss.)** Here are some other things to appreciate about Christ Jesus:

1. Jesus taught and lived the true idea of being (*Science and Health*, p. 325:7).
2. He accepted a "full life," unlimited affection, and the never-limited power of Truth.
3. He respected children at a time when children did not get much respect (Matthew 9:13–14).
4. He taught, even as Christian Science teaches, that "man is in a degree as perfect as [the Mind that forms him]" (*Science and Health*, p. 337:10–11).

5. He would not let himself be separated from **(Christ, the Messiah)**, God's idea of man, and this enabled Jesus to demonstrate his control over matter (*Science and Health*, p. 482:19–23).

6. He proved that a person has self-completeness by *choosing* to acknowledge only one God, *and refusing* to acknowledge another god (*Science and Health*, p. 201:1–6; p. 264:15).

7. He said, "If you give to others, you will be given a full amount in return. The way you treat others is the way you will be treated" (Luke 6:38, Contemporary English Version).

8. He would not let himself be drawn into the hurtful cycle of guilt and condemnation, and he refused to be discouraged by the teachings of the popular religions that man is a sinner and should be punished (John 8:3–11).

9. He taught that the kingdom of heaven (of God) is **(within)** you (Luke 17:21; *Science and Health*, p. 476:28–32).

10. He taught me to let my light shine so that everyone can see my **(good works)** and glorify not *me*, but glorify our Father **(which is in heaven)** (Matthew 5:16).

11. He teaches me about reflection. Because I have "freely received," I can "freely give." He said heal **(the sick)**, cleanse people with "contagious diseases," raise the **(dead)**, and cast out the so-called **(devils)** that cause mental problems and disturbed thinking (see Matthew 10:8 and the seal on the cover of *Science and Health*).

12. In his Sermon on the Mount, Christ Jesus asks me (Matthew 5) to publish peace; to subdue grief with comfort; to be humble; to obey God; to be merciful; to be pure; to do right even when treated badly; to make my light shine; to act like my Father in heaven; and I *say, yes, I will.*

13. Jesus looked about at the sick and the sinning, but what he saw was God's creation, whole and free. He transformed both the body and the thought of those he healed.

14. He convinces me over and over again that the Christ is with me always, in all ways and conditions, even though mortal mind's false view of the world tries to make me forget or doubt this great truth (*Science and Health*, p. 317:11).

Are there any other things you would mention in *your biography* about Christ Jesus and his healing work?

Pick a few statements that helped you the most in *getting to know more about the implications of Jesus' healings.*

18

GETTING TO KNOW MORE ABOUT MARY BAKER EDDY AND CHRISTIAN SCIENCE

Bible study and Sunday School are full of purpose. In brief, they help us get to know God and ourselves. Questions and "discussion sheets" help facilitate this purpose. All the following items draw on the Bible and the Christian Science textbook, *Science and Health with Key to the Scriptures*, by Mary Baker Eddy. Each discussion sheet ideally contains at least one example like the items listed in this chapter. Students should consider the questions and statements and you will find answers in **(boldface words or citations in the parenthesis).** What students answer is determined through looking things up, discussion, and teacher input. This process will help us get to know more about Mary Baker Eddy and Christian Science.

Why did Mary Baker Eddy write *Science and Health*? Did she have a book that helped her write her textbook? **(Yes, the Bible.)** (See *Science and Health*, p.110:13.) Why did she call it a textbook and not just a book? **(You study a textbook for the purpose of learning.)**

The first "important point or religious tenet of Christian Science" is on page 497. What is our "sufficient guide to eternal Life"? **(The inspired Word of the Bible.)** Where do we find "the Word" in order to learn it? **(In the Bible.)**

In the Scientific Statement of Being (*Science and Health*, p. 468), it says matter is **(mortal error)** and also that matter is the **(unreal)** and **(temporal).** That same statement says that Spirit is **(immortal Truth)** and also that Spirit is the **(real)** and **(eternal).** Do you think Mrs. Eddy learned these facts from the other scientists of her day? **(No.)** She learned these facts by studying the life of **(Christ Jesus).**

Nearly two thousand years after Jesus, **(Mary Baker Eddy)** said it was time to reinstate primitive Christianity and its lost element of **(healing)**. (See *Church Manual of The First Church of Christ, Scientist*, by Mary Baker Eddy, p. 17.)

Mrs. Eddy says that Truth is the way to freedom and Truth is a Science—to be proved. The "powers of this world" (**belief in matter**) will try to interrupt the proving of Science, but they cannot succeed (see *Science and Health*, p. 225:5). Why not? Through the Science of Christianity, we learn more about our dominion over m(**aterial**) s(**ense**) because it would try to cover up our s(**piritual**) s(**ense**).

St. John tells us (John 1:14) that "the Word was (**made flesh**), and dwelt among us, [and we beheld his glory, the glory as of the only begotten of the Father], full of grace and truth." Was John referring to Jesus Christ? (**Yes.**) The Word (God) is also "made flesh" when we let that Word heal the body. Is that what Jesus did? (**Yes.**)

Where in the Christian Science textbook are we reminded that "All is infinite Mind and its infinite manifestation"? (***Science and Health*, p. 468—it's from the Scientific Statement of Being.**) Infinite means un(**limited**). Manifestation means ex(**pression**). Does God see you as an unlimited expression of infinite Mind? (**Yes!**) The apostle Paul said something similar when he said, "Let this (**mind**) be in you which was also in (**Christ Jesus**)" (Philippians 2:5).

The author of *Science and Health* called the "Holy Ghost" a "Comforter, revealing the divine Principle, Love, and leading into all truth" (p. 332:19). Who was the best example of the Comforter? (**Christ Jesus.**) "It is the spiritual idea, the Holy Ghost and Christ, which enables (**you to demonstrate**), with scientific certainty, the rule of healing, based upon its divine Principle, Love, underlying, overlying, and encompassing all true being" (p. 496:15).

The Holy Ghost is also defined in the glossary of *Science and Health* as (**divine Science**).

In the preface of *Science and Health*, its author writes, "Since the author's discovery of the might of (**Mind**) in the treatment of (**disease**) as well as of (**sin**), her system has been fully tested and has not been found wanting; but to reach the heights of Christian Science, man must live in (**obedience**) to its divine Principle. To develop the full might of this Science, the discords of (**corporeal sense**) must yield to the harmony of spiritual sense, even as the science of music corrects false tones and gives sweet concord to sound" (*Science and Health*, p. vii:27).

Is physical healing the main mission of Christian Science? (**No.**) (See *Science and Health*, p. 150:4.) Metaphysical healing of physical disease is only a sign that the Christ-power is here today to take away "the (**sins of the world**)." What are some examples of "sins of the world"? (**Crime, government corruption, drug addiction...what else?**)

"The effect of Christian Science is to stir the human (**mind**) to a change of base on which it may yield to the harmony of the (**divine Mind**)" (*Science and Health*, p. 162:9).

The words of Jesus are the message of Christian Science: "Correct material belief by (**spiritual understanding**), and Spirit will form you anew" (*Science and Health*, p. 425:24–26).

Was health important to Christ Jesus? (**Yes.**) How do you know? (**Because he healed people—restored them to health.**)

Did Christ Jesus expect his followers to do something about health? (**Yes.**)

What did he tell us to do? (**Go and do likewise—see Luke 10:37.**)

Was health important to Mary Baker Eddy? (**Yes.**) How do you know? (**Because she healed, too, and wrote a book titled,** *Science and Health*.)

Material sense has a c(**ounter**)feit sense of health and body. On the other hand, S(**cience**), true knowledge and proven fact, gives a true sense of health and body. Science does great things for us. It (**destroys**) the false testimony of p(**ersonal**) sense. (See *Science and Health*, p.120:7.)

Why is Christian Science the best method in the world for treating disease? (**It's the method Christ Jesus taught and used.**) (*Science and Health*, p.162:4; 344:19–24.)

Is Christianity different from Christian Science? (**No—they're the same thing.**) (See *Science and Health*, p. 372:17–18.) What do you like most about Christian Science? (**Discuss.**)

In his youth, who taught Jesus the history of the Jews, the laws of Moses, and the prophecies of Isaiah? (**His parents and the teachers in the synagogues.**) In addition to these human teachers, who was Jesus' divine teacher? (**God.**)

Who taught Mary Baker Eddy about the Bible and about God? (**The Bible.**) Nearly two thousand years after Jesus, Mary Baker Eddy was called, like the prophet Isaiah had been called, to help the people improve their concept of God, to see God as the only cause and creator. Let's read what *Science and Health* teaches us about God (see *Science and Health*, p. 331:18–24).

Mary Baker Eddy helps Christians and Christian Scientists discover the one God through these seven synonyms she gave us, such as Principle, Mind, Soul and Spirit. Can you name the other three? (**Life, Truth, Love.**)

In the glossary of *Science and Health*, she gives us helpful definitions of things we need to understand as we get to know God and man. What familiar words do you see in the definitions of Elijah (Elias)? P(rophecy); C(hristian) S(cience). True prophets (like Elijah and Christian Science) focus on s(piritual evidence) and deny m(aterial) s(ense).

Mary Baker Eddy says, "Truth is made manifest by its effects upon the human mind and body, healing (sickness) and destroying (sin)" (*Science and Health*, p. 316:7). "Soul is the substance, Life, and intelligence of man, which is (individualized) but not in matter ... Man is the (expression) of Soul" (*Science and Health*, p. 477:22–26).

The Psalmist warns us, "Cease from (anger), and forsake (wrath): fret not thyself in any wise to (do evil)" (Psalm 37:8). Is it okay to be angry? (Discuss.) *Science and Health* (p. 406:19) says, "Resist evil—error of every sort—and it will (flee from you)." How do you "resist evil"? (Discuss.)

What do you think are very harmful attitudes and actions: anger, selfishness ... what else? Mary Baker Eddy says many things about sin, but maybe this statement sums it up: "It is a sin to believe that aught can overpower omnipotent and eternal Life, and this Life must be brought to light by the understanding that there is no death, as well as by other graces of Spirit" (*Science and Health*, p. 428:32). How are we supposed to "bring Life to light"?

Jesus reversed the evidence of material sense and healed people. What a wonderful proof of God's omni(presence), omni(potence), omni-(science) and omni-(action). (See definition of *Good* in the glossary of *Science and Health*, p. 587.)

Did everyone appreciate what Jesus did, his power to heal? (No.) Why? (They didn't understand him, and they were afraid of losing power.) Today, does everyone appreciate Christian Science for its power to heal? (No.) Why? (The same reasons.)

To feel "the mighty hand of God" lifting us up, perhaps we need a truer view of anything "pulling us down." I'm glad to have Christian Science, which shows me this true view. "We learn in Christian Science that all inharmony of mortal mind or body is (unreal), possessing neither reality nor identity though seeming to be real and identical" (*Science and Health*, p. 472:30).

Mary Baker Eddy gives us a word-picture of a baby chick coming out of its shell (see *Science and Health*, p. 552:16–19). In line 17, who is "they"? (Mortals.) The passage says we must "peck open our shells with Christian Science" and do what? (look outward and upward.)

Matter is the opposite of Spirit, but there is another meaning of the word *matter*.

"Matter" also means "subject"; for example, "Don't laugh; this is a serious matter" (subject). How does the dictionary define *matter*? Does the dictionary include a Christian Science definition of *matter*? **(Yes.)** What is it?

Is a table "substance?" **(Yes/No?)** Christian Science explains that a table is not m**(atter)** but is really the m**(anifestation)** of a right idea. See the Scientific Statement of Being (*Science and Health*, p. 468:9–11).

Every Christian Science Bible Lesson reminds us to claim and use something God gave us to demonstrate the power of Spirit. What is it? **(Dominion.)** (See Genesis 1:26.)

I think Mary Baker Eddy is reminding me of what my soul's intention and desire and motive is when she says this: "Love for God and man is the **(true incentive)** in both healing and teaching. Right **(motives)** give pinions to thought, and strength and freedom to speech and action" (*Science and Health*, p. 454:17–21).

The Lord's Prayer indicates that when Christ Jesus talked *about* God and talked *to* God, he called God **("Father")**. Christ Jesus constantly proved the caring, comforting, mothering actions of God, so Mary Baker Eddy talks about God also as **("Father-Mother")** (see *Science and Health*, p. 16:26–27).

Dictionary definitions:

Is it important to know how the dictionary defines words we see often in our Bible Lessons? Yes! How does the dictionary define these words, which we often have in our Bible Lessons: *substance, matter, scientist, spirit, reality, truth,* etc. Does the dictionary you use include a "Christian Science" definition for any of these words? (Note: I use Dictionary.com and Webster's Collegiate Dictionary, Third Edition, which is now known as *Merriam-Webster's Collegiate Dictionary* in its various editions. However, you can use any good-quality, comprehensive dictionary you choose.) In my Webster's, neither *reality* nor *sacrament* has a designated Christian Science definition. However, these are the words I have discovered so far that *do* include a Christian Science definition: *God, Christ, man, Jesus, matter, substance, intelligence, principle, mind, soul, spirit, life, truth, love, scientist,* and *baptism.*

In the Christian Science church, do we use water in baptism or bread and wine for the sacrament? **(No.)** Thank you, Mary Baker Eddy, for bringing to Christianity a more spiritual meaning of *baptism* and *sacrament.* In *Science and Health*, she defines baptism this way: "BAPTISM. Purification by Spirit; submergence in Spirit. We are 'willing rather to be absent from the body, and to be present with the Lord' (II Corinthians 5:8)" (p. 581:23). Then she says (p. 241:27), "The baptism of Spirit, washing the body of all the impurities of flesh, signifies that the pure in heart see God and are approaching spiritual Life and its demonstration." Finally, how does she further describe baptism (see p. 35:19)? **(As a "purification from all error.")**

Sacrament. "Our Eucharist (sacrament) is spiritual communion with the one God. Our bread, 'which cometh down from heaven' is **(Truth)**. Our cup is the cross" (*Science and Health*, p. 35:25–27). What do the "cup" and "cross" represent?

Science and Health says there is something more important than the "material symbols" of water, bread, and wine. Mary Baker Eddy challenges all Christians with this question: "Christians, are you drinking his cup?" (*Science and Health*, p. 33:27). What do you suppose the practical result would be if everyone was truly drinking his cup? She tells us in the following:

> If all who ever partook of the sacrament had really commemorated the sufferings of Jesus and drunk of his cup, they would have revolutionized the world. If all who seek his commemoration through material symbols will take up the cross, heal the sick, cast out evils, and preach Christ, or Truth, to the poor,—the receptive thought,—they will bring in the millennium (*Science and Health*, p. 34:13).

You and I are preaching Christ, or Truth, every time we remember to be an example of honesty, purity, faith, and l**(ove)**. God inspires us to say true words and do good deeds. What does it mean to be an example of love and purity? Tell about a time you were willing to be an example of good and Godlikeness.

What is an angel? Webster's says an angel is "a spiritual being superior to man in power and intelligence; a guardian, a messenger." Does Webster's definition include a *Christian Science* definition? **(Yes/No?)** *Science and Health* says that "angels" are "God's thoughts passing to man; spiritual intuitions, pure and perfect" (p. 581:4).

Are lions a natural enemy to man? **(No.)** A negative mental influence called **(fear)** tries to make them enemies, tries to empower a**(nimal)** m**(agnetism)**, which is another name for m**(ortal)** m**(ind)** (see *Science and Health*, p. 103:18–19). Animal magnetism/mortal mind is only a f**(alse)** belief that m**(ind)** is in m**(atter)** and is both evil and good. God, immortal M**(ind)**, protects and delivers humans and causes the lies of mortal mind to self-destruct (see *Science and Health*, p. 103:22–28). Was anyone ever safe in a lion's den? **(Yes, Daniel.)**

Competition: Do different versions of the truth compete for your attention? Sometimes it does seem they try to. Can you give some examples?

Did Jesus have any competition? (Yes.) Religious leaders (the Pharisees and Sadducees) tried to convince the Jews that they must follow religious ritual and hundreds of laws they had written. They objected strongly when Jesus "worked" on the Sabbath day by healing the woman who could not stand up straight (see Luke 13:10–17). Some of them also believed that the Jews must overthrow the Roman occupation of Israel in order to be free. But Jesus said, "Ye shall know the truth and the truth shall make you free" (John 8:32). What truth was Jesus referring to? **(Discuss.)** Mary Baker Eddy writes in *Science and Health* that "Jesus' religion had a divine Principle, which would cast out error and heal both the sick and the sinning" (p.136:1). What was the divine Principle? **(Truth.)**

Did Mary Baker Eddy have any competition? (Yes.) Leaders in the fields of theology and medicine insisted that man is sinful and material—that he gets sick and dies. But Mary Baker Eddy pursued a spiritual interpretation of the Bible which says that God saw, and still sees, everything He makes, and behold, it is very **(good)**. She said that theology and medicine are means of divine thought, and are not about matter at all. This is one of the things she said about Jesus: "As the individual ideal of Truth, Christ Jesus came to rebuke rabbinical error and all sin, sickness, and death,—to point out the way of Truth and Life" (*Science and Health*, p. 30:19–21).

In 1875, she published the first edition of *Science and Health*, the book that explains the theology of Christian Science. In that same year, other people presented a theory called "theosophy." Theosophy also teaches about God and the world, but its teachings are based on the mystical insights of *the human mind*, not on the revelations of the divine Mind.

Does the human mind help you understand and demonstrate Christian Science? **(No.)** The human mind is not a factor, because God is the only Mind. The Scientific Statement of Being says that *all* is infinite Mind and its infinite manifestation. Jesus said this about his so-called human mind: "I can of mine own self do nothing … I seek not mine own will, but the will of the Father which hath sent me" (John 5:30).

My "thinking" is clearer and more correct as I "let this Mind be in [me] which was also in Christ Jesus" (Philippians 2:5). I too say with Paul, "I can do all things through Christ which strengtheneth me" (Philippians 4:11). Mary Baker Eddy says, "The time for **(thinkers)** has come" (*Science and Health*, p. vii:13). Thinkers look to the divine Mind, not to the **(human or mortal mind)**.

Does Christian Science have any competition now, in the twenty-first century? (Yes.) Material "scientists" say that man is physical, although some say man is more than just a body and a brain. Most theologians still insist that man is material and sinful, and that the Bible says so. Does the Bible teach that man is material and sinful? One might say yes and no.

The Bible is many books, and it seems to teach many things, so how do I know what to believe? The Bible's message can be understood only through *spiritual* interpretation. A *literal* reading results in confusion. I accept the premise that God is All, God is good, man is the reflection of God, and God's works are good for man (see Genesis 1:31). The beliefs of some Jews about God grew more spiritual over the centuries, and finally a Jew named Jesus came along to raise that spiritual view even higher.

Jesus had such a spiritually unlimited view of God and man that he said this in his Sermon on the Mount: "Be ye therefore perfect, even as your Father which is in heaven is perfect" (Matthew 5:48). It was his correct understanding of perfect God and perfect man created in God's image and likeness that enabled Jesus to heal the sick and sinful, proving their unreality. If healing sin and sickness had been contrary to God's will, Jesus could never have done it.

The sixty-six books of the Bible were written over a period of almost 1,200 years. Most of the authors of these books just kept on believing that man is material and sinful. A few prophets, however, began to see that the one God is a good God who intended good for man, not evil: Abraham, Jacob-Israel, Joseph, Moses, Joshua, David, Elijah, Elisha, Isaiah, and Jeremiah. I thank God for the life work of each of these people. Their stories help me understand better what makes people "fall" for error or "hold on" to truth.

Finally, in 1875, Mary Baker Eddy published the first edition of *Science and Health with Key to the Scriptures.* This book presents the proof that God and creation are only good. People who stay focused on this truth and walk in it (that, is, live it) can always experience freedom from all limitation and evil. I am glad she established a systematic way for me, for us, to keep learning more and more about perfect God and perfect man (see *Science and Health*, p. 259:13).

What is the system she set up to teach and promulgate Christian Science? (The Mother Church and Church Manual, which establish all the activities of the church, including Christian Science branch church services and Sunday School; lectures; primary class instruction; the weekly Bible Lessons in their many forms; among other things.)

Mary Baker Eddy faced a great deal of criticism, especially from those with a competing view of God and man. It is very instructive and inspiring to read biographies of this Discoverer, Founder, and Leader of Christian Science. Over twenty were published between 1907 and 2002. A good one for young people is *The Golden Days*, by Jewel Spangler Smaus. Also, there is a new book, *A World More Bright*, by Isabel Ferguson and Heather Vogel Frederick. Another is called, *We Knew Mary Baker Eddy,* recently republished in a two-volume expanded edition. *Mary Baker Eddy: Christian Healer* (amplified edition), by Yvonne Cache von Fettweis and Robert Townsend Warneck, is still another excellent resource. And for a variation in format, watch *Soul of a Woman*, a video that first aired on New Hampshire Public Television in 1994.

Do you face any competition? **(Yes/no?)** What is the competition? **(Discuss.)** During your years in high school and college, what is likely to compete against your interest in Christian Science?

How can we face that competition and be victorious every time? See the following citations from *Science and Health*:

> We know that a desire for holiness is requisite in order to gain holiness; but if we desire holiness above all else, we shall sacrifice everything for it. We must be willing to do this, that we may walk securely in the only practical road to holiness (p. 11:22–27).

> Universal salvation rests on progression and probation, and is unattainable without them ... No final judgment awaits mortals, for the judgment day of wisdom comes hourly and continually, even the judgment by which mortal man is divested of all material error (p. 291:12–13, 28–31).

> If the disciple is advancing spiritually, he is striving to enter in. He constantly turns away from material sense, and looks towards the imperishable things of Spirit. If honest, he will be in earnest from the start, and gain a little each day in the right direction, till at last he finishes his course with joy (p. 21:9).

Pick a few statements that helped you the most in getting to know more about Mary Baker Eddy and Christian Science.

19

GETTING TO KNOW MORE ABOUT IDENTITY

When the apostle Paul wrote a letter to the church in Galatia, he said that Spirit, like a tree, bears fruit. It produces things that are useful and very desirable. Spirit is expressed, for example, as affection for others, joy, peace, patience, long-suffering, kindness, gentleness, goodness, faithfulness, and self-control (see Galatians 5:22–23).

Which "fruits of the Spirit" above do you express often? Underline them above.

Are there any fruits of the Spirit that you need to express (act out) more often than you are doing at present? Circle those above.

Why is it important for us to know all the time that we are greatly loved? **(Discuss.)** Do you think one meaning of *sense* in the dictionary is *intelligence*? **(Yes—for instance, the phrase "he has good sense.")** Can *sense* mean *judgment* and *wisdom*? **(Yes.)** God-sense, spiritual sense, intelligence, tells us that man's true senses belong to G**(od)**—to God, not to matter. God, divine L**(ove)** makes sure that my senses glorify God and bless others. Thank you, Love, for loving me in this way.

The Lord's Prayer indicates that when Christ Jesus talked *about* God and talked *to* God, he called God, Father. Christ Jesus constantly proved the caring, comforting, fathering, and mothering actions of God. It becomes more natural to prove that God, M**(ind)**, is my mind; I manifest or express or reflect divine Mind, divine intelligence. Who said, "Let this mind be in you which was also in Christ Jesus"? **(Paul.)** (See Philippians 2:5.)

The divine Mind, God, gives us all good, gives us true thoughts and feelings like patience, confidence, trust, and expectation of good. Mind wants us to know only *the facts* and *helps* us know them. Thank you, God!

Mortal-no-mind, or the carnal mind, however, claims to take over our feelings (thoughts) and make us agree to impatience, worry, fear, and doubt. In Romans, Paul explains this. He writes, "[T]he carnal mind is enmity against God" (Romans 8:7). This no-mind does not ask, "What are the facts?" We must turn away from human thoughts, which can be negative *or* positive, and turn toward the one all-knowing (**Mind**). This Mind, God, which loves us, gives us spiritual (**thoughts**), spiritual consciousness—in other words, the spiritual facts. Another word for *fact* would be t(**ruth**). Is T(**ruth**) another name for God? (**Yes!**).

Jesus was able to bless himself and others because he chose to have and use only spiritual con(**sciousness**), spiritual facts. Can you do the same? (**Yes.**) And wouldn't this be letting "this mind be in you which was also in Christ Jesus"? (Philippians 2:5).

A prophet of God is focused on listening to God and doing God's will. Are you a prophet? (**Yes.**) The prophet Elijah agreed to have the qualities of patience, confidence, trust, and expectation of good. When Elijah had no food because of a famine in the land, he did not panic. No! *Never.*

He trusted divine Mind, God, who told him to go to the home of a poor widow. She was able to feed him because Elijah helped her prove the law of God—that there is *always* enough. Later, when the widow's son suddenly died, Elijah did not panic. He prayed with confidence and expectation of good. What happened next? (**He raised the boy from the dead.**) (See I Kings 17:8–10, 17, 22–24.)

Are we always making spiritual progress as well as human progress? (**Yes.**) Each time we consider the story of Moses leading the children of Israel out of Egypt in the book of Exodus, we can have new questions about what happened and what the story has to do with each of us—if anything, since it happened so long ago. The only way we can grow in our understanding of Truth is to ask questions. What kind of questions should we ask? We cannot be content only with questions that test our memory, for example, but with questions that stimulate *new* thinking.

Does everyone have spiritual sense? (**Yes.**) Every time we use it, we gain more skill in using it. It is natural to use spiritual sense because Spirit, God, created each of us and renews us every day. It is natural to use a loving sense because divine (**Love, Spirit**) renews us every day. If we first gain a knowledge of God, we can study and learn an unlimited number of things about any other subject. Are you a genius? (**Discuss.**) Is Mind, God, unlimited intelligence? Do you manifest infinite Mind, infinite intelligence, and isn't this the truth of your being? I thank God, Love, that this is my identity. Don't you do the same?

"You are what you eat" is a popular saying. "Ye shall know the truth, and the truth shall make you free" (John 8:32). Which statement is more true, and why?

You and I are preaching Christ, or Truth, every time we remember to be an ex**(ample)** of honesty, purity, faith, and l**(ove)**. The spirit of God inspires us to *say* true words (truth) and *do* good deeds (love). What does it mean to be an example of love and purity? Tell about a time you were willing to be an example of good and Godlikeness.

What does it mean to *sacrifice* something? If we try to do everything through Love, we will not lose anything good by sacrificing. We cannot lose anything good, because Love is giving us everything good. "I know the thoughts that I think toward you, saith the Lord, thoughts of peace, and not of evil, to give you an expected end" (Jeremiah 29:11).

We seem to constantly hear through friends and TV news many things that are negative. What can we do if a voice says, "You are not succeeding"? First, we can say no! There is no liar voicing a lie, because God, Truth, makes no liars or lies. Second, we can say yes, God, I have the spiritual understanding that You are constantly expressing in me. The voice of Truth is always telling me all I need to know and do, and its message is never neg**(ative)**. Through the Christ, God directs, protects, and corrects, but never punishes.

What is the meaning of *mortal mind*? Mortal mind, or the carnal mind, is the belief that man has a separate mind from God. Is mortal mind a real thing? (**No.**) It's like a mistake in mathematics—just waiting for someone to catch the mistake and correct it. Because we are intelligent and alert as the one Mind's expression, we can be alert to mistakes and correct them. Tell about a time when you corrected a mistake.

I cannot be tricked by the mistake called m**(ortal)** m**(ind)** if I am taking the high way—the freeway—of knowing I can do what Christ Jesus and the apostle Paul tell me I can do: "Be ye therefore perfect, even as your Father which is in heaven is **(perfect)**" (Matthew 5:48). "Let this **(mind)** be in you which was also in Christ Jesus" (Philippians 2:5).

Hundreds of years before the angel message came to the Virgin Mary, it came to the prophet Isaiah. He was ready to receive a very unusual message because he was a p**(rophet)** of the Lord, and a prophet is someone who **(listens to God and speaks God's word)**. Angel thoughts come to g**(uide)** us. Do angels *make* us listen and follow? (**No.**) We hear the angel message when we are thanking God and lis**(tening)** to God.

Angels **(thoughts)** shine a light on our sp**(iritual)** sense, and in this light we see how m**(aterial)** sense would try to limit and confuse us. As we say, "Yes, thank you, God," for every angel **(thought)**, the beliefs of discord and disease lose their influence.

When you are g**(overned)** by G**(od)**, you know that "with God all things are possible" (Matthew 19:26). God, Spirit, preserves you by giving you *spiritual substance* and *divine intelligence*.

"God guards you from every evil, he guards your very life. He guards you when you leave and when you return, he guards you now, he guards you always" (Psalm 121:7–8, *THE MESSAGE: The Bible in Contemporary Language*, NavPress, copyright 2002, by Eugene Peterson).

Can you think of a time when God guarded and guided you? What temptation do you have to resist?

Is it safe to ignore evil and danger? (**No.**) If you try to pretend that evil and danger are not a problem, then they will seem to have more presence and more power until you *denounce* them as untrue because they are not created by Truth, God.

I am safe at all times if I am remembering that God, good, is all p(**ower**), all p(**resence**), and all action.

Many people over hundreds of years have written stories—histories—of creation from their own point of view. *Point of view* means "opinion or attitude" (Dictionary.com).

For hundreds of years, people have been asking, Who was the first man? Who was the first woman? These people already had a point of view (which is an opinion or belief) before they asked the question. They believed that man is mortal, material, disobedient and "fallen" with a mind of his own. As a result, the creation stories they wrote expressed these beliefs.

The Adam and Eve story was probably written about 1000 BCE. At that time, the Hebrews were a strong nation, and D(**avid**) was their king. Over the next nine hundred years, prophets faithful to the one God gave the Hebrew people a better understanding of God. Who were some of these prophets?

A spiritual account of creation, included in the Bible in Genesis 1, was written in late 500 BCE, according to many scholars. In this true history, God, Spirit, reveals a spiritual expression of itself, a spiritual creation where man and woman have d(**ominion**) and are declared to be g(**ood**), not evil or fallen (see verses 26, 27, 31).

Would our good parent, God, divine Spirit, let His/Her children become *mortal, sinful* or *fallen*? (**No.**) *Mortal-no-mind* is the star of the untrue history and tries to get people to believe it. Do most people believe they are mortal and fallen? (**Yes.**) *Mortal-no-mind* believes itself, but woman/man (like Abraham) looks higher for a heavenly view. Do you remember how Abraham became the first man to look for a heavenly view, to know and serve the one God? You will recall that God told him to leave (**his country**) and go to ("**a land I will show you**") (Genesis 12:1).

I don't want to sin. Do you? Of course not. If I don't want to sin, then I need to acknowledge that I am the child of God and cannot sin. To demonstrate immortality is to be always ready to say *no* to the belief of being separated from God, divine Life, and saying *yes* to your oneness with God.

Your thinking is what makes you, *you*! Do you want to think bad, do bad, feel bad? **(No!)** Do you want to punish others? **(No!)** Love is a name for **(God)**. Does Love want to punish? **(No.)** Why not? So is it okay to think bad, do bad, and feel bad, since God does not punish? **(No.)** Why?

Does God love you? **(Yes.)** How do you know? **(Discuss.)** Do *you* love you? Why?

Sin punishes itself and seems to punish the person who expects to ignore God and try, like *a mad scientist*, to prove that being *sinful* is the normal nature of man. What is sin? Sin is the lazy, incorrect, harmful belief that **(man is a fallen, sinful mortal)**. Is sin necessary? **(No.)** Why? **(Because God takes care of us—if we listen to Him.)** The Psalmist put it this way: "The steps of a good man are ordered by the Lord" (Psalm 37:23).

In Psalm 23, the Psalmist knew that he was being protected and guided by God, his Shepherd, and he saw a much brighter path. Instead of dark shadows, he saw abundance of food, drink, and safety that his enemies could not steal. In his expanding view of God as the great Shepherd (defender and guide), he could see that kindness and love ("goodness and mercy") would be with him every day ("all the days of [his] life") and that he actually lived in God's "house." What is this house? Spiritual **(consciousness)**. Is that where you live? **(Yes.)** No matter where you live now—or may live twenty years from now—you always live in consciousness.

We are God's image and **(likeness)**. We are at-one with God, but we can know what this means only as we know the life and teachings of Christ Jesus. He proved what is true and dismissed what is untrue. He said, "I and my Father are one" (John 10:30). And you can say the same thing about your relationship to God.

Is it your duty and purpose in life to receive healing and offer healing truths to others? **(Yes.)** How do you know? **(Jesus told us to do so.)** (See Matthew 10:1, 5, 8.) Can you tell about a healing you had or were a witness to?

Then and now, it takes certain qualities of thought to experience Christ-healing. Jesus talked about these qualities in Matthew 5 when he gave us the Beatitudes.

The Beatitudes give us the qualities that bless and bring blessing, such as humility, o**(be-dience)**, mercy, p**(urity)**, and peacemaking.

"Who do you think you are, anyway?" You might have heard this negative reaction to your self-expression. Does self-expression include "showing off"? **(No.)** Your first response to this question needs to be thought, not words. In thought you might ask yourself, "Am I feeling or acting superior to others? Putting myself ahead of others in importance?"

It takes honesty and humility to ask and answer such questions, but you need to move on from the question to the answer. Is your Parent Mind always showing you how to be and do good? **(Yes.)** You are learning how to be a real Christian, an actual follower of Christ Jesus. The Bible tells you to quickly take a spiritual direction in thought, to remember who you really are. Who or what are you really, according to God? **(Discuss.)**

Did people ask Jesus, Who do you think you are, anyway? **(Yes.)** Religious leaders criticized Jesus for doing things they couldn't do and didn't understand. People were afraid …and jealous, too. They could have said, Teach us more. Instead, they said, This is not what we have always believed, so how could it be true? (See Mark 3:1–6, for instance.)

The Bible writers made many statements about *man*. What did the prophet Isaiah say? (See Isaiah 43, verses 5 and 21.) What did the prophet Jeremiah say? (See Jeremiah 31:3.) What did the apostle Paul say? (See Romans 8:16.) What did Christ Jesus say? (See Matthew 5:48.) Let's find some phrases that are strong statements of truth about man (like the ones Christ Jesus made).

"I am God Almighty: be fruitful and multiply" (Genesis 35:11). A tree is fruitful. Are you a fruitful tree? **(Yes/no?)** What does it mean to be fruitful? God also wants us to multiply. Does that mean God wants more than one of you? **(No.)** What does God want you to multiply? **(Good.)**

We could say your individuality is your total self. Do you have the same individuality now that you will have twenty years from now? **(Yes.)**

We could say *Soul* is the synonym for God that creates and nurtures your spiritual individuality. *Soul* as used in the book of Psalms, however, often refers to the longing state of human thought as it yearns to know the true spiritual status of man. The Psalmist wrote (107:8,9), "Oh that men would praise the Lord for his goodness, and for his wonderful works to the children of men! For he **(satisfieth)** the longing soul, and **(filleth)** the hungry soul with goodness."

Spirit, Soul, gives us spiritual understanding; then we accept it and practice using it. Where in the Bible does it say, "God created man in his own image, in the image of God created he him; male and female created he them"? **(In Genesis 1:27.)**

Various prophets in the Old Testament, especially A(**braham**) and J(**acob/Israel**), heard God say, "Be fruitful and multiply" or were promised that they would be "exceeding fruitful." In the New Testament, Jesus completely accepted God's invitation to be fruitful and multiply. What did he multiply when thousands of people were hungry? (**Loaves and fishes.**) Jesus also multiplied the calm when a storm threatened the boat he was in (see Matthew 8:8, 23–27). Jesus multiplied harmony and wholeness as he went about teaching and preaching and healing (see Matthew 9:35). Jesus and the prophets knew that the one S(**oul, God**) was creating and nurturing all individuality—every one of us.

Human consciousness is sometimes afraid or uncertain, but it always has access to understanding and wisdom. A psalmist said, "Thou art my portion, O Lord" (Psalm 119:57). God is All-in-all. If I say that God is my "portion," it means that I have (**all or every spiritual idea I need**).

You are making choices now, and you will always be making choices—about friends and schoolwork and activities and new adventures. How can you make wise choices that satisfy your desire to *be the unlimited you* and *do unlimited good*? (**Discuss.**)

One who makes wise choices has a wise guide. One name for such a guide in the Bible is *shepherd*. Let's look at Psalm 23. This Psalmist chose the Lord as his Shepherd. What were the good results? (**Discuss.**)

A person could have knowledge, talent, and success. A person would probably feel good about having these and sharing these, but the prophet Jeremiah described something even more important in Jeremiah 9:23, 24. What was it? (**Glorifying God.**) Indeed, every person *does* have knowledge, talent, and success.

A *witness* is someone who (**saw what happened**). A *servant* is someone who (**serves**). According to the prophet Isaiah, God, Love, makes you a witness and a servant so that you can do what? (**Know, believe, and understand God.**) (See Isaiah 43:10.)

As a witness and a servant, are you separate from God? (**Yes/no?**) Can you always overcome evil with good? (**Yes.**) Why and how? (**Discuss.**)

Look at John 3:1–7. Is Christ Jesus saying something to Nicodemus about identity? What is he saying? Perhaps Jesus was saying to Nicodemus, You have sp(**iritual**) identity. Accept it, and you will understand more about doing the works of God.

There are three kinds of questions:

1. A question that can be answered with yes or no.

2. A question that can be answered with a statement of fact.
3. And a question that can be answered with thoughtful opinion.

Is Soul a name for God? **(Yes.)**

How does the dictionary define *soul*? Dictionary.com defines soul this way: "(1) the principle of life, feeling, thought, and action in humans, regarded as a distinct entity separate from the body, and commonly held to be separable in existence from the body; (2) the spiritual part of humans regarded in its moral aspect, or as believed to survive death and be subject to happiness or misery in a life to come; (3) the animating principle; (9) the embodiment of some quality; (10) (initial capital letter) [In] Christian Science. God; the divine source of all identity and individuality."

What then does soul mean to you? I like to define *Soul* (capital *S*) as the truth about identity.

Does everyone have their own soul? No. Does a single ray of sunshine have its own sun? No, all the individual rays reflect the one sun. Likewise, we all *reflect* the one Soul, God, but we do not have our own individual *soul*. God is the Soul of everyone's being. Each individual has a Soul—the same Soul; that is, God. Jesus knew and proved for himself and others that a sense of "separate" identity or "flawed" identity is not true, and each one must replace—accept replacement of—the false sense by the *true* sense of being, or Soul.

Are qualities exclusively masculine or feminine? Are the following qualities masculine or feminine, or both? Love, purity, tenderness, strength, beauty, intelligence, courage, decisiveness, sensitivity. These are *qualities* and therefore are spiritual and not related to gender. You and I embody these qualities, express these qualities as individual man, the image and likeness of God.

What do you have that has infinite resources for blessing mankind? I have identity. My *spiritual* identity reflects and expresses infinite resources for meeting every challenge to myself or to others. As a so-called separate "material identity," I seem to lack the resources for helping myself and others.

Does everyone you know have questions about identity? Yes. But it's nice to know that a question isn't necessarily a doubt; it's simply a desire for more understanding.

Pick a few statements that helped you the most in *getting to know more about identity*.

20

GETTING TO KNOW MORE ABOUT PRAYER, PRAY-ER, AND THE LORD'S PRAYER

Mary Baker Eddy gives us a simple prayer that can guide and guard our rising thought. Titled, "A Verse," the first stanza is subtitled, "Mother's New Year Gift to the Little Children":

> Father-Mother God,
> Loving me,—
> Guard me when I sleep;
> Guide my little feet
> Up to thee.

> (*Miscellaneous Writings 1883–1896*, p. 400)

Prayer is usually associated with religion, often as a church ritual. Christian Science takes seriously the command, "Pray without ceasing" (I Thessalonians 5:17). People study Christian Science because they believe and want to understand *healing through prayer*. Individual and ceaseless prayer characterizes the practice of Christianity—and of Christian Science. In *Science and Health*, there are dozens of references to words related to "pray" and "praying."

During worship in most other religions, a pastor or priest verbalizes the prayer and prays aloud on behalf of the congregation. I grew up in a church where the minister took the lead in vocalizing a prayer for the congregation, thanking and petitioning God on our behalf. Only after I learned more about prayer through the study of Christian Science did I make this observation, that pastors' prayers not only thanked God for His presence and blessing but also asked God to *do things*: bless these particular people, guide this particular endeavor, remember this particular promise.

Occasionally I am with Christian friends who like to offer grace before a meal. When saying grace, one such friend asks God to do a number of things in terms of correcting social problems and restoring mankind's spiritual health; then finally she asks God to "bless this food to our use and our lives to Thy service." This observation prompts me to wonder, What is the role of verbalized prayer?

When I am asked to offer the prayer in such a setting, I'm perplexed about what to do. Sometimes I make a series of "thank you" statements. Sometimes I offer this Daily Prayer from the *Church Manual*, by Mary Baker Eddy (article VIII, section 4):

> 'Thy kingdom come;'
> let the reign of divine Truth, Life, and Love
> be established in me,
> and rule out of me all sin;
> and may Thy Word enrich the affections
> of all mankind, and govern them!

The Lord's Prayer indicates that when Christ Jesus talked *about* God and talked *to* God, he called God *Father*. Christ Jesus constantly proved the caring, comforting, fathering, and mothering actions of God, and so Mary Baker Eddy talks about God as Father-Mother.

And what is the foundation for asking God to *do things*? I can think of several examples from the Lord's Prayer: Give us, Forgive us, Lead us not, Deliver us. Shall I pray, Please do these things, or Thank you for doing these things?

How is prayer incorporated into Christian Science church services? A Sunday church service is conducted by two readers rather than by a pastor or minister. The first reader, who conducts the service, invites the congregation to pray silently and then join together in praying aloud the Lord's Prayer. After silent prayer, the second reader leads the congregation in praying the Lord's Prayer. Following each line in the prayer, the first reader reads from *Science and Health with Key to the Scriptures* the "spiritual sense" of that line (p. 16–17):

> Our Father which art in heaven,
> > *Our Father-Mother God, all-harmonious,*
> Hallowed be Thy name.
> > *Adorable One.*
> Thy kingdom come.
> > *Thy kingdom is come; Thou art ever-present.*
> Thy will be done in earth, as it is in heaven.

Enable us to know,—as in heaven, so on earth,—God
is omnipotent, supreme.
Give us this day our daily bread;
    Give us grace for to-day; feed the famished affections;
And forgive us our debts, as we forgive our debtors.
    And Love is reflected in love;
And lead us not into temptation, but deliver us from evil;
    And God leadeth us not into temptation, but
    delivereth us from sin, disease, and death.
For Thine is the kingdom, and the power, and the glory,
forever.
    For God is infinite, all-power, all Life, Truth, Love,
    over all, and All.

In Sunday School, students and teachers pray the Lord's Prayer together after silent prayer, but the superintendent does not interject the "spiritual sense" of each line. During silent prayer,

- Are you just waiting for the service to continue?
- Are you asking God for something?
- re you thanking God for something?

What is our purpose in praying together? On page 42 of the *Church Manual*, Mary Baker Eddy says this about prayer in church: "The prayers in Christian Science churches shall be offered for the congregations collectively and exclusively."

The "pray-er" asks, Can God help me? Is God helping me? Will God help me? As a Christian and a Christian Scientist, I know the spiritually correct answer is *yes*. What brings on such questions? Sometimes a persistent and painful problem seems to elicit such questions. The pray-er has prayed and prayed, yet the problem persists. Thank God, the Lord hears, helps us to be receptive, comforts us, and heals us.

I read an article in the *Christian Science Sentinel* where the author also questioned her ability to know and connect with God through prayer. So she decided to change her usual approach of affirmation and denial and instead used a simple, sincere prayer.

Part of the definition of *angels* given by Mary Baker Eddy in *Science and Health* is, "God's thoughts passing to man" (p. 581:4). The angel says to us, "God never sends or permits painful problems." Christ speaks to the human consciousness, and you might hear an angel message like this: "Dear precious child, I created you beautifully, perfectly, and completely. Know this, and you will realize all that I know you to be."

"I am also teaching you," says the heavenly director and protector, "to guard your house—your consciousness—with the might, light, and wisdom I've given you. I renew these gifts and capabilities every day because I love the way they lift you up as you lift up your thanks to Me. I also give you hymns of hope and joy. Pray with some of these hymns. It's always my whole design, 'thy dross to consume and thy gold to refine.' (Hymn No. 123, adaptation by Rippon, Keith and Keene, *Christian Science Hymnal*, ©1932, renewed 1960, The Christian Science Board of Directors. Used with permission.) My will *is* done," says the one Almighty God.

Whatever form of prayer we choose, there is a way to determine if our prayers are effective. Mary Baker Eddy tells us in the Christian Science textbook (p. 9:5) the following about prayer:

> The test of all prayer lies in the answer to these questions: Do we love our neighbor better because of this asking? Do we pursue the old selfishness, satisfied with having prayed for something better, though we give no evidence of the sincerity of our requests by living consistently with our prayer? If selfishness has given place to kindness, we shall regard our neighbor unselfishly, and bless them that curse us; but we shall never meet this great duty simply by asking that it may be done. There is a cross to be taken up before we can enjoy the fruition of our hope and faith.

The Congregation's Prayer

In a Wednesday evening meeting, as in the Sunday church service, the first reader invites the congregation to pray silently and then join together in praying aloud the Lord's Prayer. For the Wednesday evening meeting, the spiritual interpretation is not included. Christian Scientists pray the Lord's Prayer much more slowly and with more time for deliberation than in other churches. Prayer in Christian Science is almost entirely individual and silent, but when we pray together, the tone of deliberation and sincerity is apparent.

Many Christians are accustomed to the Lord's Prayer given in the 1611 version of the King James Bible. More than two hundred years earlier, in 1382, John Wycliffe prepared an English Bible—the first European translation done in nearly one thousand years. Here is John Wycliffe's translation of the Lord's Prayer (Matthew 6:9–13):

> Oure fadir that art in heuenes, halewid be thi name;
> thi kyngdoom come to; be thi wille don 'in erthe as in heuene;
> yyue to vs this dai oure 'breed ouer othir substaunce;
> and foryyue to vs oure dettis, as we foryyuen to oure dettouris; and lede vs
> not in to temptacioun, but delyuere vs fro yuel. Amen.

There have been many translations of the Lord's Prayer. Will there be more? A list of fourteen versions of the Lord's Prayer is given in the next chapter of this book, titled, "Getting to Know the Many Versions of the Lord's Prayer."

Daily Prayers

Many Christians pray daily. In the *Church Manual*, Article VIII—Guidance of Members, Mary Baker Eddy articulates three "daily" prayers: A Rule for Motives and Acts; the Daily Prayer; and Alertness to Duty. These prayers, whether spoken or thought, illustrate the individual nature of prayer in Christian Science. Do these prayers ask God to do something?

Church Manual, p. 40: A Rule for Motives and Acts

> Neither animosity nor mere personal attachment should impel the motives or acts of the members of The Mother Church. In Science, divine Love alone governs man; and a Christian Scientist reflects the sweet amenities of Love, in rebuking sin, in true brotherliness, charitableness, and forgiveness. The members of this Church should daily watch and pray to be delivered from all evil, from prophesying, judging, condemning, counseling, influencing or being influenced erroneously.

Church Manual, p. 41: Daily Prayer

> It shall be the duty of every member of this Church to pray each day: "Thy kingdom come"; let the reign of divine Truth, Life, and Love be established in me, and rule out of me all sin; and may Thy Word enrich the affections of all mankind, and govern them!

Church Manual, p. 42: Alertness to Duty

> It shall be the duty of every member of this Church to defend himself daily against aggressive mental suggestion, and not be made to forget nor to neglect his duty to God, to his Leader, and to mankind. By his works he shall be judged,—and justified or condemned.

In preparing Sunday School discussion sheets, I try to include a question about or a reference to prayer, especially the Lord's Prayer. For example, Which lines in the Lord's Prayer (*Science and Health*, p. 16–17) show that Jesus did not regard matter as the real thing ... reality?

Here are four examples from discussion sheets:

1. How did the wise men know to go to Bethlehem? (See Matthew 2:1–2.)
   Wise people had been looking for a "king" because the prophet Isaiah had told them that "the (**government**) shall be upon his shoulder" (Isaiah 9:6).
   Was the Lord already their King? (See Isaiah 43:15: "I am the Lord, your Holy One, the creator of Israel, (**your King.**") Why were the children of Israel looking for a king? (**Discuss.**)
   Do you and I pray for a King to come? (**Yes/no?**) There is a prayer in the *Church Manual*, page 41, that uses the words *kingdom, reign, rule,* and *govern*. It is called the (**Daily**) Prayer.

2. When sin, sickness, or death seem real to us, we can pray. As we pray we can think and say words like these:
   > Teach me to do Thy will. I am Thy servant; I do Thy will.
   > Create in me a clean heart. I will listen for Thy voice.
   > I am one of your perfect ideas. I thank you, God, for being All-in-all.
   What are some words you say as you pray?

3. Before, during, and after our prayer, God, Love, gives us thoughts like these:
   > I have saved you, and you are my witness.
   > I have called you by name, and you are mine.
   > You are my loved son and daughter.
   > I have put a new song in your mouth.
   > I am the Lord, and there is none else; there is no other god called sin, sickness, or death.
   > I, Spirit, created you; you are a spiritual idea including all right ideas.
   What does God say to you?

4. Write your name in the blanks:
   _____ prays to the Lord; _____, praise the Lord.

Pick out few statements from the above that helped you the most.

21

GETTING TO KNOW THE MANY VERSIONS OF THE LORD'S PRAYER

Matthew 6:9–13
Translations 1382–2008

John Wycliffe prepared the first translation of the English Bible in 1382—the first European translation done in over one thousand years.

Here is John Wycliffe's translation of the Lord's Prayer (Matthew 6:9–13):

> Oure fadir that art in heuenes, halewid be thi name;
> thi kyngdoom come to; be thi wille don `in erthe as in heuene;
> yyue to vs this dai oure `breed ouer othir substaunce;
> and foryyue to vs oure dettis, as we foryyuen to oure dettouris; and
> lede vs not in to temptacioun, but delyuere vs fro yuel. Amen.

Over the next several hundred years, many other English translations appeared. Some translations end with a version of "Thine is the kingdom," which was not in the original Greek. Most modern translations conclude the prayer with a version of "Lead us not into temptation, but deliver us from evil." Mary Baker Eddy says of evil in *Science and Health*, "the one evil … declares that man begins in dust or as a material embryo" (p. 476), and she further explains on page 71 that "evil is neither person, place, nor thing."

Myles Coverdale prepared *The Great Bible* in 1538. It was the first authorized edition of the Bible in English, authorized by King Henry VIII of England to be read aloud in the church services of the Church of England. It went through over thirty editions, the last edition appearing in 1569. Coverdale's *New Testament* is a revision of Tindale's 1534 Bible, which was based on the Latin Vulgate and Luther's German version.

The Bible appears in hundreds of new translations. The King James Version is only one of them. A good place to compare translations is the Lord's Prayer. And a good verse to use for this purpose is the traditional line, "And forgive us our debts, as we forgive our debtors." Most people when praying this verse aloud emphasize the words *debts* and *debtors*. However, some of the translations below suggest the emphasis should more naturally fall on *our*, *we*, and *our*.

Notice the J. B. Phillips translation (#6) below. He writes, "Forgive us what we owe to you, as we have also forgiven those who owe anything to us." Don't you naturally emphasize *you* and *us*? Several other translations suggest this as well. Note the New English Version (#7): "Forgive us the wrong we have done, as we have forgiven those who have wronged us." Here, the natural emphasis would be on the first *we* and the last *us*.

Using this approach with our traditional King James Version, it would be read like this (italicized words are emphasized): "And forgive us *our* debts, as *we* forgive *our* debtors." Interestingly, members of the Institute of Analytical Reading (www.analyticalreading.org), a group of reading professionals who train others in the art and science of reading aloud *conversationally*, also support this emphasis as an alternative to the traditional way.

1. *Book of Common Prayer*—1559 (modern spelling, ed. Booty, 1976)
   Our Father which art in heaven, hallowed be thy name.
   Thy kingdom come. Thy will be done in earth as it is in heaven.
   Give us this day our daily bread.
   And forgive us our trespasses, as we forgive them that trespass against us.
   And lead us not into temptation, but deliver us from evil. Amen.

2. King James Version (Luke 11:2–4)—1611
   Our Father which art in heaven, Hallowed be thy name.
   Thy kingdom come. Thy will be done, as in heaven, so in earth.
   Give us day by day our daily bread.
   And forgive us our sins; for we also forgive every one that is indebted to us.
   And lead us not into temptation; but deliver us from evil.

3. King James Version (Matthew 6:9-13)—1611
   Our Father which art in heaven, Hallowed be thy name.
   Thy kingdom come. Thy will be done in earth, as it is in heaven.
   Give us this day our daily bread.
   And forgive us our debts, as we forgive our debtors.
   And lead us not into temptation, but deliver us from evil:
   For thine is the kingdom, and the power, and the glory, for ever. Amen.

4. *Science and Health with Key to the Scriptures,* by Mary Baker Eddy, which was first published in 1875. On page 16 she writes, "Here let me give what I understand to be the spiritual sense of the Lord's Prayer."

Our Father which art in heaven,
Our Father-Mother God, all-harmonious,
Hallowed be Thy name.
Adorable One.
Thy kingdom come.
Thy kingdom is come; Thou art ever-present.
Thy will be done in earth, as it is in heaven.
Enable us to know,—as in heaven, so on earth—God is omnipotent, supreme.
Give us this day our daily bread;
Give us grace for to-day; feed the famished affections;
And forgive us our debts, as we forgive our debtors.
And Love is reflected in love;
And lead us not into temptation, but deliver us from evil;
And God leadeth us not into temptation, but delivereth us from sin, disease, and death.
For Thine is the kingdom, and the power, and the glory, forever.
For God is infinite, all-power, all Life, Truth, Love, over all, and All.

5. James Moffatt Translation—1954
Our Father in heaven, thy name be revered,
thy Reign begin, thy will be done on earth as in heaven!
give us to-day our bread for the morrow,
and forgive us our debts as we ourselves have forgiven our debtors,
and lead us not into temptation but deliver us from evil.

6. J. B. Phillips, *The New Testament in Modern English*—1958
Our Heavenly Father, may your name be honored;
May your kingdom come, and your will be done on earth as it is in Heaven.
Give us this day the bread we need,
Forgive us what we owe to you, as we have also forgiven those who owe anything to us.
Keep us clear of temptation, and save us from evil.

7. *New English Bible—1961*
Our Father in heaven, thy name be hallowed;
Thy kingdom come, thy will be done, on earth as in heaven.
Give us today our daily bread.
Forgive us the wrong we have done, as we have forgiven those who have wronged us.
And do not bring us to the test, but save us from the evil one.

8. *Good News for Modern Man: Today's English Version—1966*
   Our Father in heaven: May your name be kept holy,
   May your Kingdom come, May your will be done on earth as it is in heaven.
   Give us today the food we need;
   Forgive us the wrongs that we have done,
   As we forgive the wrongs that others have done us;
   Do not bring us to hard testing, but keep us safe from the Evil One.

9. *New Jerusalem Bible—1985*
   Our Father in heaven. May your name be held holy.
   Your kingdom come. Your will be done on earth as in heaven.
   Give us today our daily bread.
   And forgive us our debts, as we have forgiven those who are in debt to us.
   And do not put us to the test, but save us from the Evil One.

10. The New Revised Standard Version—1989
    Our Father in heaven, hallowed be your name.
    Your kingdom come. Your will be done, on earth as it is in heaven.
    Give us this day our daily bread.
    And forgive us our debts, as we also have forgiven our debtors.
    And do not bring us to the time of trial, but rescue us from the evil one.

11. *The Message: The Bible in Contemporary Language—1993*, Eugene Peterson
    Our Father in heaven,
    Reveal who you are.
    Set the world right;
    Do what's best—as above, so below.
    Keep us alive with three square meals.
    Keep us forgiven with you and forgiving others.
    Keep us safe from ourselves and the Devil.
    You're in charge!
    You can do anything you want!
    You're ablaze in beauty!
    Yes. Yes. Yes.

12. Today's New International Version—2001
    Our Father in heaven, hallowed be your name,
    your kingdom come, your will be done on earth as it is in heaven.
    Give us today our daily bread.
    And forgive us our debts, as we also have forgiven our debtors.
    And lead us not into temptation, but deliver us from the evil one.

13. *Discoverer's Bible for Young Readers*—2002
    Our Father in heaven,
    may your name be honored.
    May your kingdom come.
    May what you want to happen be done on earth as it is done in heaven.
    Give us today our daily bread.
    Forgive us our sins, just as we also have forgiven those who sin against us.
    Keep us from falling into sin when we are tempted.
    Save us from the evil one.

14. *The Chronological Study Bible, New KJV*—2008
    Our Father in heaven,
    Hallowed be Your name.
    Your kingdom come.
    Your will be done
    On earth as it is in heaven.
    Give us this day our daily bread.
    And forgive us our debts,
    As we forgive our debtors.
    And do not lead us into temptation,
    But deliver us from the evil one.
    For Yours is the kingdom and the power and the glory forever. Amen.

Most of the modern translations of the Lord's Prayer managed to avoid the problem of substituting "who" for "which" in reference to God. I have attended services in a number of other Christian churches where the pray-ers substitute "who" for "which," as in "Our Father *who* are in heaven."

However, "Our Father who art in heaven" is not Biblical. Both Matthew and Luke record Jesus as saying, "which," not "who." So what's the difference?

The word *which* indicates a spiritual entity, such as creator or Principle, whereas "Our Father who" personalizes the divinity. The word *who* might indicate to some people a reference to the person named Jesus. Jesus never indicated that he was God, as has already been pointed out in this book. A study of Jesus' use of the word *father* shows clearly that he regarded God as Father and himself as the son of God and the son of man.

22

GETTING TO KNOW MORE ABOUT THE POEMS WE SING AS HYMNS

On a Sunday I've said to my Sunday School students, "We gather twice in the center of the room to … sing! Did you ever wonder why we sing *twice*?" It's good to wonder, to ask questions. It's the best way to learn new things. Why do you think we sing two hymns every Sunday morning?

My contribution to a discussion about singing might sound like this: Let's look at different settings, other than Sunday School. What do people do at a concert or a sports event when they are really thrilled with what they are hearing or seeing? Right! They stand up and clap or cheer! If it's a school game, the band may start playing—and the crowd may start singing—the school song.

Does any organized cheering go on in church? Yes, singing and … testimonies at Wednesday meetings. Singing is a way of raising a cheer. Whom are we cheering when we sing Hymn No. 1 in the *Christian Science Hymnal*?

> Be Thou, O God, exalted high;
> And as Thy glory fills the sky,
> So let it be on earth displayed,
> Till Thou art here and now obeyed.

Besides singing three hymns at Wednesday meetings, those present do another kind of cheering and praising—they listen to and give testimonies.

At this service, the first reader presents a reading on a topic of general interest based on citations selected from the Bible and *Science and Health with Key to Scriptures*, by Mary Baker Eddy. For example, the subject might be "prayer" or "safety." Then after the congregation sings the second hymn, the reader will say something like, "It is now your opportunity to share testimonies of healing or remarks based on your study of Christian Science."

Through prayer and the study of Christian Science, people experience the love and guidance and protection of God. So they want to tell about it, to raise a cheer for God, as well as for the teachings of Christ Jesus and the "Science" of Christianity. These teachings are helping them know God better and live as individualized expressions of Life, Love, God.

The words to our hymns are poems. What is a poem? Is it just words that rhyme? No. A poet wants to say something important, so the poet carefully selects just the right words, often choosing words that rhyme. Hymn No. 9 says, "He knows the angels that you need, and sends them to your side, to comfort, guard and guide." Christian Science helps us understand that *angels* are thoughts from God.

One time I asked students for examples of common uses of the word *love*—for example, I *love* ice cream. One mentioned, "Love makes the world go 'round." Popular songs ask, Where is love? Is this love? Can I love? Why did my love go away? *Love* is a verb as well as a noun, as in Hymn No. 179:

> Love one another,—word of revelation;
> Love frees from error's thrall,—Love is liberation.
> Love's way the Master trod;
> He that loves shall walk with God.
> Love is the royal way.

Later, I looked up *God* in my hymnal concordance to find out what God says and does. For example, the third verse of Hymn No. 123 says,

> Fear not, I am with thee, O be not dismayed,
> For I am thy God, I will still give thee aid;
> I'll strengthen thee, help thee, and cause thee to stand,
> Upheld by My gracious, omnipotent hand;

Also, in Hymn No. 375 God says, "Rejoice for thou art whole."

In Hymn No. 30, another poem by Mary Baker Eddy, titled "Love," God commands, "Let there be light, and there was light ..."

And Hymn No. 19 praises God's messengers of Love and Life, and God saith, "These are Mine."

Several hundred hymns ascribe actions to God. I found more than two dozen examples of actions, such as *loves, lives, gives, comes, hears, helps, brings, supplies, bids, works, promises,* and *comforts.*

Is there singing in the Bible? Yes, there are many cheers for God in the Bible, especially in the book of Psalms. The dictionary tells us that a psalm is a sacred song or poem. Open your Bible to the book of Psalms and find an example for us. A "pray-er" (as in, one who prays) praises God with psalms and poems.

Is *Science and Health* full of singing? Its author says of Christian Science that "[W]hen understood, it is Truth's prism and praise." She also says this: "God is not moved by the breath of praise to do more than He has already done, nor can the infinite do less than bestow all good, since He is unchanging wisdom and Love. We can do more for ourselves by humble fervent petitions, but the All-loving does not grant them simply on the ground of lip-service, for He already knows all" (p. 2:8–11, emphasis added).

From her youth, Mary Baker Eddy wrote poems, and many were published in the local newspaper and in magazines. Just after publishing *Science and Health*, she wrote the words to Hymn 298, titled "Communion Hymn," in 1867. The last verse is full of praise:

> Strongest deliverer, friend of the friendless,
> Life of all being divine:
> Thou the Christ, and not the creed;
> Thou the Truth in thought and deed;
> Thou the water, the bread, and the wine.

Her poems are very thankful and affirmative appeals to God, whom she praises in her writings as Life, Truth, Love, Mind, Soul, Spirit, and Principle. She writes in Hymn 161, "Satisfied,"

> Who doth His will—His likeness still—
> Is satisfied.

These questions might prompt some discussion:

1. What do you like about singing hymns?
2. What ideas or images do you like to sing about?
3. Can you tell about a time when the words or music of a hymn made you feel closer to God?

God, Love, does not cause us to be sinners, live as sinners, and die. No. God, Father-Mother Love, causes us to be the sinless children of God and live forever as sons and daughters of God. Here is the way we sing it Hymn No. 218 from the *Christian Science Hymnal*, which is a poem by Samuel Longfellow:

> O Life that maketh all things new,
> The blooming earth, the thoughts of men;

Our pilgrim feet, wet with Thy dew,
In gladness hither turn again.

From hand to hand the greeting flows,
From eye to eye the signals run,
From heart to heart the bright hope glows,
The seekers of the Light are one:

One in the freedom of the truth,
One in the joy of paths untrod,
One in the heart's perennial youth,
One in the larger thought of God;—

The freer step, the fuller breath,
The wide horizon's grander view;
The sense of Life that knows no death,—
The Life that maketh all things new.

Pick a few statements that helped you the most in *getting to know about the poems we sing as hymns.*

The following hymns used in this chapter are from the *Christian Science Hymnal,* © 1932, renewed 1960, The Christian Science Board of Directors. Used with permission.

Hymn 123, adaptation by Rippon, Keith, and Keene
Hymn 179, by Margaret Morrison
Hymn 375, by John Randall Dunn

The following hymns used in this chapter are used courtesy of The Mary Baker Eddy Collection:

Hymn 19, based on the Danish of Hans A. Brorson
Hymn 30, by Mary Baker Eddy
Hymn 161, by Mary Baker Eddy
Hymn 218, by Samuel Longfellow
Hymn 298, by Mary Baker Eddy

23

GETTING TO KNOW THE PSALMS

The Christian Science textbook, *Science and Health*, states that "The Bible contains "the recipe for all healing" (p. 406:1). Many of the psalms tell us how to follow that recipe. The psalms are songs of praise, petition, and promise. In Psalm 23, its writer says, "The Lord is my shepherd, *I* shall not want." "Yea, though *I* walk through the valley of the shadow of death, *I* will fear no evil." *I* will listen to what the Psalmist says *I* can do. *I* will listen to what the Lord is saying to me in the language of the New English Translation of the Bible (1996). In most, but not all, of the chapters of the book of Psalms, the Psalmist speaks for me as "I."

Psalm 3
4 To the Lord I cried out, and he answered me from his holy hill. 5 I rested and slept; I awoke, for the Lord protects me.

Psalm 4
1 When I call out, answer me, O God who vindicates me! Though I am hemmed in, you will lead me into a wide, open place. Have mercy on me and respond to my prayer! 3 the Lord responds when I cry out to him. 8 I will lie down and sleep peacefully, for you, Lord, make me safe and secure.

Psalm 5
2 Pay attention to my cry for help, my king and my God, for I am praying to you! 3 Lord, in the morning you will hear me;

Psalm 6
2 Have mercy on me, Lord, for I am frail! Heal me, Lord, for my bones are shaking!

Psalm 7
1 O Lord my God, in you I have taken shelter. Deliver me from all who chase me! Rescue me!

Psalm 8

3 When I look up at the heavens, which your fingers made, and see the moon and the stars, which you set in place, 4 Of what importance is the human race, that you should notice them?

Psalm 9

1 I will thank the Lord with all my heart! I will tell about all your amazing deeds! 2 I will be happy and rejoice in you! I will sing praises to you, O sovereign One!

Psalm 13

5 I trust in your faithfulness. May I rejoice because of your deliverance! 6 I will sing praises to the Lord when he vindicates me.

Psalm 16

1 Protect me, O God, for I have taken shelter in you. 2 I say to the Lord, "You are the Lord, my only source of well-being." 7 I will praise the Lord who guides me; yes, during the night I reflect and learn. 8 I constantly trust in the Lord; because he is at my right hand, I will not be upended.

Psalm 17

6 I call to you for you will answer me, O God. Listen to me! Hear what I say! 15 As for me, because I am innocent I will see your face; when I awake you will reveal yourself to me.

Psalm 18

1 I love you, Lord, my source of strength! 2 The Lord is my high ridge, my stronghold, my deliverer. My God is my rocky summit where I take shelter, my shield, the horn that saves me, and my refuge. 3 I called to the Lord, who is worthy of praise, and I was delivered from my enemies. 6 In my distress I called to the Lord; I cried out to my God. From his heavenly temple he heard my voice; he listened to my cry for help. 21 For I have obeyed the Lord's commands; I have not rebelled against my God. 23 I was innocent before him, and kept myself from sinning. 49 So I will give you thanks before the nations, O Lord! I will sing praises to you!

Psalm 23

1 The Lord is my shepherd, I lack nothing. 4 Even when I must walk through the darkest valley, I fear no danger, for you are with me; your rod and your staff reassure me. 6 I will live in the Lord's house for the rest of my life.

Psalm 25

1 O Lord, I come before you in prayer. 5 Guide me into your truth and teach me. For you are the God who delivers me; on you I rely all day long.

Psalm 26

3 I am ever aware of your faithfulness, and your loyalty continually motivates me. 8 O Lord, I love the temple where you live, the place where your splendor is revealed.

Psalm 27

1 The Lord delivers and vindicates me! I fear no one! 4 I have asked the Lord for one thing—this is what I desire! I want to live in the Lord's house all the days of my life, so I can gaze at the splendor of the Lord and contemplate in his temple. 6 Now I will triumph over my enemies who surround me! I will offer sacrifices in his dwelling place and shout for joy! I will sing praises to the Lord! 7 Hear me, O Lord, when I cry out! Have mercy on me and answer me! 13 Where would I be if I did not believe I would experience the Lord's favor in the land of the living?

Psalm 28

1 To you, O Lord, I cry out! My protector, do not ignore me! 7 The Lord strengthens and protects me; I trust in him with all my heart. I am rescued and my heart is full of joy; I will sing to him in gratitude.

Psalm 30

1 I will praise you, O Lord, for you lifted me up, and did not allow my enemies to gloat over me. 2 O Lord my God, I cried out to you and you healed me. 8 To you, O Lord, I cried out; I begged the Lord for mercy:

Psalm 31

5 Into your hand I entrust my life; you will rescue me, O Lord, the faithful God. 7 I will be happy and rejoice in your faithfulness, because you notice my pain and you are aware of how distressed I am. 14 But I trust in you, O Lord! I declare, "You are my God!" 21 The Lord deserves praise for he demonstrated his amazing faithfulness to me ...

Psalm 34

1 I will praise the Lord at all times; my mouth will continually praise him. 2 I will boast in the Lord; let the oppressed hear and rejoice!

Psalm 38

15 Yet I wait for you, O Lord! You will respond, O Lord, my God!

Psalm 40

1 I relied completely on the Lord, and he turned toward me and heard my cry for help. 5 O Lord, my God, you have accomplished many things; you have done amazing things and carried out your purposes for us. No one can thwart you! I want to declare them and talk about them, but they are too numerous to recount! 10 I have not failed to tell about your justice; I spoke about your reliability and deliverance; I have not neglected to tell the great assembly about your loyal love and faithfulness.

Psalm 41

4 As for me, I said: "O Lord, have mercy on me! Heal me, for I have sinned against you! 11 … I know that you are pleased with me, for my enemy does not triumph over me.

Psalm 42

1 As a deer longs for streams of water, so I long for you, O God! 2 I thirst for God, for the living God. I say, "When will I be able to go and appear in God's presence?" 5 Why are you depressed, O my soul? Why are you upset? Wait for God! For I will again give thanks to my God for his saving intervention.

Psalm 56

3 When I am afraid, I trust in you. 4 In God—I boast in his promise—in God I trust, I am not afraid. What can mere men do to me? 9 My enemies will turn back when I cry out to you for help; I know that God is on my side.

Psalm 57

1 Have mercy on me, O God! Have mercy on me! For in you I have taken shelter. In the shadow of your wings I take shelter until trouble passes. 2 I cry out for help to the sovereign God, to the God who vindicates me. 7 I am determined, O God! I am determined! I will sing and praise you! 8 Awake, my soul! Awake, O stringed instrument and harp! I will wake up at dawn! 9 I will give you thanks before the nations, O Master! I will sing praises to you …

Psalm 59

16 As for me, I will sing about your strength; I will praise your loyal love in the morning. For you are my refuge and my place of shelter when I face trouble. 17 You are my source of strength! I will sing praises to you! For God is my refuge, the God who loves me.

Psalm 61

1 O God, hear my cry for help! Pay attention to my prayer! 2 From the most remote place on earth I call out to you in my despair. Lead me up to an inaccessible rocky summit! 4 I will be a permanent guest in your home; I will find shelter in the protection of your wings. 8 Then I will sing praises to your name continually, as I fulfill my vows day after day.

Psalm 62

1 For God alone I patiently wait; he is the one who delivers me. 2 He alone is my protector and deliverer. He is my refuge; I will not be upended. 8 Trust in him at all times, you people! Pour out your hearts before him! God is our shelter!

Psalm 66

13 I will fulfill the vows I made to you, 14 which my lips uttered and my mouth spoke when I was in trouble. 16 Come! Listen, all you who are loyal to God! I will declare what he has done for me. 17 I cried out to him for help and praised him with my tongue.

Psalm 69

30 I will sing praises to God's name! I will magnify him as I give him thanks!

Psalm 70

5 I am oppressed and needy! O God, hurry to me! You are my helper and my deliverer! O Lord, do not delay!

Psalm 71

1 In you, O Lord, I have taken shelter! Never let me be humiliated! 2 Vindicate me by rescuing me! Listen to me! Deliver me! 3 Be my protector and refuge, a stronghold where I can be safe! For you are my high ridge and my stronghold. 14 As for me, I will wait continually, and will continue to praise you. 15 I will tell about your justice, and all day long proclaim your salvation, though I cannot fathom its full extent. 22 I will express my thanks to you with a stringed instrument, praising your faithfulness, O my God! I will sing praises to you accompanied by a harp, O Holy One of Israel! 23 My lips will shout for joy! Yes, I will sing your praises! I will praise you when you rescue me!

Psalm 73

23 I am continually with you; you hold my right hand. 24 You guide me by your wise advice, and then you will lead me to a position of honor. 25 Whom do I have in heaven but you? I desire no one but you on earth. 28 But as for me, God's presence is all I need. I have made the sovereign Lord my shelter, as I declare all the things you have done.

Psalm 77

1 I will cry out to God and call for help! I will cry out to God and he will pay attention to me. 2 In my time of trouble I sought the Lord. I kept my hand raised in prayer throughout the night. 11 I will remember the works of the Lord. Yes, I will remember the amazing things you did long ago! 12 I will think about all you have done; I will reflect upon your deeds!

Psalm 84

2 I desperately want to be in the courts of the Lord's temple. My heart and my entire being shout for joy to the living God.

Psalm 86

1 Listen O Lord! Answer me! For I am oppressed and needy. 2 Protect me, for I am loyal! O my God, deliver your servant, who trusts in you! 3 Have mercy on me, O Lord, for I cry out to you all day long! 4 Make your servant glad, for to you, O Lord, I pray! 7 In my time of trouble I cry out to you, for you will answer me. 11 O Lord, teach me how you want me to live! Then I will obey your commands. Make me wholeheartedly committed to you! 12 O Lord, my God, I will give you thanks with my whole heart! I will honor your name continually!

Psalm 88

1 O Lord God who delivers me! By day I cry out and at night I pray before you. 9 I call out to you, O Lord, all day long; I spread out my hands in prayer to you.

Psalm 89

1 I will sing continually about the Lord's faithful deeds; to future generations I will proclaim your faithfulness. 2 For I say, "Loyal love is permanently established; in the skies you set up your faithfulness."

Psalm 101

2 I will walk in the way of integrity. 3 I will not even consider doing what is dishonest. I hate doing evil; I will have no part of it. 4 I will have nothing to do with a perverse person; I will not permit evil. 5 I will not tolerate anyone who has a cocky demeanor and an arrogant attitude. 6 I will favor the honest people of the land, and allow them to live with me.

Psalm 102

2 Do not ignore me in my time of trouble! Listen to me! When I call out to you, quickly answer me! 6 I am like an owl in the wilderness; I am like a screech owl among the ruins. 7 I stay awake; I am like a solitary bird on a roof.

Psalm106

4 Remember me, O Lord, when you show favor to your people! Pay attention to me, when you deliver, 5 so I may see the prosperity of your chosen ones, rejoice along with your nation, and boast along with the people who belong to you.

Psalm 108

1 I am determined, O God! I will sing and praise you with my whole heart. 2 Awake, O stringed instrument and harp! I will wake up at dawn! 3 I will give you thanks before the nations, O Lord! I will sing praises to you …

Psalm 116

1 I love the Lord because he heard my plea for mercy, 2 and listened to me. As long as I live, I will call to him when I need help. 4 I called on the name of the Lord, "Please Lord, rescue my life!" 9 I will serve the Lord in the land of the living. 10 I had faith when I said, "I am severely oppressed." 12 How can I repay the Lord for all his acts of kindness to me? 13 I will celebrate my deliverance, and call on the name of the Lord. 14 I will fulfill my vows to the Lord before all his people. 16 Yes, Lord! I am indeed your servant; 17 I will present a thank offering to you, and call on the name of the Lord. 18 I will fulfill my vows to the Lord before all his people …

Psalm 118

6 The Lord is on my side, I am not afraid! What can people do to me? 7 The Lord is on my side as my helper. I look in triumph on those who hate me. 17 I will not die, but live, and I will proclaim what the Lord has done. 19 Open for me the gates of the just king's temple! I will enter through them and give thanks to the Lord. 21 I will give you thanks, for you answered me, and have become my deliverer.

Psalm 119

8 I will keep your statutes. 10 With all my heart I seek you. Do not allow me to stray from your commands! 11 In my heart I store up your words, so I might not sin against you. 14 I rejoice in the lifestyle prescribed by your rules as if they were riches of all kinds. 15 I will meditate on your precepts and focus on your behavior. 16 I find delight in your statutes; I do not forget your instructions. 18 Open my eyes so I can truly see the marvelous things in your law! 24 Yes, I find delight in your rules; they give me guidance. 26 I told you about my ways and you answered me. Teach me your statutes! 27 Help me to understand what your precepts mean! Then I can meditate on your marvelous teachings. 30 I choose the path of faithfulness; 31 I hold fast to your rules. O Lord, do not let me be ashamed! 32 I run along the path of your commands, for you enable me to do so. 33 Teach me, O Lord, the lifestyle prescribed by your statutes, so that I might observe it continually. 34 Give me understanding so that I might observe your law, and keep it with all my heart. 35 Guide me in the path of your commands, for I delight to walk in it. 40 I long for your precepts. Revive me with your deliverance! 41 May I experience your loyal love, O Lord, and your deliverance, as you promised. 44 Then I will keep your law continually now and for all time. 45 I will be secure, for I seek your precepts. 47 I will find delight in your commands, which I love. 48 I will lift my hands to your commands, which I love, and I will meditate on your statutes. 55 I remember your name during the night, O Lord, and I will keep your law. 56

This has been my practice, for I observe your precepts. 57 The Lord is my source of security. I have determined to follow your instructions. 58 I seek your favor with all my heart. Have mercy on me as you promised! 59 I consider my actions and follow your rules. 60 I keep your commands eagerly and without delay. 63 I am a friend to all your loyal followers, and to those who keep your precepts. 70 I find delight in your law. 77 May I experience your compassion, so I might live! For I find delight in your law. 80 May I be fully committed to your statutes, so that I might not be ashamed. 81 I find hope in your word. 88 Revive me with your loyal love, that I might keep the rules you have revealed. 93 I will never forget your precepts, for by them you have revived me. 94 I belong to you. Deliver me! For I seek your precepts. 97 O how I love your law! All day long I meditate on it. 98 Your commandments make me wiser than my enemies, for I am always aware of them. 99 I have more insight than all my teachers, for I meditate on your rules. 100 I am more discerning than those older than I, for I observe your precepts. 101 I stay away from the evil path, so that I might keep your instructions. 111 I claim your rules as my permanent possession, for they give me joy. 112 I am determined to obey your statutes at all times, to the very end. 114 You are my hiding place and my shield. I find hope in your word. 116 Sustain me as you promised, so that I will live. Do not disappoint me! 117 Support me, so that I will be delivered. Then I will focus on your statutes continually. 121 I do what is fair and right. 125 I am your servant. Give me insight, so that I can understand your rules. 127 For this reason I love your commands more than gold, even purest gold. 129 Your rules are marvelous. Therefore I observe them. 145 I cried out with all my heart, "Answer me, O Lord! I will observe your statutes." 146 I cried out to you, "Deliver me, so that I can keep your rules." 147 I am up before dawn crying for help. I find hope in your word. 148 My eyes anticipate the nighttime hours, so that I can meditate on your word. 152 I learned long ago that you ordained your rules to last. 159 See how I love your precepts! O Lord, revive me with your loyal love! 166 I hope for your deliverance, O Lord, and I obey your commands. 167 I keep your rules; I love them greatly. 168 I keep your precepts and rules, for you are aware of everything I do. 174 I long for your deliverance, O Lord; I find delight in your law. 175 May I live and praise you! 176 I have wandered off like a lost sheep. Come looking for your servant, for I do not forget your commands.

Psalm 120

1 In my distress I cried out to the Lord and he answered me. 7 I am committed to peace …

Psalm 122

1 I was glad because they said to me, "We will go to the Lord's temple." 8 For the sake of my brothers and my neighbors I will say, "May there be peace in you!" 9 For the sake of the temple of the Lord our God I will pray for you to prosper.

Psalm123

1 I look up toward you, the one enthroned in heaven.

Psalm 130

1 From the deep water I cry out to you, O Lord. 2 O Lord, listen to me! Pay attention to my plea for mercy! 5 I rely on the Lord, I rely on him with my whole being; I wait for his assuring word. 6 I yearn for the Lord, more than watchmen do for the morning, yes, more than watchmen do for the morning.

Psalm 131

1 O Lord, my heart is not proud, nor do I have a haughty look. I do not have great aspirations, or concern myself with things that are beyond me. 2 Indeed I am composed and quiet, like a young child carried by its mother; I am content like the young child I carry.

Psalm 138

1 I will give you thanks with all my heart; before the heavenly assembly I will sing praises to you. 2 I will bow down toward your holy temple, and give thanks to your name, because of your loyal love and faithfulness, for you have exalted your promise above the entire sky. 3 When I cried out for help, you answered me. You made me bold and energized me. 7 Even when I must walk in the midst of danger, you revive me.

Psalm 139

1 O Lord, you examine me and know. 2 You know when I sit down and when I get up; even from far away you understand my motives. 3 You carefully observe me when I travel or when I lie down to rest; you are aware of everything I do. 7 Where can I go to escape your spirit? Where can I flee to escape your presence? 8 If I were to ascend to heaven, you would be there. If I were to sprawl out in Sheol, there you would be. 9 If I were to fly away on the wings of the dawn, and settle down on the other side of the sea, 10 even there your hand would guide me, your right hand would grab hold of me. 11 If I were to say, "Certainly the darkness will cover me, and the light will turn to night all around me" ... 14 I will give you thanks because your deeds are awesome and amazing. You knew me thoroughly; 17 How difficult it is for me to fathom your thoughts about me, O God! How vast is their sum total! 18 If I tried to count them, they would outnumber the grains of sand. Even if I finished counting them, I would still have to contend with you.

Psalm 140

6 I say to the Lord, "You are my God." O Lord, pay attention to my plea for mercy! 12 I know that the Lord defends the cause of the oppressed and vindicates the poor.

Psalm 141

1 O Lord, I cry out to you. Come quickly to me! Pay attention to me when I cry out to you! 8 Surely I am looking to you, O sovereign Lord. In you I take shelter. Do not expose me to danger!

Psalm 142

1 To the Lord I cry out; to the Lord I plead for mercy. 2 I pour out my lament before him; I tell him about my troubles. 5 I cry out to you, O Lord; I say, "You are my shelter, my security in the land of the living." 6 Listen to my cry for help, for I am in serious trouble! Rescue me from those who chase me, for they are stronger than I am. 7 Free me from prison, that I may give thanks to your name. Because of me the godly will assemble, for you will vindicate me.

Psalm 143

5 I recall the old days; I meditate on all you have done; I reflect on your accomplishments. 6 I spread my hands out to you in prayer; my soul thirsts for you in a parched land. 8 May I hear about your loyal love in the morning, for I trust in you. Show me the way I should go, because I long for you. 9 Rescue me from my enemies, O Lord! I run to you for protection. 12 I am your servant.

Psalm 144

9 O God, I will sing a new song to you! Accompanied by a ten-stringed instrument, I will sing praises to you ...

Psalm 145

1 I will extol you, my God, O king! I will praise your name continually! 2 Every day I will praise you! I will praise your name continually! 5 I will focus on your honor and majestic splendor, and your amazing deeds! 6 They will proclaim the power of your awesome acts! I will declare your great deeds!

Psalm 146

1 Praise the Lord! Praise the Lord, O my soul! 2 I will praise the Lord as long as I live! I will sing praises to my God as long as I exist!

In conclusion, Hymn No. 114 from the *Christian Science Hymnal*, verses by John Burton, summarizes what the Bible does for you and me.

> Holy Bible, book divine,
> Precious treasure, thou art mine:
> Mine to tell me whence I came;
> Mine to tell me what I am;
>
> Mine to chide me when I rove,
> Mine to show a Saviour's love;
> Mine thou art to guide and guard;
> Mine to give a rich reward;

Mine to comfort in distress,
With a Saviour's tenderness;
Mine to show, by living faith,
Man can triumph over death.

(Hymn No. 114, by John Burton, *Christian Science Hymnal*, © 1932, renewed 1960, The Christian Science Board of Directors. Used with permission.)

We've just seen many instances of the Psalmist speaking to God as "I." In the following verses from the King James Version of the Bible (1611) the Psalmist also addresses God as "Thou" and "Thy" and describes many actions that show God blessing man.

Psalm 3
3 thou, O LORD, art a shield for me; my glory, and the lifter up of mine head.

Psalm 4
1 Hear me when I call, O God of my righteousness: thou hast enlarged me when I was in distress; Thou hast put gladness in my heart, I will both lay me down in peace, and sleep: for thou, LORD, only makest me dwell in safety.

Psalm 5
3 My voice shalt thou hear in the morning, O LORD; in the morning will I direct my prayer unto thee, and will look up. 4 For thou art not a God that hath pleasure in wickedness: neither shall evil dwell with thee. 11 But let all those that put their trust in thee rejoice: let them ever shout for joy, because thou defendest them: let them also that love thy name be joyful in thee. 12 For thou, LORD, wilt bless the righteous; with favour wilt thou compass him as with a shield.

Psalm 8
3 When I consider thy heavens, the work of thy fingers, the moon and the stars, which thou hast ordained; 4 What is man, that thou art mindful of him? and the son of man, that thou visitest him? 5 For thou hast made him a little lower than the angels, and hast crowned him with glory and honour. 6 Thou madest him to have dominion over the works of thy hands; thou hast put all things under his feet:

Psalm 9
4 For thou hast maintained my right and my cause; 5 Thou hast rebuked the heathen, thou hast destroyed the wicked, thou hast put out their name for ever and ever.

Psalm 10

17 LORD, thou hast heard the desire of the humble: thou wilt prepare their heart, thou wilt cause thine ear to hear:

Psalm 16

10 thou wilt not leave my soul in hell; neither wilt thou suffer thine Holy One to see corruption. 11 Thou wilt shew me the path of life: in thy presence is fulness of joy; at thy right hand there are pleasures for evermore.

Psalm 17

3 Thou hast proved mine heart; thou hast visited me in the night; thou hast tried me, and shalt find nothing; 6 I have called upon thee, for thou wilt hear me, O God: incline thine ear unto me, and hear my speech. 7 Shew thy marvellous lovingkindness, O thou that savest by thy right hand them which put their trust in thee from those that rise up against them.

Psalm 18

28 thou wilt light my candle: the LORD my God will enlighten my darkness. 35 Thou hast also given me the shield of thy salvation: and thy right hand hath holden me up, and thy gentleness hath made me great. 36 Thou hast enlarged my steps under me, that my feet did not slip. 39 For thou hast girded me with strength unto the battle: thou hast subdued under me those that rose up against me.

Psalm 19

12 Who can understand his errors? cleanse thou me from secret faults.

Psalm 21

13 Be thou exalted, LORD, in thine own strength: so will we sing and praise thy power.

Psalm 22

1 My God, my God, why hast thou forsaken me? why art thou so far from helping me, and from the words of my roaring? 2 O my God, I cry in the daytime, but thou hearest not; and in the night season, and am not silent. 3 But thou art holy, O thou that inhabitest the praises of Israel. 4 Our fathers trusted in thee: they trusted, and thou didst deliver them.

Psalm 25

5 Lead me in thy truth, and teach me: for thou art the God of my salvation; on thee do I wait all the day.

Psalm 27

8 When thou saidst, Seek ye my face; my heart said unto thee, Thy face, LORD, will I seek. 9 Hide not thy face far from me; put not thy servant away in anger: thou hast been my help; leave me not, neither forsake me, O God of my salvation.

Psalm 30

1 I will extol thee, O LORD; for thou hast lifted me up, and hast not made my foes to rejoice over me. 2 O LORD my God, I cried unto thee, and thou hast healed me. 3 O LORD, thou hast brought up my soul from the grave: thou hast kept me alive, that I should not go down to the pit. 10 Hear, O LORD, and have mercy upon me: LORD, be thou my helper. 11 Thou hast turned for me my mourning into dancing: thou hast put off my sackcloth, and girded me with gladness; 12 To the end that my glory may sing praise to thee, and not be silent. O LORD my God, I will give thanks unto thee for ever.

Psalm 31

3 thou art my rock and my fortress; therefore for thy name's sake lead me, and guide me. 5 Into thine hand I commit my spirit: thou hast redeemed me, O LORD God of truth. 14 I trusted in thee, O LORD: I said, Thou art my God. 19 Oh how great is thy goodness, which thou hast laid up for them that fear thee; which thou hast wrought for them that trust in thee before the sons of men! 20 Thou shalt hide them in the secret of thy presence from the pride of man: thou shalt keep them secretly in a pavilion from the strife of tongues. 22 For I said in my haste, I am cut off from before thine eyes: nevertheless thou heardest the voice of my supplications when I cried unto thee.

Psalm 71

3 Be thou my strong habitation, whereunto I may continually resort: thou hast given commandment to save me; for thou art my rock and my fortress. 5 For thou art my hope, O Lord GOD: thou art my trust from my youth. 7 I am as a wonder unto many; but thou art my strong refuge.

Psalm 118

28 Thou art my God, and I will praise thee: thou art my God, I will exalt thee. 29 O give thanks unto the LORD; for he is good: for his mercy endureth for ever.

Psalm 119

114 Thou art my hiding place and my shield: I hope in thy word. 132 Look thou upon me, and be merciful unto me, as thou usest to do unto those that love thy name.

Psalm 132

8 Arise, O LORD, into thy rest; thou, and the ark of thy strength.

Psalm 139

7 Whither shall I go from thy spirit? or whither shall I flee from thy presence? 8 If I ascend up into heaven, thou art there: if I make my bed in hell, behold, thou art there. 9 If I take the wings of the morning, and dwell in the uttermost parts of the sea; 10 Even there shall thy hand lead me, and thy right hand shall hold me.

As we have seen, the Psalmist speaks to God as "I" and speaks to God as "Thou."

"The Lord saith" appears multiple times without any reference to "I." In the following verses from the New King James Version (1982), however, God speaks as "I."

Psalm 2
7 Today I have begotten You. 8 Ask of Me, and I will give You The nations for Your inheritance, and the ends of the earth for Your possession.

Psalm 46
10 Be still, and know that I am God; I will be exalted among the nations, I will be exalted in the earth!

Psalm 50
7 "Hear, O My people, and I will speak … 15 Call upon Me in the day of trouble; I will deliver you, and you shall glorify Me."

Psalm 91
14 "Because he has set his love upon Me, therefore I will deliver him; I will set him on high, because he has known My name. 15 He shall call upon Me, and I will answer him; I will be with him in trouble; I will deliver him and honor him. 16 With long life I will satisfy him, And show him My salvation."

God and the Psalmist speak not only in verses from the Bible but also as "I" in the two following hymns from the *Christian Science Hymnal* and *Hymnal Supplement*:

Hymn No. 123

How firm a foundation, ye saints of the Lord,
Is laid for your faith in His excellent Word.
What more can He say than to you He hath said,
To you who to God for your refuge have fled:

Fear not, I am with thee, O be not dismayed,
For I am thy God, I will still give thee aid;
I'll strengthen thee, help thee, and cause thee to stand,
Upheld by My gracious, omnipotent hand;

When through fiery trials thy pathway shall lie,
My grace, all sufficient, shall be thy supply;
The flame shall not hurt thee; I only design
Thy dross to consume and thy gold to refine.

(Hymn No. 123, adaptation by Rippon, Keith, and Keen, *Christian Science Hymnal*, © 1932, renewed 1960, The Christian Science Board of Directors. Used with permission.)

Hymn No. 444

I am the Lord, there is none else;
There is no God beside Me.
I girded thee, I girded thee,
Though thou hast not even known Me.
But know that from the rising sun
To the west there is none beside Me,
For I am the Lord, there is none else;
There is no God beside Me.

I am the Truth, there is none else;
There is no Truth beside Me.
Infinite light, bountiful, bright,
Is ever present to guide thee.
Beloved and free, eternally,
Perfect peace and joy I provide thee,
For I am the Lord, there is none else;
There is no God beside Me.

Innocent one, sinless and pure,
Nothing can ever divide thee.
Governed by Love, you're safe and secure;
I am forever beside thee.
So rest and know wher-e'er you go,
Home and heav'n cannot be denied thee,
For I am the Lord, there is none else;
There is no God beside Me.

(© 2008 Lightchild Publishing, Desiree Goyette. Used by permission.)

In many other hymns God speaks as Himself or through the Christ; for example, see Nos. 44, 76, 172, 188, 290, 296, 298, 318, 337, 382, 396, 404, and 412 (*Christian Science Hymnal*); 439, 453 (*Hymnal Supplement*).

Here also is God speaking as "I" in the poem "I Am Holding You," by Susan Mack.

I Am Holding You

Verse 1
Is there a God, a mind besides Me?
There's no other god, none else to see!
I am the first, and I am the last.
I command and creation, creation, stands fast!

Chorus:

I am holding you, I am knowing you.
I am minding you, and causing you.
I am blessing you, and cherishing you,
My own image, expression, reflection so true.

Verse 2
I am in control of all I create.
My works are true. My thoughts are great.
And you are embraced in such infinite care,
No thought goes astray, no moment of fear.

Chorus

Verse 3
My power and strength are a law to each day.
I'm guiding and guarding each step of the way.
No accident, chance, untoward event
Can ever disturb My all good intent.

Chorus

Bridge
I take unto me my great power and I reign.
I govern creation without stress or strain.
I delight in the glory of all that I am—
And you are the joy I'm reflecting as man.
Chorus

(© 2009 The Solo Committee, Susan Mack. Used with permission.)

24

GETTING TO KNOW MORE ABOUT OTHER CHRISTIAN RELIGIONS

I appreciate the way Stephen Prothero describes the world's eight major religions in his book *God is Not One: The Eight Rival Religions That Run the World—and Why Their Differences Matter* (HarperCollins Publishers, New York, 2010). He makes the point that each religion sees a different human problem and a different solution, summarized this way in the book's dust jacket:

- Islam: the problem is pride/the solution is submission
- Christianity: the problem is sin/the solution is salvation
- Confucianism: the problem is chaos/the solution is social order
- Buddhism: the problem is suffering/the solution is awakening
- Judaism: the problem is exile/the solution is to return to God

In its textbook, *Science and Health with Key to the Scriptures*, by Mary Baker Eddy, Christian Science presents a concept of one infinite God, or good, and what He does in the world and for the world this way (p. 340:23):

> One infinite God, good, unifies men and nations; constitutes the brother-
> hood of man; ends wars; fulfils the Scripture, "Love thy neighbor as thyself";
> annihilates pagan and Christian idolatry,—whatever is wrong in social, civil,
> criminal, political, and religious codes; equalizes the sexes; annuls the curse
> on man, and leaves nothing that can sin, suffer, be punished or destroyed.

Christians. This term refers to the early followers of Jesus Christ. They believed that Jesus was the Son of God, who helped people understand God better. This term, *Christian*, also refers to people today, in all parts of the world, who want to understand God and Jesus Christ and the Holy Spirit.

Many Christian denominations teach about "Jesus' atonement for sin," believing that man is *separate* from God and that he shares the guilt of Adam and Eve. Yet Jesus promised, "He that believeth on me, the works that I do shall he do also; and greater works than these shall he do; because I go unto my Father" (John 14:12). He commanded his followers, "Heal the sick, cleanse the lepers, raise the dead, cast out devils" (Matthew 10:8). These are not acts performed by sinners, but by those who have ceased to *identify themselves* as sinners. The Master said, "Be ye therefore perfect, even as your Father which is in heaven is perfect" (Matthew 5:48).

Christian Science corrects and uplifts the belief that man is a miserable sinner. Jesus taught man's innocence and oneness with God, and he was willing to endure the crucifixion in order to prove it. Jesus proved that sin, disease, and death have no power and told us to do likewise (see Matthew 10:8).

For thousands of years, people have believed that man fell away from God into sin, disease, and death. Writers made up a story about when and how this happened. When that story began to spread around (like a false rumor) some psalmists did not believe it and gave this good bit of advice instead: "Mark the perfect man, and behold the upright: for the end of that man is peace" (Psalm 37:37).

Did the author of Genesis 1:27, 31 believe the story about "fallen man"? (**No.**)

Did St. Paul believe the story? (**No.**) (See Ephesians 1:4–6.)

Did Christ Jesus believe the story? (**No.**) He said, "Be ye therefore perfect, even as your Father which is in heaven is perfect" (Matthew 5:48).

Did Mary Baker Eddy believe the story? (**No.**) She writes in *Science and Health*, "man in God's image is unfallen and eternal" (p. 476–477; see also her definition of man, p. 591).

Do you believe the story of "the fall of man" (see Genesis 2:4 to Genesis 4:24)? (**We hope not!**) If someone criticized you for not believing the story, what would you say? (**Discuss.**) Mary Baker Eddy writes in *Science and Health*, "Whatever indicates the fall of man or the opposite of God or God's absence, is the Adam-dream, which is neither Mind nor man, for it is not begotten of the Father" (p. 282:28–31).

Most Christian churches teach that God knows *good and evil* and so does man, because they believe that both good and evil are real. Christian Science teaches what Christ Jesus taught: that God is (**perfect**) and man is therefore (**perfect**). Remember he said in Matthew 5:48, "Be ye therefore perfect, even as your Father which is in heaven is perfect."

When she was a young girl, Mrs. Eddy honored the pastors of her church. As a grown woman, still searching for a God she could believe in, she discovered *God's law*, the *Science* of being. What does this Science teach? In *Science and Health* she writes, "This Science teaches man that God is the only **(Life)**, and that this Life is **(Truth)** and **(Love)**; that God is to be **(understood)**, adored, and demonstrated; that **(divine)** Truth casts out suppositional error and heals the sick" (p. 471:31).

Many Christians believe that *Jesus is God*, because Jesus said things, such as "He that hath seen me hath seen the Father" (John 14:9). But Jesus said, "The Father hath sent me" (John 5:36); "My Father is greater than I" (John 14:28); and "The Son of man shall come in the glory of his Father" (Matthew 16: 27). So Christian Science teaches that God is Father/Mother and Christ Jesus is the ideal man (see *Science and Health*, p. 338:31).

When the Bible says, "The Word was made flesh" (John 1:14), couldn't this mean that the Word of God was made practical right here and now as *healing*, rather than as matter or a corporeal person? In *Unity of Good*, Mary Baker Eddy writes, "When 'the Word' is 'made flesh' among mortals, the Truth of Life is rendered practical on the body. Eternal Life is partially understood; and sickness, sin, and death yield to holiness, health, and Life,—that is, to God" (p. 39:1–5).

It seems like what we *can see* is matter and what we *can't see* is idea, but a spiritual thinker *can* see idea. Jesus looked at matter, saw the perfect spiritual idea, and healed mind and body.

Christian Science presents a Godlike man, but other theologies present a manlike God, an anthropomorphic god. What is the difference? **(Discuss.)**

Did Jesus think that man and the universe were "governed in general by material laws" (*Science and Health*, p. 83:16), but that God could set aside these laws when He wanted to? **(No.)** Is this what you think? Is this what many people think? **(Discuss.)**

God's unchangeable law is called Science. Science is an angel saying to us, "Here, take this idea and prove it. It will bless you." The study of matter and its changing conditions is not S**(cience)**, but only s**(cience)** or human knowledge. Can you explain the difference? **(Hint: metaphysics versus physics; divine Science versus physical science.)**

An angel (a good thought) does not offer an opinion or suggestion. It offers truth. Angels (good thoughts) bring good messages of freedom and do good. "The Science of being reveals man as perfect, even as the Father is perfect …" (*Science and Health*, p. 302:19).

Mortal mind (or, *mortal-no-mind*, as I like to call it) is the star of the untrue history of man; it tries to get people to *believe* that history. Is it successful? (**Sometimes.**) Do many (or most) people believe they are mortal? (**Yes.**) Mortal-no-mind believes itself, but we look higher for a heavenly view, as Abraham did. Do you remember that Abraham became the first man to look for a heavenly view, to know and serve the one God? God told him to leave his (**country**) and go to (**a land**) that He would show him (see Genesis 12:1). If we think of this command spiritually, couldn't it mean that God was telling Abraham to leave his present state of thinking—and pagan view—and adopt a new view, a more spiritual view?

Why is the atonement "a hard problem in theology"? (See *Science and Health*, p. 23:7.) Perhaps it's because most people in the special field of God study (or *theo-logy*) believe that man is a sinner, separated from God. Did God create or permit sinners? How could He if everything He saw "was very good" as it tells us in Genesis 1:31. The Science that belongs to all theology (God study) says, "You can do this. You can believe that Jesus was being practical when he said, 'Be ye therefore perfect, even as your Father which is in heaven is perfect.'" Where in Matthew is this command? (**Matthew 5:48.**) You are one with God, your creator, and you will get to prove this scientifically many times.

Christ Jesus did not come to earth to show people how sinful they were. So why did he come? *Science and Health* states, "Christ came to destroy [the belief] of sin" (p. 473:6–7). Why didn't he come to destroy sin? (**Because it is only a *belief*, not a reality.**) But Mary Baker Eddy makes this important point in the third tenet of Christian Science: "We acknowledge God's forgiveness of sin in the destruction of sin and the spiritual understanding that casts out evil as unreal. But the belief in sin is punished so long as the belief lasts" (p. 497:9).

Theology and physics teach that matter is real and good. What is theology? What is physics? The apostle Paul says, Don't keep looking at matter: it is t(**emporal**) (hint: means temporary). Do keep looking at idea: ideas are e(**ternal**) (hint: means forever). How about *heaven* and *earth*? Theology and physics say that matter is where we live now, and heaven is where we go when we die. What does the Lord's Prayer say about heaven and earth?

Maybe you know the names of some other Christian denominations; for example, P(**resbyterian**), M(**ethodist**), E(**piscopal**), B(**aptist**), and L(**utheran**). As I understand them, these denominations teach that God became flesh, in the form of Jesus. Christian Scientists do not believe this. In the Bible, John says, "The Word was made flesh" (John 1:1, 14). Again, couldn't this mean that the Word of God was made practical right here and now as *healing*, rather than as matter or a corporeal person?

If God makes sin, disease, and death, then why should we try to overcome them? Some theologians (people who study to learn about God and religion) say this: God did not *make* sin, disease, and death, but God *allows* them! I don't think so! Would *you* allow something, like bullying, that you are totally against? No!

I'd say a "God" that allows what He totally disapproves of is not a God of love, intelligence, and authority! What do you say? God is not just a super-sized mortal who believes that mistakes are made. The nature of God is infinite good, harmonious, loving, and spiritual. **(Write down four more attributes that describe God's nature, other than the seven prominent synonyms of God.)**

Not only sin but disease and death must also be destroyed. We need to outgrow and set aside the belief in a creation and power opposed to God, good.

Most people could name thoughts and actions that would be called *sins*. But what is sin itself? Here's a short but accurate definition: *Sin is the belief that man is separated from God.* So the opposite of sin would be the conviction that man is **(one with God, or inseparable from God).**

Jesus said that to commit sin is to be the servant of sin (see John 8:31–36). A person is "committing sin" if he or she does what? You cannot commit sin if you are "born of God" (see I John 3:9).

Science and Health says, "To hold yourself superior to **(sin)**, because God made you superior to it and governs man, is true **("wisdom")** (p. 231:20–21). I cannot fear sin if I let spiritually inspired thinking help me hold to the fact that man is s**(inless)**. Write down five words that describe spiritual man: **(sinless, holy, good, pure, and strong).**

Some people try to reject Christian Science as a real religion by calling it a "cult". Is it a cult, according to the dictionary definition? "1. a particular system of religious worship, especially with reference to its rites and ceremonies. 2. an instance of great veneration of a person, ideal, or thing, especially as manifested by a body of admirers: 3. the object of such devotion" (Dictionary.com).

Do Christian Scientists "worship" Mary Baker Eddy? **(No—absolutely not.)** Mary Baker Eddy says that we should overcome evil with good, abound in good works, obey the laws of the land, and follow her only so far as she follows Christ. Here is what she says specifically: "Finally, brethren, wait patiently on God; return blessing for cursing; be not overcome of evil, but overcome evil with good; be steadfast, abide and abound in faith, understanding, and good works; study the Bible and the textbook of our denomination; obey strictly the laws that be, and follow your Leader only so far as she follows Christ" (*Message to The Mother Church for 1901*, p. 34:20–26).

Destiny means "something that is to happen or has happened to a particular person or thing; the predetermined, usually inevitable or irresistible, course of events." A *destination* is "the place to which a person travels" (Dictionary.com).

*Pre*destination refers to God's unchanging purpose concerning you and everyone and everything. In the true theology of Christian Science, that purpose is *good*, transplanting "the affections from sense to Soul … materiality giving place to man's higher individuality and destiny" (*Science and Health*, p. 265:32).

We've all heard the expression "It was meant to be." Does this mean that *God* meant it to be? (**Discuss.**) What does Christian Science say?

> Jesus rendered null and void whatever is unlike God; but he could not have done this if error and sin existed in the Mind of God. What God knows, He also predestinates; and it must be fulfilled. Jesus proved to perfection, so far as this could be done in that age, what Christian Science is today proving in a small degree, — the falsity of the evidence of the material senses that sin, sickness, and death are sensible claims, and that God substantiates their evidence by knowing their claim (Mary Baker Eddy, *No and Yes*, p. 37:27–5).

More than twenty-five hundred years ago, the Old Testament prophet Jeremiah said in Lamentations, "It is of the Lord's mercies that we are *not consumed*, because his (**compassions**) fail not. They are new (**every morning**)" (Lamentations 3:22, 23; emphasis added). Not death, but rather Life, Truth, and Love are "meant to be."

Around two thousand years ago, the apostle (**Paul**) wrote letters of encouragement to the brand-new Christian churches in Asia Minor. He told the people in the church at Ephesus that God has blessed us and chosen us, "that we should be holy and (**without blame**) before him in love" (Ephesians 1:3–4); and "We are his (**workmanship**), created in Christ Jesus unto (**good works**), which God hath before ordained that we should walk in them" (Ephesians 2:10).

What is *your* destiny? (**Discuss.**)

Since the time of Jesus more than two thousand years ago, leaders of the Christian church have been preaching—are still teaching—that the sins of the world caused Jesus to suffer. One might ask, *did* the sins of the world cause Jesus to be crucified? How did the crucifixion, resurrection, and ascension of Jesus change the world forever? Mary Baker Eddy writes, "The crucifixion and resurrection of Jesus served to uplift faith to understand the allness of (**Soul, Spirit**) and the nothingness of (**matter**)" (*Science and Health*, p. 497:20).

Is there a real "fallen man" as represented by Adam in the allegory presented in the second chapter of Genesis? **(No.)** In the garden of Eden, Adam and Eve turned away from the Lord's command not to eat from the tree containing knowledge of **(good)** *and* **(evil)**. We read in Genesis 1:31, "And God saw every thing he had made, and, behold, it was very good." Could the knowledge of *evil* be very good?

According to the story, the Lord condemned Adam and Eve and punished them by expelling them from their home. Did the writer of Genesis 3: 22–24 imply that they would be able to return? **(No.)** This writer apparently believed that their *false sense* of the Lord and of themselves caused them to fall, and they were fallen. Period. But *no*. Now we know about the rising and multiplying of good "through the knowledge of **(God)** and **(Jesus our Lord)**" (II Peter 1:2).

Adam and Eve had a third son (Seth) and a grandson (Enos), and then something wonderful happened: "then began men to call upon **(the name of the Lord")** (Genesis 4:25–26). Thought was rising; concepts were growing more spiritual.

After a few more generations, Enoch was born. He must have had a strong spiritual sense. What happened to Enoch? (See Genesis 5:24.) And later, Noah was born. Noah also **("walked with)** God" (see Genesis 6:9). Did that walk save his life? **(Yes.)**

Did Jesus come to destroy sin or to fulfill God's will? **(To fulfill.)** (See *Science and Health*, p. 474:16.) So what is "God's will?" **(Discuss.)**

What about evil? Do most people believe that evil is real? **(Yes.)** Here is a dictionary definition of evil: Something that is "morally wrong or bad"; that produces "misfortune or suffering; … the force in nature that governs and gives rise to wickedness and sin" (Dictionary.com).

God is not the parent of evil. Evil has a supposititious parent. What is its parent? *Science and Health* says that "the supposititious parent of evil is **(a lie)**" (p. 480:24).

Textbooks in school have assumptions and statements about the creation and evolution of humans. The Christian Science Bible Lesson deals with this topic every week, and particularly in lessons titled, "Is the Universe, Including Man, Evolved by Atomic Force?" and "God the Only Cause and Creator." The weekly Bible Lesson will help students compare what they are exposed to in daily school with what they learn in Sunday School.

Do you believe in *creationism or evolution* as explanations for how mankind came to be on earth? *Creationism* asserts that six thousand years ago, God created a material world in six days; for example, a Monday through a Saturday. Most religious creationists are fundamentalist Christians. *Evolution* asserts that simple life forms, like sea and land creatures, gradually evolved or changed until they became mortal man. The theory of biological evolution is associated with Charles Darwin around 1860.

A third option would be called sp**(iritual)** evolution, which means what? *Spiritual evolution* asserts that "Spirit and its formations are the only realities of being" (*Science and Health*, p. 264:20). What books teach us about spiritual evolution? (**The Bible and *Science and Health with Key to the Scriptures*.**)

Is spiritual evolution going on in your life? (**Yes.**) I am perfect now, and my demonstration of this will evolve and expand. Mary Baker Eddy writes in *Science and Health*, "Spiritual evolution alone is worthy of the exercise of divine power" (p.135:9).

What is a *sermon?* In many Christian churches, a minister or pastor preaches a sermon on Sunday. In a Christian Science church the "pastor" and "sermon" take on a different form. What is the sermon in a Christian Science church (**the weekly Bible Lesson**), and who presents it? (**The readers.**) Mrs. Eddy chose something other than a minister as pastor of the Christian Science Church. What did she choose? (**The two books, the Bible and *Science and Health*.**)

Mary Baker Eddy is the pastor emeritus of the Christian Science Church (see the title page of *Science and Health*). She wrote *Science and Health with Key to the Scriptures* and ordained the Bible and *Science and Health* as pastor of every Church of Christ, Scientist (see *Church Manual*, Article XIV, p. 58).

Prior to the reading of the lesson sermon on Sunday, the first reader reads this introduction, approved by Mary Baker Eddy. It's called the "Explanatory Note" because it explains who and what the pastor is in a Christian Science service:

> Friends: The Bible and the Christian Science textbook are our only preachers. We shall now read Scriptural texts, and their correlative passages from our denominational textbook; these comprise our sermon. The canonical writings, together with the word of our textbook, corroborating and explaining the Bible texts in their spiritual import and application to all ages, past, present, and future, constitute a sermon undivorced from truth, uncontaminated and unfettered by human hypotheses, and divinely authorized.

Do we have the same pastor in Sunday School? (**Yes.**)

What very important thing does Mary Baker Eddy say about sermons? (See *Science and Health*, p. 201:1–3.) She also says that clergymen (ministers, pastors) "should uplift the standard of Truth. They should so raise their hearers **(spiritually)**, that their listeners will love to grapple with a **(new, right idea)** and broaden **(their concepts)**" (p. 235:28–32). What "new idea" or "broadened concept" about sermons did you receive today? Are we doing the same thing in Sunday School that adults are doing in church? How? **(Discuss.)**

Pick a few statements that helped you the most in *getting to know more about other Christian religions.*

25

A MESSAGE TO TEACHERS AND STUDENTS OF THE BIBLE

I have endeavored to present to you a fresh, more spiritual view of the Bible than many other books typically provide, based on my many years of studying it, praying with it, and living it as best I can. I have found that it is only this spiritual view that inspires, uplifts, and heals.

So many works focus on the historical aspects of the Bible—who did what and when. While the chronological and historical aspects are certainly interesting and important, it is only by understanding the *spiritual* message of the Bible—God's Word—that lives and characters are transformed and real spiritual growth follows. In other words, it is not the letter of the Bible—all the facts, figures, and characters—but the spirit of the Bible that is most beneficial.

Paul bluntly explains it this way: "the letter killeth, but the spirit giveth life" (II Corinthians 3:6).

A spiritual approach to the Bible helps me learn about God and man's relationship to Him. Each character, event, and teaching also helps me learn about who I am. It is this spiritual view of the Bible, and its stories, verses, and characters, that I hope I have helped you see and appreciate spiritually as much as I do.

Throughout, I have provided sometimes provocative ideas and statements that challenge traditional assumptions. This is intentional. We all need to think and challenge ourselves—teachers and students alike—and be able to answer the tough questions that Sunday School students, especially teenagers, ask these days.

In most chapters, I have also provided a list of questions and answers that will provide teachers and students alike an organized study method to help review the material presented in each chapter. Teachers can reproduce the question pages and make these available as work sheets for students while keeping the answer pages for themselves.

And in the next section that follows this chapter, titled, "Part IV: Useful Information and Tools," are additional study resources that teachers may find helpful in bringing fresh new insights and learning tools to their classes.

Finally, this book is a starting point. I hope you will continue to develop existing teaching tools of your own to help and challenge your students to find those ageless truths in the Bible that give fundamental meaning and value to life.

PART IV

USEFUL INFORMATION AND TOOLS

26

WOMEN IN THE OLD AND NEW TESTAMENTS

Here is a list of some of the women in the Old Testament and New Testament of the Bible. We acknowledge them and thank those and the hundreds of women not named who were willing to serve the purposes of God.

Old Testament

Abigail helped David when he was hiding from Saul; later became David's wife.

Bathsheba. Wife of Uriah the Hittite, then wife of David and mother of Solomon.

Daughter of Pharaoh. She found the baby Moses in an ark made of bulrushes among the flags on the riverbank, and she raised him as her own son, a prince.

Deborah. The fifth judge of Israel and the only female judge; a prophet.

Esther. A Jewish queen who saved her people from destruction.

Eve. First woman, wife of Adam; acted on the suggestion of the serpent, evil.

Hagar. Wife of Abraham; mother of Ishmael.

Hannah dedicated her son Samuel to the Lord; he became an important prophet in Israel.

Huldah. A prophet during the same time that Jeremiah was a prophet.

Little Maid. She told the wife of Naaman that Elisha the prophet could heal Naaman of his leprosy, and he did.

Miriam. Sister of Moses and Aaron.

Rahab. He hid two Hebrew spies in Jericho; ancestor of David and Jesus.

Rebekah. Wife of Isaac; mother of Esau and Jacob.

Ruth. From Moab, a pagan country; great-grandmother of David.

Sarah. Wife of Abraham; mother of Isaac.

Shunammite woman. Helped the prophet Elisha; he healed her barrenness.

Tamar. A Canaanite (pagan) wife of Judah, one of the sons of Jacob-Israel; one of the descendants of Judah and Tamar was Jesus.

Widow of Zarephath. Widow with son, willing to give Elijah their last bit of food.

New Testament

Anna saw the baby Jesus and realized that he was the long-awaited Messiah.

Dorcas. Raised from the dead by Peter; also called Tabitha.

Elisabeth. Mother of John the Baptist; her husband was Zacharias.

Lois and Eunice. Lois was Eunice's mother; Eunice was the mother of Timothy, one of Paul's helpers.

Lydia. Wealthy tradeswoman from Thyatira; heard Paul speak and became the first convert to Christianity in Europe. She invited Paul into her house; the first Christian community met in her household.

Martha and Mary. Sisters of Lazarus and followers of Jesus.

Mary. Mother of Jesus, called the Virgin Mary.

Mary Magdalene. She may have been the Mary out of whom Jesus cast seven demons; she became one of Jesus' followers. She brought spices to Jesus' tomb and was the first witness to the resurrected Jesus. She reported to the apostles that Jesus was risen, but they did not believe her.

Mary. Mother of James and John. Follower of Jesus; present at Jesus' crucifixion.

Mary. Mother of John Mark, who is regarded by some as the author of the Gospel of Mark.

Phoebe. A wealthy businesswoman who helped Paul.

Pilate's wife defended Jesus and said he shouldn't be condemned and crucified.

Priscilla. She and her husband, Aquila, helped Paul spread the gospel of Christianity. She mentioned Christianity in at least one Roman synagogue and was expelled from Rome. Coworker with Paul who later returned to Rome and set up a house church.

Rhoda. Joyfully welcomed Peter at the house of Mary, mother of John Mark, after Peter was delivered by an angel from prison.

Salome. Follower of Jesus; present at crucifixion.

Woman of Canaan. She approached Jesus asking for help for her daughter. When she proved her humility, not willfulness, her daughter was healed.

Woman of Samaria. Gave Jesus a drink at the well; accepted Jesus' statement that he was the Christ.

For further study of women in the Bible, you might enjoy this book by *New York Times* best-selling author Francine Rivers: *A Lineage of Grace: Five Stories of Unlikely Women Who Changed Eternity*. In this compilation of the five books in the best-selling Lineage of Grace series by Francine Rivers, we meet the five women whom God chose—Tamar, Rahab, Ruth, Bathsheba, and Mary. Each was faced with extraordinary—even scandalous—challenges. Each took great personal risk to fulfill her calling. And each was destined to play a key role in the lineage of Jesus Christ, the Savior of the world.

- Tamar shows the story of a woman betrayed, yet a woman determined to do what is right in the eyes of God.
- Rahab, a harlot, shows that no matter the sin God can still do wonderful things in each of our lives.
- Ruth, a love story of epic proportions ... we see love given from daughter-in-law to mother-in-law, but we also see love shown from man to woman as Ruth takes her rightful place as the wife of Boaz.
- Bathsheba—we again see how God can turn a sin into something that is for His glory, if only the participants are willing.

- Mary gives us an interpretive look into the life of Jesus' mother and the struggles she went through watching her son, whom she knew to be the Christ, grow up and be rejected by a world that was supposedly waiting for his arrival. We see with Mary how God can take the most illogical person to be someone who is important to His plan.

27

MEN IN THE OLD TESTAMENT

Here is a list of some of the men in the Old Testament. We acknowledge them and thank those and the hundreds of men not named who were willing to serve the purposes of God.

Aaron. Brother of Moses. He went with Moses to speak with Pharaoh.

Abraham had the faith to go to a new land and have only one God; Father of many nations.

Absalom. Son of David who tried to kill David.

Adam. First human; did not obey God; banished from Garden of Eden; in spite of this, after the birth of his grandson Enos, "then began men to call upon the name of the Lord" (Genesis 4:26).

Ahab. King of Israel; he and his wife, Jezebel, worshipped Baal.

Daniel refused to worship the idol set up by the king, so he was thrown into a den of lions; the lions did not hurt Daniel, for he was obeying God.

David. As king, he united Israel and Judah into one nation; wrote many psalms; an ancestor of Joseph, the husband of Mary, mother of Jesus.

Elijah. God's prophet who destroyed the "prophets of Baal"; ran away from Jezebel's death threat; witnessed earthquake, wind, and fire; heard God as a still, small voice; restored a widow's son to life; did not die but was taken up into heaven.

Elisha succeeded the prophet Elijah; advised kings, preached the Word of God; he sweetened the bitter waters for drinking and healed Naaman of leprosy.

Esau. Twin brother of Jacob. Sold his birthright to his brother for a mess of pottage.

Gehazi. Elisha's servant.

Gideon. A prophet; delivered Israel from the Midianites with only three hundred men.

Isaac. Abraham and Sarah's son; Isaac and Rebekah were parents of Jacob and Esau.

Isaiah. A prophet; warned the Israelites that they were not living up to their purpose, but that God would send a savior.

Jeremiah. A prophet during the years that Israel was in captivity in Babylon.

Jacob/Israel. Had to flee from home after deceiving his father and tricking him into giving him his brother Esau's birthright. Later promised by God in a dream that he and his children would inherit land and be blessed.

> **Twelve sons of Jacob/Israel** settled in Canaan. These sons were the foundation of the Twelve Tribes of Israel: Gad, Reuben, Simeon, Judah, Dan, Levi, Asher, Joseph, Benjamin, Issachar, Zebulon, and Naphtali.

Job lived an honest life before God; "Satan" took everything away from him, but Job remained faithful and would not "curse God." "And the Lord turned the captivity of Job, when he prayed for his friends: also the Lord gave Job twice as much as he had before" (Job 42:10).

Jonah ran away from God's directive, spent three days in the belly of a great fish, and then went forward to "cry against" and "preach unto" the Ninevites, as God had directed him to do.

Joseph. Jacob's favorite son; he became a prince in Egypt and saved his brothers, who had sold him into slavery because of their jealousy.

Joshua led the children of Israel into Canaan, conquering the city of Jericho.

Lot. Abraham's nephew; left Abraham to live in the city of Sodom.

Melchizedek. King of Salem; priest of the Most High God; a "Christ" figure. He blessed Abraham.

Moses. Called by God to lead the children of Israel out of slavery in Egypt; received the Ten Commandments; did not cross the Jordan River into the Promised Land.

Nehemiah rebuilt the walls of Jerusalem after the children of Israel returned from captivity in Babylon.

Noah followed God's directions to build an ark and save mankind from the flood.

Samson. Last judge of Israel; destroyed many pagan Philistines by breaking the pillars that held up the roof of the temple of Dagon.

Samuel. First prophet of the Hebrew nation; anointed Saul, then David, as king of Israel.

Saul. First king of the nation of Israel; the children of Israel insisted on having a king because the nations around them had kings.

The servant. Servants play significant roles in the lives of Bible characters.

Solomon. David's son; second king of Israel; built the temple in Jerusalem; a wise king. Proverbs 1:1 attributes the book of Proverbs to Solomon: "The proverbs of Solomon the son of David, king of Israel."

28

MEN IN THE NEW TESTAMENT

The **Disciples of Jesus** were Simon Peter, Andrew, James the son of Zebedee, John, Philip, Bartholomew, Thomas, Matthew, James the son of Alphaeus, Thaddaeus, Simon the Zealot, and Judas Iscariot.

Eutychus. It would seem that Paul's lecture bored him to death, but Paul raised him to life after he dozed off and fell to the ground from a third-floor window.

Gamaliel. A Pharisee who was a doctor of the law and was an advocate for Paul, saving his life.

Jesus. The Son of God; the Messiah. Through parables and healings, he taught the people that God is all-powerful and that the real man is not material but is also the son of God. His teachings were summed up in the two great commandments, "Thou shalt love the Lord thy God with all thy heart, and with all thy soul, and with all thy mind," and "Thou shalt love thy neighbour as thyself" (see Matthew 22:37–40).

John. A disciple of Jesus; a strong leader of the disciples after Jesus ascended; banished to the isle of Patmos, where he wrote the book of Revelation. In "An Introduction to the Gospels," its author writes in *The New Oxford Annotated Bible*, "John's account of the passion ... differs markedly: there is no agony. Conscious of his unity with the Father and the cross as his exaltation and return to preexistent glory, Jesus controls all the events; he engages Pilate, the Roman governor, in an ironic discussion of kingship ..." (p. 1745). The "disciple whom Jesus loved," presumed to be John, stayed at the cross with Jesus' mother, his mother's sister, and Mary Magdalene, and he took Jesus' mother to his own home "from that hour" (John 19:27).

John the Baptist preached in the wilderness; called the Jewish people to repent; baptized Jesus.

Julius. The centurion who prevented the Roman soldiers from killing Paul after the shipwreck in Acts 27.

Lazarus. Raised from the dead by Jesus.

Luke helped the apostle Paul; wrote about the healings of Jesus in the book of Luke and the healings of the apostles in the book Acts of the Apostles.

Mark wrote the first story of Jesus' life several decades after Jesus' ascension.

Matthew. A tax collector called to be Jesus' disciple; the book of Matthew was written by a Greek-speaking educated Jew in the city of Antioch who recorded many of Jesus' parables and healings.

Paul. In many cities, he established churches based on Jesus Christ as the Son of God; he wrote letters to encourage these churches. Some of those letters are books in the New Testament and were the earliest Christian writings. He raised Eutychus from the dead.

Peter. A disciple of Jesus; witnessed the transfiguration, together with James and John; denied Jesus before the crucifixion but later raised Dorcas from the dead; he and the apostle Paul spread Christianity after Jesus ascended.

Philip preached the gospel and healed people.

Publius. Chief of the island of Malta; Paul healed the father Publius.

The servant. Servants play significant roles in the lives of Bible characters.

Zacharias. Father of John the Baptist. Saw Gabriel in a vision in the temple and was told he would have a son.

For further study of men in the Bible, you might enjoy this book by *New York Times* best-selling author Francine Rivers: *Sons of Encouragement*. In this five-book compilation of the Sons of Encouragement series, author Francine Rivers illuminates the lives of five Biblical men who stood behind the heroes of the faith and quietly changed eternity. Aaron, Caleb, Jonathan, Amos, and Silas each faithfully sought after God in the shadows of His chosen leaders. They answered God's call to serve without recognition or fame. And they gave everything, knowing their reward might not come until the next life. Behind the men who shaped history are the heroes who changed it forever.

- Aaron: The priest who stood in Moses' shadow but had the courage to cover his brother's fears.
- Caleb: The warrior whose words stirred men's hearts and brought God's people to the Promised Land.
- Jonathan: The prince whose humility led him to befriend the man who would become king in his place.
- Amos: The prophet who heard when God called and spoke to a nation unwilling to listen.
- Silas: The scribe who surrendered his wealth to record God's word, even as those around him were silenced.

29

DATES WHEN OLD TESTAMENT BOOKS WERE WRITTEN

All dates are BCE

Proverbs	1020–500	Habakkuk	605
Psalms	1000–165	Ezekiel	593–573
Genesis	950–500	Lamentations	580–550
Exodus	950–500	Leviticus	550–500
Numbers	950–500	Song/Solomon	550–300
Joshua	950–500	Haggai	520
Judges	950–500	Zechariah	520–518
I & II Samuel	950–650	Jonah	510–380
Amos	750	Malachi	500–450
Hosea	745	Obadiah	490
I Isaiah	742–700	Esther	486–465 or 400–322
II Isaiah	540–525	Job	450–400
III Isaiah	538–300	Joel	430
Micah	731	I & II Chronicles	400
Deuteronomy	650	Ezra	400
I & II Kings	650	Nehemiah	400
		Ruth	400–325
		Ecclesiastes	250–200
		Daniel	168–164

30

DATES WHEN NEW TESTAMENT BOOKS WERE WRITTEN

All dates are CE

I Thessalonians	49–50	II Timothy	66–67
II Thessalonians	49–50	Mark	70
Galatians	53–54	Matthew	80 or 85
Philippians	54–55 or 58–60	Luke	85–100
I Corinthians	54–55	Acts	85–100
II Corinthians	55–56	I Peter	90–95
Colossians	55–56 or 58–60	Revelation	90–95
Romans	56–57	I, II, & III John	90–100
Ephesians	58–60	John	90–100
Philemon	58–60		
James	60 or 75–100		

31

A Chronology of the Life of Mary Baker Eddy, Discoverer of Christian Science, Author of *Science and Health with Key to the Scriptures*, and Founder of The First Church of Christ, Scientist

1821   Mary Baker is born on a small farm in Bow, New Hampshire. She is the youngest of six children.

1830s   At this time, women are not typically formally educated. When her health permits, Mary sporadically attends a local school. Her brother, Albert, a graduate of Dartmouth, introduces her to the classics. He serves in the office of Franklin Pierce and is elected to the New Hampshire Statehouse. Mary is home-schooled and very much engaged with the times. She is privy to the lively conversations of her father and those who come to discuss politics, religion, and science.

1843   She marries George Washington Glover.

1844   The Glovers move to Wilmington, North Carolina. Mary begins writing antislavery articles and is concerned about other social topics as well.

George dies of yellow fever. Mary returns to her parents' home in New Hampshire.

Her son, George Washington Glover II, is born, and a period of invalidism of more than twelve years begins for Mary.

1851   Relatives who are providing a home for Mary are no longer willing to allow her son to stay with her. They send him to live with another family, about twenty-five miles away.

1850s	She studies homeopathy and practices it. Gradually she learns that it is the faith of the doctor, the patient, or the person administering the remedy, not the remedy itself, that relieves the symptoms of disease.
	She heals dozens of people and pursues her study of the Scriptures.
1853	She marries Dr. Daniel Patterson, an itinerant dentist.
1855	The Pattersons move to a four-room cottage in North Groton, New Hampshire, to be near her son, George.
1856	Her son, almost twelve years old, is taken to Minnesota, and he doesn't see his mother again until 1879.
1866	Mary Baker Patterson falls on the ice and is seriously injured. The doctor and friends consider the injuries fatal. Upon reading from the New Testament, she is completely healed. Mary cannot explain to others what has happened, but she knows her healing is the result of what she is reading in the Bible.
	Writing about her discovery of Christian Science, she states that she "searched the Scriptures and read little else, kept aloof from society, and devoted time and energies to discovering a positive rule" (*Science and Health with Key to the Scriptures*, by Mary Baker Eddy, p. 109:12-15). She applies this positive rule to healing many individuals throughout her lifetime.
1867	She begins to teach others to heal through prayer.
1868	She heals a woman dying of pneumonia, and one of the doctors in attendance urges her to write a book about her system of healing.
1872	She begins writing *Science and Health with Key to the Scriptures*, which explains Christian Science as a system of healing and reformation.
1873	She obtains a divorce from Dr. Patterson on the grounds of his desertion and adultery.
1875	She formally withdraws from the Congregational Church and publishes the first edition of *Science and Health*. She heals Asa Gilbert Eddy of a heart condition, and he becomes the first person to advertise himself as a Christian Science practitioner. Later he founds the Christian Science Sunday School for children and teenagers.
1877	She marries Asa Gilbert Eddy.
1870s	She teaches Christian Science in her home and gives public lectures on Christian Science.
1879	Mary Baker Eddy and some of her students organize a church "designed to commemorate the word and works of our Master, which should reinstate primitive Christianity and its lost element of healing." (This statement subsequently appears in the *Church Manual* on page 17.)

1880s	Eddy regularly preaches on Sundays in public venues and gradually appoints other people to preach the sermons.
1881	Mary Baker Eddy establishes the Massachusetts Metaphysical College in Boston, where she teaches classes on Christian Science. The college is chartered by the Commonwealth of Massachusetts, the first and only charter for a metaphysical medical college (see *Miscellaneous Writings 1883–1896*, by Mary Baker Eddy, p. 382).
1882	Asa Gilbert Eddy dies. Mrs. Eddy begins seven years of teaching, preaching, lecturing, writing, and publishing.
1883	The first issue of the *Journal of Christian Science* is published bimonthly by the Christian Scientists' Publishing Company, with Eddy as editor and publisher.
1884	The *Journal of Christian Science* becomes a monthly publication.
1885	Eddy changes the name to *The Christian Science Journal*.
1887	Eddy arranges with the Boylston Hotel in Boston to display her published writings. She wants to make her works easily accessible to the public by putting them in such a public place.
	Her poems "Christ My Refuge" and "Feed My Sheep" are copyrighted. These are the first two of seven poems written by Mary Baker Eddy that later become hymns (see *Poems*, by Mary Baker Eddy, and the *Christian Science Hymnal*).
1889	Eddy dissolves the Massachusetts Metaphysical College and eliminates the congregational-business-meeting format of church organization. She desires to devote greater time and effort to revising *Science and Health*.
1890	She establishes the *Christian Science Quarterly Bible Lessons* to be studied daily, used in adult Sunday Schools, and discussed at Friday-night meetings.
1891	Eddy requests that church members better meet the nursing needs of Christian Scientists. This intention comes to fruition in 1908 when she formalizes the requirements for the Christian Science nurse with a bylaw in the *Church Manual*.
	Eddy publishes the fiftieth edition of *Science and Health*.
	Retrospection and Introspection, her autobiography, is published.
1892	She reorganizes her church as The First Church of Christ, Scientist, "designed to be built on the Rock, Christ; even the understanding and demonstration of divine Truth, Life, and Love, healing and saving the world from sin and death; thus to reflect in some degree the Church Universal and Triumphant" (*Church Manual*, p. 19).

She establishes the Christian Science Board of Directors, which administers the business of The Mother Church in accordance with the *Church Manual.*

1893   She publishes her poem *Christ and Christmas* in book form, with illustrations by James Gilman.

1894   The cornerstone is laid for the The First Church of Christ, Scientist, in Boston, Massachusetts (The Mother Church). This edifice seats approximately one thousand people. Eddy ordains the Bible and *Science and Health with Key to the Scriptures* as Pastor of The Mother Church. The first service is held on Sunday, December 30th —a communion service.

1895   She publishes the first edition of the *Church Manual*, with bylaws relative to the organization of The Mother Church.

She ordains the Bible and *Science and Health with Key to the Scriptures* as pastor in branch churches worldwide.

1896   Her poems "Communion Hymn," "Love," and "Mother's Evening Prayer" are copyrighted.

1897   Eddy publishes *Miscellaneous Writings 1883–1896.* This is a compilation of her contributions to *The Christian Science Journal* and includes sermons and other articles. This book is based on the author's own experiences in putting her system of healing into practice. Another compilation of individually published writings is published as *Prose Works* in 1925.

1898   Eddy teaches her last formal class on Christian Science, and she establishes several significant avenues for the promotion and protection of Christian Science:

- In January, she establishes the Board of Lectureship, which authorizes individuals to give public lectures about Christian Science and the life of its Discoverer.
- In February, she establishes the Board of Education, which prepares and certifies teachers of Christian Science.
- She establishes The Christian Science Publishing Society.
- Eddy launches *The Christian Science Weekly.* Four months later it is renamed *Christian Science Sentinel.*
- Eddy establishes the Committee on Publication. This office answers questions from the public, news media, and other sources. The purpose of the Committee on Publication is "to correct in a Christian manner impositions on the public in regard to Christian Science ..." (*Church Manual*, p. 97).
- She designates twenty-six topics for weekly lesson-sermons for use in individual Bible study and as sermons in Churches of Christ, Scientist.

1900	The first Christian Science Reading Room opens in Boston. As required in the *Church Manual,* all Christian Science churches are to provide a place—a reading room—where the public can read or purchase Christian Science literature.
1902	Eddy publishes the 226th and last major edition of *Science and Health.*
1903	*The Herald of Christian Science* is launched in German as *Der Herold der Christian Science,* the first publication in a language other than English. Published in thirteen languages, the *Herald* presents articles and testimonies of healing and a directory of Christian Science churches, practitioners, and other listings for many countries. Her poem "Christmas Morn" is copyrighted.
1904	She establishes Christian Science Organizations for Colleges and Universities. The cornerstone of the Extension of The Mother Church is laid. This edifice seats over five thousand people.
1905	Mary Baker Eddy and student Alice Longyear discuss the great need for trained Christian Science nurses in the movement. Eddy states that there is a pressing need for the establishment of a Christian Science facility as part of the worldwide beneficence she wishes to carry out. In 1908, she would formalize the requirements for the Christian Science nurse with a bylaw in the *Church Manual.*
1906	She writes in the final edition of *Science and Health,* "An ill-tempered, complaining, or deceitful person should not be a nurse. The nurse should be cheerful, orderly, punctual, patient, full of faith—receptive to Truth and Love" (p. 395:15). The first service in the Extension of The Mother Church is held on June 10, 1906, and is both a communion service and a dedication service.
1907	Sibyl Wilbur, a journalist and not a Christian Scientist, publishes the first biography, titled, *The Life of Mary Baker Eddy.* In the *Christian Science Sentinel* of March 12, 1910, Mrs. Eddy thanks Miss Wilbur "for [her] unselfed labors in placing this book before the public ..." Subsequently, many biographies of Mary Baker Eddy are published by The Christian Science Publishing Society.
1908	She requests the trustees of the Publishing Society to publish a daily newspaper to be called *The Christian Science Monitor.* The first issue appears on November 25th. She includes a new bylaw, "Christian Science Nurse," in the *Church Manual.* She also requests that the Board of Directors establish a facility for the purpose of nursing.

1910	She authorizes the first translation of *Science and Health* into another language, German. Subsequently, *Science and Health* is translated into sixteen languages.
	She makes last revisions to *Science and Health with Key to the Scriptures* and the *Church Manual*.
	Her poem "Satisfied" is copyrighted.
	She publishes a collection of her poems in *Poems*.
	She passes on December 3rd at her home in Chestnut Hill, Massachusetts. Her last written words are, "God is my life."

32

THE "NO JEOPARDY" GAME

Through this game, our Sunday School students (and teachers!) can learn and review their knowledge of the Bible, *Science and Health*, Christian Science, and Mary Baker Eddy.

I made a list of answers and questions, and it was several pages long. After each "A:" and after each "Q:" I gave an example.

A: These four books of the Bible are sometimes called the Gospels.
Q. What are Matthew, Mark, Luke, and John?

A. God told this man to build a big boat even though he didn't live by the water and didn't have a trailer.
Q: Who was Noah?

I would put approximately five A/Q couplets on a page. This will result in many pages. I would pull a page at random and ask the students to use the index card I had given them to cover up the five examples. Then I would say, Uncover the first capital A. Read it aloud. Then state the question that would match it.

Because I would be using a different set of A and Q couplets each time, the students would really have to think in order to answer. Sometimes I would have them cover all five examples with their index card and ask the students to begin at the bottom with a capital Q. They would read the Q aloud and then provide the A.

For example,

A: This woman left her pagan country to follow the true God.
Q: Who was Ruth?

A: This prince was a friend of David.
Q: Who was Jonathan?

A: This book was written in 1875 to explain Christian Science.
Q: What is *Science and Health with Key to the Scriptures*?

A: This woman devoted her life to explain the spiritual concept of God and man as found in the Bible.
Q: Who was Mary Baker Eddy?

Jeopardy Questions and Answers

A: These four books of the Bible are sometimes called "the Gospels."
Q: What are Matthew, Mark, Luke, and John?

A: This man had a name, but then God gave him a new name (multiple answers possible).
Q: Who was Abram (or Saul, or Jacob, or Simon)? (Abraham, Paul, Israel, Peter)

A: This man and woman were key players in a make-believe story, or allegory, about how humans are created.
Q: Who were Adam and Eve?

A: This boy was a good friend of David and the son of a king who wanted to kill David.
Q: Who was Jonathan?

A: This woman left her own family and country to follow the true God. One of the books in the Bible is about this woman.
Q: Who was Ruth?

A: God told this man to build a big boat even though he did not live near the water (and didn't even have a boat trailer!).
Q: Who was Noah?

A: This city was the capital of Israel.
Q: What was Jerusalem?

A: These people crossed a big desert to find freedom from slavery.
Q: Who were the children of Israel?

A: Only this man had more power in Egypt than Joseph did.
Q: Who was Pharaoh?

A: This man was put in prison on an island, but there God gave him a vision of the future and he wrote the last book of the Bible.
Q: Who was Saint John?

A: This man had the job of making tents, but he also traveled around helping groups of Christians start churches.
Q: Who was Paul?

A: This man almost died from a wound in his hip, but Mary Baker Eddy healed him.
Q: Who was Mr. Clark?

A: Mary Baker Eddy wrote *Science and Health* for something other than a particular denominational group.
Q: Who are honest seekers for Truth?

A: This person wrote the Pauline Epistles to Christian churches in Rome, Corinth, and other cities.
Q: Is Pauline the twin sister of Paul? No! Pauline is the adjective form of Paul.

A: Many of the chapters in this book of the Bible were written by King David.
Q: What is the Psalms?

A: This book is made of sixty-six other books written by different people.
Q: What is the Bible?

A: These books of the Bible were written by prophets whose names begin with *I* and *J*.
Q: Who was Isaiah? Who was Jeremiah?

A: This woman was suffering from a serious injury caused by a slip on the ice when she read about one of Jesus' healings and a great truth came to her thought. She later wrote a book explaining this truth.
Q: Who was Mary Baker Eddy?

A: This boy heard God calling him by name, but he thought it was the priest calling him.
Q: Who was Samuel?

A: This young man had an opportunity to kill his enemy, but instead he just cut off a piece of his robe while his enemy slept.
Q: Who was David?

A: This is where you can find the true story of creation.
Q: What is the first chapter of Genesis?

A: This psalm describes God's tender guidance and care.
Q: What is Psalm 23? Or, What is Psalm 91?

A: Mary Baker Eddy started this newspaper because so many newspapers in her day practiced wrong and harmful journalism.
Q: What is *The Christian Science Monitor*?

A: King Nebuchadnezzar tried to kill these three boys because they were faithful to the true God.

Q: Who were Shadrach, Meshach, and Abednego?

A: This familiar passage from *Science and Health* tells us that "all is infinite Mind and its infinite manifestation for God is All-in-all."

Q: What is the Scientific Statement of Being?

A: This chapter in *Science and Health* has definitions of many words.

Q: What is the *Glossary*?

A: This is the best book for helping someone understand the Bible's spiritual meaning.

Q: What is *Science and Health with Key to the Scriptures*?

A: It took many people nearly one thousand years to write this book.

Q: What is the Bible?

A: This book has been translated into seventeen different languages.

Q: What is *Science and Health with Key to the Scriptures*?

A: This store has many copies of *Science and Health* for sale.

Q: What is a Christian Science Reading Room? Or, what is a Reading Room?

A: People attend this Christian Science church service during the week to give gratitude for healing and share spiritual insights.

Q: What is a Wednesday testimony meeting?

A: Mary Baker Eddy named twenty-six subjects, one of which we study each week, in order to learn more about perfect God and God's perfect creation.

Q: What is the weekly Bible Lesson?

A: God gave these two people the job of taking care of the baby Jesus and helping him grow up.

Q: Who are Mary and Joseph?

A: Mary Baker Eddy says this prayer covers all human needs.

Q: What is the Lord's Prayer?

A: This group of religious leaders was so focused on their traditions that they couldn't understand what Jesus was teaching them. Later they tried to kill Jesus.

Q: Who were the Pharisees?

A: This is a type of simple story Jesus often used when teaching his followers about God and God's creation.
Q: What is a parable?

A: This man said we can heal ourselves and others if we obey the guidance, "Ye shall know the truth, and the truth shall make you free."
Q: Who was Christ Jesus? Or, who was Jesus?

A: This woman said that anyone can learn this Science, which helps them help others.
Q: Who was Mary Baker Eddy?

A: This very important Science was discovered in 1866.
Q: What is Christian Science?

A: This word describes the process of asking a question, stating a theory, and testing the theory again and again in order to prove it true.
Q: What is a science?

A: This teaching of Jesus in his Sermon on the Mount tells people they feel good and blessed when they show mercy and purity.
Q: What are the Beatitudes?

A: These two books of the Bible were written *before Genesis.*
Q: What are Proverbs and Psalms?

A: These people did not react to, or hate, the public leaders who told lies about them.
Q: Who was Christ Jesus? Who was Mary Baker Eddy? Who was the apostle Paul? Who was Martin Luther King? Who was Mahatma Gandhi?

A: This book in the Old Testament was written by a "cool dude."
Q: What is Deuteronomy?

A: This woman founded an award-winning international daily newspaper when she was eighty-seven years old.
Q: Who was Mary Baker Eddy?

ABOUT THE AUTHOR

Dr. Lincoln began teaching the Bible to teenagers several decades ago, which led her to delve more deeply into the Scriptures. She has also studied *Science and Health with Key to the Scriptures* by Mary Baker Eddy, a companion book to the Bible, because she believes that book opens up the spiritual meaning of the Bible in a way that no other book about the Bible does. She writes, "I appreciate the first tenet of Christian Science: As adherents of Truth, we take the inspired Word of the Bible as our sufficient guide to eternal Life (*Science and Health*, p. 497:3-4)."

Dr. Lincoln began her career teaching music and second grade in Los Angeles and primary grades for the Department of Defense Overseas Schools in Germany and Japan. She taught English briefly at colleges in California and Michigan and for six years at Principia College in Illinois. In addition, at several colleges she taught courses about challenging sex discrimination in education. For seventeen years, she was employed by the State of Michigan, first as the sex equity coordinator and then as a professional development consultant, retiring in 1995.

During her professional career as a teacher of young children and college students, she learned much about interactive teaching methods and used these same methods extensively in teaching the Bible.

For twenty-five years, Dr. Lincoln organized and conducted tours of Great Britain, Norway, Australia, New Zealand, and Japan. In addition, she has traveled to Mexico, the Philippines, Taiwan, and most of the European countries.

Dr. Lincoln taught Sunday School for about twenty years, mostly in classes of high school and college students. She started an independent adult Bible study group in 2004, and later she initiated an additional evening Bible study group. A friend remarked that she had "a singular and practical approach" to Bible study and urged her to write a book. She writes, "What I offer here is simply an angle on the Bible, sent by an angel. The writing of *BibleAlive: A Guide to Discovering the Ageless Vitality of the Bible for Teachers and Students* enriched my knowledge and appreciation of the Bible. I hope this book will enrich your reading of it, too."

Dr. Lincoln received a bachelor of music education degree from Northwestern University, a master of arts degree in English from the University of Chicago, and a doctor of arts degree in English and women's studies from the University of Michigan.

There is one additional "degree" she likes to think about: a "BC"—Bible commentator. She writes, "There is a high degree of commentary in this book. This degree was not bestowed by an institution you would recognize but was earned by GMA—Good Motives and Acts."

Sara Ann Lincoln
4599 Avery Road
Hilliard, Ohio 43026
614.876.0084 ext. 601
Sara.lincoln@sbcglobal.net

Alternate contact:
Mike Hedge
Bingham Farms, MI
mhedge@hedgeco.com

INDEX

W

Y

Z